# Grassley:
## Senator from Iowa

# Grassley:
## Senator from Iowa

Eric Woolson

Foreword by
Senator Robert Dole

Mid-Prairie Books
Parkersburg, Iowa
1995

Book Composition by:
Ireland Design & Publishing, Cedar Falls, Iowa

Published by:

Mid-Prairie Books
P.O. Box C
Parkersburg, Iowa  50665
(319) 346-2048

ISBN 0-931209-59-5 - cloth
ISBN 0-931209-60-9 - paper

# Table of Contents

# Preface

This project could not have come together without the inspiration, guidance, and wherewithal of my publisher, Bob Neymeyer of Mid-Prairie Books. He is a true credit to the entrepreneurial spirit of today's small publishing trade.

It is equally true that it never would have been possible to write with any real degree of depth without the cooperation of Charles Grassley and his wife, Barbara. They welcomed me into their home and graciously tolerated many questions and intrusions. They encouraged their friends and family, political supporters and colleagues to candidly offer their recollections and opinions of events in their lives. Senator Grassley was forthright, warm, and always generous with his time, despite his genuine bemusement and humility that anyone would want to write his life's story. Interviewing Mrs. Grassley was a delightful experience.

I am not a scholar, a historian, nor a psychologist. Lacking such qualifications, I neither attempt to fix Grassley's place in history nor offer a psychoanalysis of what makes him work. I am a journalist who lays out the facts as they have been told to me, attempts to organize them in a coherent manner, and allows the reader to come to his or her own conclusions. This approach is the path I have attempted to follow since my career as a professional writer began in 1976. It is equally important to emphasize that this book is not an authorized biography over which the subject had veto power.

Instead, the Senator, in offering his full cooperation and his influence on several occasions to assist me in securing interviews, exhibited an extraordinary faith that all would turn out well. That's not to say that he, or members of his staff, did not keep tabs on the process every once in awhile; Charles Grassley did not achieve his durable political success by being inattentive to details. He took great pains to steer me in the direction of those whom he felt know him best and, perhaps, would reflect him in the best light. At the same time, Grassley possesses a small-town humility and simplicity that refuses to die. Even when he finally accepted the notion that a biography was not some sort of joke, he continued to ask with a genuine and amusing astonishment, "Do you really think someone would want to buy a book about *me*?"

1

Thankfully, I was not presented with any agonizing decisions about omitting or doctoring up a raft of personal stories about the "private Charles Grassley." His life has been a remarkable journey of civility and forthrightness; he lives by the rule that he never says anything anywhere that he would not be willing to see in print or hear on the nightly news. As one political intimate said, "A bunch of us would be in this office talking over strategy and some rough language would start flying around. But that stuff just stopped when he came in the room. We knew by the way he presented himself that he didn't go for that. You just behave differently around him."

Indeed, several people who were gracious enough to grant interviews called me later, noting with deep chagrin that they believed they had used what most newspeople consider mild profanity. They wanted to know if I would change the offending word because they did not want to be associated with language that would offend the Senator in a book written about him. (For the record, I agreed to the changes because they were not of factual importance.)

Even without talking to all of Grassley's thousands of ardent fans, the interviewing process was an involved one. Very special thanks also to the Senator's sister, Bunnie Grassley Wiegmann, for her priceless recollections of her early family years.

Special thanks to Senate Republican Leader Robert Dole; Senators Joseph Biden, Phil Gramm, Tom Harkin, Orrin Hatch, David Pryor, and Arlen Specter; former Grassley aides Pete Conroy, John Maxwell, and Bev Hubble Tauke, who were so generous with their time and insights into their former boss; Grassley press secretary Jill Hegstrom, who went above and beyond the call of duty; and to my editors on this project, Shellie Robson and Marianne Abel.

Thanks also to former President George Bush, Brent Appel, Mary Jo Archibold of Grassley's staff, Mary Ann Baker of Biden's staff, Larry Ballard, Judge Robert H. Bork, Bob Bradsell, Gov. Terry Branstad, Joyce Campbell of Senator Dole's staff, Ben Campney, Scott Cawelti, former state Sen. Joseph Coleman, Roxanne Conlin, Ken Cunningham, A. Arthur Davis, Kolan Davis, Mark Farnen, Allen Finch, Len Froyen, Chuck Gifford, former Sen. Barry Goldwater, Jim Gritzner, Bob Haus, Jack Hovelson, Jackie Howell at Common Cause, Kris Kolesnik, Dr. Lawrence Korb, Elizabeth Law, Susan Lamontagne of Specter's staff, Jeremy R. T. Lewis, J. W. "Bill" Lynes, Judy McCoy, Caran Kolbe McKee, Ally Milder, former state Rep. Floyd Millen, Bob Molinaro, David Oman, Larry Orth, Bob Ostrem, Tim Raftis, David Ransom, Steve Rapp, former state Sen. Robert Rigler, John Roehrick, Luke Roth, Michael Schreuers, Luverne Schroeder, Fred Schuster of Grassley's staff, former Iowa Democratic Party spokesman Joe Shannahan, my editor and colleague at the *Waterloo Courier*, Saul Shapiro, Jodie Silverman of Harkin's staff, former state Sen. Art Small, Paul Smith of Hatch's staff, Wendy Grassley Speckerman, David Stanley, Tom Stoner, Ken Sullivan, Tom Synhorst, Curt Sytsma, Eric Tabor, Damon Thompson of Pryor's staff, Dick Thornton, Jack Warren, Caspar Weinberger, Heather Wiegand, David Yepsen, and Dean Zerbe.

Deepest gratitude is reserved for my wife, Debora Blume, and our son, Brooks, for their patience, good humor, and support on the home front. This book is dedicated to the two of them and the memory of Bob Case, a top-notch newsman who had a truly uncommon appreciation and knowledge of American government, politics, and politicians.

September 8, 1995
Waterloo, Iowa

# Foreword

Chuck Grassley is the most popular politician in Iowa history. If there were ever any doubts about the truth of that statement, they were removed in 1992. It was a year in which voters were turning against any candidate with the words "incumbent" or "experienced" attached to their name. Yet, it was also the year when a remarkable 72 percent of Iowans voted to reelect Chuck Grassley to a third term in the United States Senate.

What explains Chuck Grassley's enduring popularity and an unbroken streak of election victories that stretches over three decades? Having travelled across Iowa with him on many occasions, and having served beside him his entire Senate career, I have a few insights which might help answer that question.

There are 99 counties in Iowa, and Chuck Grassley knows everything there is to know about each one of them. Who are the community leaders? How's business on Main Street? Was the harvest a success? What are they discussing down at the local coffee shop? Chuck can tell you all this and more.

Just as important as knowing what Iowans are thinking, is translating that knowledge into a set of principles. And the principles that have guided Chuck throughout his public service career spring from common sense midwestern values: Government is too big and spends too much. The national deficit is a national disgrace. The family farm should be preserved. Criminals should face swift and sure punishment. It is these principles that Americans overwhelmingly endorsed in November 1994.

Another reason behind Chuck's success is his perseverance—a quality that all farmers must possess. Whether it's shaking every hand at a county fair, or shaking up bureaucrats in Washington, the man simply does not know how to give up.

For many years, Chuck conducted what was almost a one-man crusade to force Congress to comply with the laws we impose on everybody else. To some in Washington, this seemed like a radical concept. To Chuck, it was just plain common sense. And the fact that the first bill passed by the 104th Congress in January 1995 was Chuck's "Congressional compliance" legislation is a tribute to both his perseverance and his common sense.

I also remember many advising Chuck to back off his effort to reform the purchasing practices of the Pentagon, saying that it was not wise to criticize the military. But Chuck knew that a coffee maker which cost taxpayers $7,600 did nothing to improve our national defense. And he forced the Pentagon to change its spending habits.

When Chuck came to the Senate, there were some in Washington who wrote him off as someone who would never be part of the "Washington scene." And they were right. Chuck Grassley didn't come to Washington to attend parties, he came to attend to the business of the people of Iowa, and the people of America.

And it didn't take long for the "inside the Beltway" crowd to realize that those who underestimated Chuck Grassley did so at their own risk.

He is a public servant of great intelligence, and even greater integrity. America and Iowa are better places because of him. I am proud to call him my friend.

Senator Robert Dole

# More Than Meets The Eye

Washington, D.C. *(May 3, 1994)*—Charles Grassley was in the hallway of his office in the sleek Senate Hart Office Building, a stone's throw from the Capitol, when he got word late in the afternoon that Treasury Secretary Lloyd Bentsen was backing out of the deal.

Grassley, ranking member of the Senate Subcommittee on Private Retirement Plans and Oversight of the Internal Revenue Service, and Sen. David Pryor, the Arkansas Democrat who was the panel's chairman, had agreed to give the agency another 5,000 agents to sic on the unsuspecting American public. In exchange, Grassley and Pryor wanted passage of legislation they called the Taxpayers' Bill of Rights II.

Four weeks earlier, everything seemed cut and dried. Now, Bentsen was calling the Iowa Republican to say the agents were staying in the budget conference report, and the Taxpayers' Bill of Rights II was not.

"I'd like to talk to Pryor before I talk to Bentsen," Grassley told aides Kolan Davis and Dean Zerbe. "I think Pryor and I ought to be going the same direction."

Grassley wouldn't find much support from his colleague. "He didn't want to cave," Zerbe said, "but he caved. The problem is everybody is looking for you to be the pillar."

A pained expression flashed across the tall, slender senator's weathered face. "In other words, I've got to be the bad boy," Grassley declared, irritation and genuine astonishment simultaneously reflected in his deep drawl.

"Right. But what you need to do . . ." Zerbe started.

"Well, that's pretty difficult when you talk to Bentsen," Grassley interrupted, sounding for a moment as if he doubted he was up to the challenge.

"If you call Pryor now he'll say, 'We'll work it out, we'll do all this stuff,'" Zerbe said, "and I don't think you ought to do that. I think you ought to dig in your heels."

"And tell Bentsen a deal's a deal," Grassley said adamantly.

"Absolutely," Zerbe agreed.

The discussion went on for several minutes, centering on a parliamentary maneuver that Grassley could use to protect the Taxpayers' Bill of Rights II.

"You've got some righteous indignation you can exercise with Bentsen and Pryor," Zerbe counseled. "Say, 'Look, the word is they were going to try to strip this from the beginning, and I don't like to do business that way. We had a deal. And I'd be happy to work with you and them, but this isn't the way to do it.'"

Davis interjected, "The problem is, Pryor's already agreed not to stand in the way."

"So I'm the guy that's going to stand in the way," Grassley said, resigned. He paused a moment. His tone was one of acceptance. "OK."

Then he was off to his next appointment, putting the long-distance touch on big-money party contributors from a phone bank in the Ronald Reagan Republican Center just a few blocks from his office. Walking down Second Street, N.E., Grassley, dressed in a dark gray, three-piece suit accentuated by a gold vest chain, filled in the details of the unfolding mini-drama between himself, Bentsen, and Pryor.

"The IRS wants to hire 5,000 more agents based upon the proposition that you hire x-number of agents and you get x-amount more revenue. I don't necessarily buy that argument but I didn't want to argue it, and I was working with Pryor anyway. So it's finally worked out that we will agree to it, if what we call the Taxpayers' Bill of Rights II passes.

"In other words, they get the 5,000 agents but they don't get the money for them until we get the Taxpayers' Bill of Rights because we're always fighting the bureaucracy at [the] IRS to get the Taxpayers' Bill of Rights," Grassley said. "Now it's appearing that Treasury agrees to all that to get it through the Senate to get it to 'conference' with the idea that [House Ways and Means Committee chairman Dan] Rostenkowski would come back and raise a squawk that we're doing something that constitutionally belongs to the Ways and Means Committee. So, then they come back and say, 'We've got all these problems with Rostenkowski. You've got to back off, but we'll work with you in the future.'"

After 20 years in Washington, D.C., Grassley had seen the legislative equivalent of the old shell game before. And he wasn't falling for it this time. "The point we're talking about," Grassley reiterated, "is a deal's a deal." He was, however, acutely sensitive to his colleague's dilemma. "Evidently Senator Pryor finds himself in a difficult position, which I could have been in, too, if we'd had a Republican president." The question, then, was whether Grassley would hold Pryor's feet to the fire—remind him, too, that "a deal's a deal"—or let him off the hook.

"Oh, I let Pryor off the hook because he's a friend of mine," Grassley shrugged. "He would probably do the same for me because he was my ranking member when I was chairman of the subcommittee. Yes, Pryor's a friend of mine." Besides, he noted, he could still raise a point of order if push came to shove with Bentsen. "They've got to have 60 votes to override me, and they won't be able to override me. They won't put it in there unless they're sure I'm not going to object in the first place. On the other hand, if I didn't object, some other Republican could. There's a lot of people that don't like the IRS."

It was, in the grand scheme of life, just another day at the office for Chuck Grassley. But the vignette summed up the simple values that seem to have guided him through 60 years of his life and more than 35 years of public service.

Stick to your word.

Stick by your friends, even when they can't stick by you.

Stick up for your principles and the ordinary people you represent.

Those guiding lights helped Grassley become only the second U.S. Senator from Iowa to win reelection in the Twentieth Century and go on to win a third term by the greatest percentage in state history.

"If old Chuck Grassley ever did anything dishonest, it wouldn't be because he was trying," said Pryor, sitting in his office in Room 267 of the Senate Russell Office Building, knowing that Grassley would not hold a grudge against him even after taking the heat from Bentsen. "I don't think he knows how to be dishonest."

Pryor, who first started working with Grassley on military spending reform in 1981, believes his colleague is "pretty well the same all the time. I don't think he veers much from threads of common sense. I think he stays right in that road. He has a lot of ethics about him. He's a very common sense type of person. And, by the way, he's very populistic. The IRS issues are deeply rooted in populism. Weapons that work. I mean, that sounds kind of goofy, but that's kind of a populistic idea."

A. Arthur Davis, the Iowa Democratic Party chairman from 1985 to 1988, brings Grassley's electoral appeal closer to home.

"He looks and sounds like what most of us kind of think Iowans are like, but not ourselves, and I think that's very important to the image of Charles Grassley. There's another significant thing going for Grassley: he does not aspire to more than he has. He neither aspires to the presidency or the vice presidency nor, do I imagine, does he aspire to be the Republican minority leader or majority leader, if they ever get control again. And that is an advantage."

Davis, whose name appears first in the title of the state's largest law firm, believes that lack of desire for higher office has set Grassley free to operate as he wishes. "He is a United States Senator; that's a very exalted position in and of itself. I think he's honored greatly. He will be a part of history. I think he's got security. He's got a life job as long as he wants it. He knows that. He's not reaching. He's doing his job well. I think probably in the private circles of the Republican Party he's probably as conservative as anybody . . . but he doesn't have to push the conservative button all the time when he's out talking in general. He doesn't need that to get elected. I don't think he's trying to change the direction of the country on a day-to-day basis. He's relatively content in voting the way he votes but not trying to lead the charge. Therefore, not very many people are unhappy, and the Democrats don't say, 'Why, that dim wit,' or 'We've got to get rid of that son of a gun.'"

The recurring description of Grassley, though, uttered by friend and foe alike, is "What you see is what you get." That's what strikes so many people about Grassley, the gut-level feeling that he's that rare, genuine article in a world of image makers, artificial issues, and smoke and mirrors. So much of his personal and political being—and so much of his success—is his genuineness. From his "aw shucks" drawl to his ballyhooed tight-fistedness, nothing faked, nothing phony.

That is "Chuck" Grassley.

The guy who can't wait to get out of Washington and get back to work on his New Hartford, Iowa, farm.

The guy whose friends fondly tease him for his vocabulary that includes the words "garsh" and "gol darned."

The guy whose wife and kids buy new, trendy clothes for him because his preferred duds look like thrift store rejects. Torn jeans and old T-shirts prove standard garb for a U.S. Senator who still mows his own large rural lawn on summer weekends.

The guy who touts simple, black-and-white solutions such as a constitutional balanced budget amendment to cure what ails America.

The guy who epitomizes rural American friendliness and familiarity.

Beverly Hubble was Grassley's press secretary when she began to date Tom Tauke, a young Congressman from Iowa. "The Senator was dying to know who I was seeing, and I said, 'I'm not going to tell you. You'll tell everybody.' I was leaving one evening to get something to eat and then come back to the office. . . . Thirty minutes later, I was having dinner in the House Dining Room with Tom, and here's Grassley with his glasses down on his nose and his nose pressed against the window. He's like one of those small town people who just have to know everything. It was great! He's a romantic. He's always trying to fix people up. Usually it's a terrible mix, but he does think of himself as this giant Cupid. . . . If somebody's single on his staff, and he thinks it's past time they get cooking, he tries to maneuver. It doesn't work, though, so he shouldn't give up his job and go into full-time matchmaking."

Pete Conroy, a former aide and long-time friend, recounts a favorite story that illustrates Grassley's constant, laserlike focus on his state and its people. "Charlton Heston came into the office one day, and the women were going bananas. He used Betty Burger's phone, and she said she'd never wash it again, all that stuff. Well, Chuck looked at the schedule that day and he said, 'Charlton Heston. Heston.' Everybody said, 'You should know who he is!' Chuck thought a moment, and said, 'Heston. He's the coach at Mason City High School.' *Bob* Heston was the football coach at Mason City. So, you understand, he didn't know who Charlton Heston was, but he sure as heck knew there was a Heston he knew in Iowa. I tell you, that's out of the blue, but if you don't know anything else about him, it's that kind of linkage that tells you he's always thinking of Iowa."

Yet, there is so much of Grassley that isn't seen, or seen very often, anyway.

Doctoral student in political science, on the road to a college professorship when he was elected to his first legislative term.

Astute strategist.

World traveler.

Human rights activist on behalf of Soviet refuseniks.

This is the other Grassley. Charles Grassley.

Shrewd. Cagey. Tenacious.

The Grassley underestimated time and again by people who prejudge his simple mannerisms, lack of guile, and country twang as proof positive that here is a dull-witted bumpkin, ripe for the picking, in their midst.

The Grassley who wouldn't play ball with his own team, confounding Reagan Administration officials to the point that White House political adviser Ed Rollins once sputtered, "I wish that son-of-a-bitchin' Grassley would die."

The Grassley who, deliberately or not, deflected intense heat off himself and onto his Iowa colleague, Roger Jepsen, during the 1981 vote on the sale of Airborne Warning and Control Systems (AWACS) radar planes to Saudi Arabia, a controversy that proved to be a political disaster for Jepsen.

"I think he's a lot like President Truman was," Sen. Arlen Specter, a Pennsylvania Republican, said. "He has a very uncommon common sense."

In part, Grassley's qualities remain unappreciated by the general public merely because he chooses not to flaunt them. John Maxwell, a political consultant and former aide said, "To him, it's not what you've done, it's who you are. And those things are not as important to him as they are to other people. He doesn't make a big deal about stressing those things. He doesn't have to prove to anybody that he's well-educated."

Mike Schreuers, a Des Moines creative consultant who produced advertising for Grassley's first and some subsequent campaigns, said, "I don't know any better way, probably, to define somebody than to say they do what they promise they'll do, and there are times when he can step out and be the roaring, booming voice of the heartland, and there are other times when he's just the quiet, gentle, hard-working example of the heartland. In a lot of senses, Chuck Grassley represents the best of us, but you have to look beyond the surface to see it."

Those who have worked for Charles Grassley—and many who have worked against him—come equipped with their own personal stories about how he wins out in the end by allowing himself to temporarily lose the constant image game that drives so many politicians and their agents.

"He's a complex guy. He's plain spoken, so in that sense, what you see is what you get. The complexity is in his actions and his interests," said Ally Milder, an attorney on Grassley's Judiciary subcommittee staff for seven years before returning to Nebraska in 1987 to run for Congress. "Grassley goes on gut feeling. His gut feeling is right because it's the gut feeling of Iowa. How to take that feeling and turn it into legislation or positions on issues is where his head comes in. The White House would call him down to talk and try to pressure him, first with carrots, then sticks. It just rolled off him. 'You don't want to come to my state, fine, that's OK with me.' He wouldn't turn down an accolade from them, but he certainly wouldn't go solicit them, and sometimes he very much enjoyed seeing them squirm. You'd say, 'The White House has this position, and they'd like you to do that,' and he'd look up and say, 'So?'"

In Milder's two congressional races, Grassley "gave me more help than I had a right to expect. He has a real sense of loyalty. He works hard on keeping people and takes it personally if you leave. I think he has a sense of defeat if you leave."

Loyalty begets loyalty.

Grassley's Senate office, by all accounts, rates high on the list of fun, rewarding places to work. Frequently on the agenda are lunches, breakfasts, or parties for staffers with birthdays or for other special occasions. There have even been "non-retirement" parties for two long-time, valued employees. In return, employees are expected to be as oblivious to the time clock as their workaholic boss whose demand from them is satisfied constituents. "We were always the envy of the other staffs," Milder said. "They would come up after the executive committee meeting and say, 'What's it like to work for Grassley, he seems so nice.' There's no air of importance about him. He doesn't think he's more important than anyone else, and that comes across."

She recalled one particular act of kindness that occurred when Grassley traveled to Israel. "He planted a tree for one of Senator [Howell] Heflin's staffers, Arthur Briskman. Arthur had helped him, and we'd worked on a lot of legislation together, and Senator Grassley just wanted to do something for him. He planted the tree and had a picture taken with a sign saying it was Arthur's tree. Arthur still has the picture on his wall. You can't fake stuff like that when you do it all the time. It's a genuine warmth and sincerity and caring about people."

Neither staff nor colleagues can recall a single incident in which Grassley has blown his top. In fact, he used to instruct close friend and former aide Pete Conroy not to visit with some groups. "He told me, 'I don't want you talking to the bankers because they know you don't like them. They can tell.' That's the thing you notice about Chuck. He never shows any anger. They can't read that he's antagonistic to them or anything else. That's an unbelievable asset."

Milder did see tears of sadness in Grassley's eyes during a 1983 trip to Moscow as he listened to Russian dissidents talk about religious persecution. "I could see he was thinking, 'What if it was me and I couldn't worship God in my way, or if I did my children would suffer.' To me, it's hard to become involved in issues and fight for them unless there's a strong emotional connection, and I saw that with him. Not only on human rights, but the attitude he has about protection of taxpayers when you're talking about $900 Allen wrenches. The emotion that generates is anger, but he doesn't necessarily show it. People may not think he's a very emotional guy, but he is."

Her connection between religion and fiscal responsibility was not casually tossed out. Besides a consuming conservatism instilled as a youngster—by a father who said United Mine Workers of America President John L. Lewis and war-time strikers should be shot for treason—Grassley got a dose of old-fashioned Baptist fervor from his mother.

If there is a wellspring of strength in Charles Grassley, it is in a set of religious values quietly practiced each day. His straightlaced code of personal conduct seems always to steer him clear of the rocky shoals of alcohol, affairs, and avarice that have battered and destroyed so many political careers.

Conroy, over more than 20 years, has never heard Grassley say anything in private that he would be ashamed to say in public. "The thing about Chuck not drinking is that I've never seen him or heard him look down his nose at people drinking. . . . Never. Never once," Conroy said. "It was at Protivin one year, I think; we were in a parade and this drunk came up and was hanging on him. Chuck's marching in the parade, doesn't look down his nose at the guy, tries to engage him in conversation. He never says afterward anything adverse about it."

John Maxwell, a political consultant and former aide, said, "He has a strong, real faith. He's answering to a higher purpose than himself, which causes him to be selfless in the things he does. He also has somewhat of a fatalistic attitude, that kind of

14

'what will be will be.' From that standpoint, he sometimes doesn't worry about the consequences, that if he's doing what's right it's all going to be the way God intended it in the end. I think Grassley does an exemplary job of living his life as Jesus taught people to live by His own example. Jesus taught not to be judgmental. Many people who are Christians don't follow that."

Charles Grassley is never far from a Bible, whether in his office, his private hideaway in the Capitol, Room S-140, his car or his home. There is no proselytizing or glazed-eyed sermonizing, but aides and associates are not uncomfortable talking about religion. For his own part, Grassley said he tends to "be a little more low-key about what I believe. Even though I'm more open than most people, I don't want to be so dogmatic. If there is a proper opening, I think I would talk very freely. . . . It's not something I would discuss because I think you have to be very diplomatic about this stuff, because if you're not diplomatic you can turn people off, and it's not for me to bring discredit to the gospel of Jesus Christ. . . . I suppose my decision making is more guided by private reflections on my religious convictions, and they're essentially guideposts for me, but they aren't entirely black-and-white."

He recalls a 1981 visit to Tel Aviv in which he discussed the Scriptures and the Biblical boundaries of Israel with Prime Minister Menachem Begin. Israel opposed the sale of sophisticated AWACS planes to Saudi Arabia; Grassley ultimately voted in favor of the deal. "There's a general admonition in the Old Testament that says, in effect, those who bless Israel will be blessed, and those who curse Israel will be cursed. In a general way, if you look at the history of mankind for 2,000 years or longer, I'm not so sure you can't see that. That's not a dogmatic expression of my support for Israel, but at least it's a starting point. It's a consideration—it's not a ruling consideration—but from a behavorial standpoint, it's a way to approach some of these issues."

Specifically, Grassley's spiritual philosophy is not based simply on the Bible, but on the interlocking foundations of four scriptural passages that manifest his deep reflection.

For all have sinned, and come short of the glory of God. (Rom. 3:23)

For God so loved the world, that He gave His only begotten Son, that whosoever believeth in Him should not perish, but have everlasting life." (John 3:16)

Now then we are ambassadors for Christ, as though God did beseech *you* by us: we pray *you* in Christ's stead, be ye reconciled to God. (2 Cor. 5:20)

If my people, which are called by my name, shall humble themselves, and pray, and seek my face, and turn from their wicked ways; then will I hear from heaven, and will forgive their sin, and will heal their land. (2 Chron. 7:14)

"I think they're pretty tied together," Grassley reflected. "I would say it this way: First of all, every individual who [may believe] in the eternity of the soul has to be impressed with the fact nobody's perfect except Christ. If you didn't come to the realization that everybody's born with the burden of sin to be forgiven, you're in no position to believe in Jesus Christ and the shedding of His blood. Man's not perfect. Jesus Christ is the plan of God for personal salvation, for renewal of life and forgiveness of sin. For a person just concerned about self and eternal salvation and their relationship with God, that would probably take care of it, but God had a plan going back to Abraham and Israel. They were chosen from Abraham and David through Mary for the birth of Jesus Christ. So as God had a plan for His own people, the Israelites, to provide for His own people, it can't end with your own personal salvation. You have a responsibility to carry the message to others, the message of love for your fellow man and woman. There's a Greek word for it, *agape* love, a deep sincere interest in the welfare of fellow men and women, even more so, an intense concern about men and women in relationship to Christ, but also in personal, social needs, even to the extent of helping people who have basic needs of food.

"You do that by being an ambassador. In the political world, an ambassador is a lifelike representative of the strange people in another country. It's the same way in the Christian world, you're supposed to be a lifelike representative of Christ. That's impossible, but you're supposed to try to be a lifelike representative of Christ to people outside of Christ. That's a spiritual representative."

Regarding America, he added that he did not necessarily believe God worked with nations as a whole. "But I believe the United States has been an especially blessed nation, the economic wealth. Are we going to use the freedoms we have and that economic wealth to spread the gospel of *agape* love? I think that it's important that a nation think in terms of how it's been blessed, and if it's out of fellowship, get in fellowship. That's not something I'd have the government dictate."

With gentle prodding, he took aim at that cornerstone of American etiquette that dictates politics and religion are two of the three subjects that should not be discussed in polite circles. "How stupid! We ought to want to, and force ourselves to talk about religion and politics all the time because there's no two subjects that have more influence, or ought to have more influence, on our lives. We ought to be able to do it without being emotional or confrontational. We should be able to do it in a spirit of brotherhood. It's idiotic and stupid, that rule in society. People hide themselves and they pride themselves on that, and I think, 'How ignorant.'"

Despite his knowledge of the Scriptures and personal relationship with Christ, the only other profession Grassley ever considered outside of public service was as a professor of political science. "I never thought about being a minister. I don't think even to this day I'd be happy as a full-time minister or even as a part-time minister. I'm just not very good at writing," he said, modestly. "I've got five sermons, which means I can't go back to the same church more than five times. I don't think I would want to give 52 sermons a year."

He has, however, allowed aides and even *Des Moines Register* political reporter David Yepsen to accompany him to churches where he spoke from the pulpit. "There's more than one pastor in Iowa who thinks his church is Grassley's second church," Conroy smiled, realizing the political benefit. "It's nothing done deliberately or with mischievous intent; Chuck just shows up at the church."

His faith, however, prompted one colleague, former Senate Judiciary Committee chairman Joseph Biden of Delaware, to suggest that "Chuck is not a Barry Goldwater conservative. My impression working with him all these years is that Chuck is sort of a morals-based conservative. Remember Barry Goldwater's quote about [evangelist] Jerry Falwell? Goldwater said,

'Somebody should give Jerry Falwell a swift kick in the ass. He's not going to tell me what I have to believe.' That's true conservatism. It means government should stay out of people's hair."

Grassley's political credentials, however, received the seal of approval from none other than Mr. Conservative himself, former Sen. Barry Goldwater, who wrote, "I would always call him a Conservative. I don't base Conservatism on whether a man is conservative in the fiscal field, but I pay a lot of attention to what he thinks, and how he reacts to our Constitution, and his beliefs. I hold him in great respect."[1]

Grassley's list of favorite writers—John Stuart Mill, John Locke, Alexis de Tocqueville, Plato, and Dante—reflect more than his love of history. The common thread is a belief in individual freedom and meritocracy, the lifting up of the lower-middle class against the upper classes that control the marketplace.

Mike Schreuers draws an analogy to another conservative, former Housing and Urban Development secretary Jack Kemp, in his attempt to define Grassley. "They're both always pushing to the edge in terms of understanding a situation and not just pushing for velocity or frequency of impact. It's like 'what's the real issue here? What is the essence? How do I get as close as possible?' The two are a lot alike, which as much as anything says to me there is a successful profile of a politician out there. That almost sounds dirty to say it that way, but Chuck Grassley has so many of the inherent qualities that should be in the model of a political representative. Those qualities are honesty, integrity, hard work, belief in responsive government, not just the code words of a history class type of thing. He really believes them."

In Grassley's mind, government doesn't need to be big to be responsive. Schreuers said, "He believes he is the representative, the way it was designed to be, that if somebody needs a voice he is their voice. I heard somebody say he's a lot like a patriot, like Patrick Henry, 'Give me liberty or give me death.' That's the extreme example of how America was represented for greatness. Chuck Grassley brings some of those same kinds of qualities.

"We haven't faced the same kinds of issues being faced at that time, but all you have to do is take a look at the Persian Gulf situation. Clearly, he went against the trend and the tide on that one, and he did it simply and purely as a matter of conscience. He went out and visited with common ordinary people, saw the stress and strain and torment they were going through, and he said, 'Is this war something worthy of our men, our boys, to lose their lives over?' He made the call based on that. I doubt that very many of our elected officials anguished over that the way Chuck did."

The product of his upbringing, Grassley proved early on to have the formula to keep himself humble. Schreuers said, "He's the kind of a guy that doesn't want good news. 'Tell me something I can work on. What are we not doing well?' I guess that's how he keeps his head on straight. He seeks out and genuinely encourages that critical view."

Sen. Phil Gramm, a Texas Republican, said Grassley was better at "keeping his ear to the ground in his home state than anybody" in the Senate. "He works at it, for one thing, he comes back home. He listens to people. He is constantly working on Iowa problems. He keeps his focus on things that are important to Iowa."

Tim Raftis, a Capitol Hill lobbyist and former Iowa Democratic operative, also chalks up Grassley's longevity in part to that unique ability to keep his finger on the pulse of Iowa. "If a charge is made that he votes against funding for senior citizens, not only has he done 20 forums with senior citizens, but he's done his mailings and he's helped gain funding for some specific programs," Raftis said. "It's the localized Charles Grassley that's remembered instead of the voting record out here. That's the testimony to his own political smarts. After 35 years in politics, you either refine those abilities and capacities in forward planning or you perish."

Grassley has proven in four primary contests and 14 general elections, spanning from the end of the 1950s to the late 1990s, that he is not the kind of politician to perish by a mistake of his own making.

# Growing Up in New Hartford

Louis A. Grassley was around 18 years old when he stepped off the train from Michigan City, Indiana, in 1910 and started a new life in Ackley, a Hardin County town surrounded by rich, black earth and prospering farms. It was not his first trip to central Iowa.

His father, who had come to America from Germany, died when Louis was seven years old. The boy's mother, Bertha, made ends meet by taking in boarders and serving meals to railroadmen. She remarried seven years later, and Louis' relationship with his new stepfather, Gottlieb Herzog, was strained from the beginning. Soon, Louis received his mother's permission to spend the summer with his half-sister Anna, one of two daughters from their father's first marriage, which ended when his wife died.

Anna, married and with the last name Fitzgerald, had offered to help Louis find a job when he decided to settle in Iowa. Employment was secured with Henry Heitland, who had a bustling brood of nine children and operated one of the most successful farms in the area. Fitzgerald and the Heitland family met Louis at the train depot. The young man, who had no knowledge of or experience in farming, quickly settled into a routine and began what would prove to be more than the average employer-employee relationship. He worked long and hard, and those first days and weeks quickly gave way to months, and then years, on the Heitland farm.

In Louis' sixth year with the Heitlands, a young woman named Ruth Corwin arrived on the nearby farm of her aunt and uncle, Mame and Otis Nicholas, who had a friendly rivalry with the Heitland family. Ruth was born in Grundy County on November 17, 1897, to George and Italene Corwin. Italene's unique first name was chosen by her mother from a storybook character. Sometimes her father farmed near New Hartford in neighboring Butler County. At other times, the family lived in nearby Cedar Falls, located to the east in Black Hawk County, and he worked for the city. Ruth, who had skipped fifth grade because she was ahead of her peers, attended the Iowa State Teachers College in Cedar Falls. It was her job as the new teacher at a little country school near Ackley that took her to the Nicholas farm.

Exactly how Louis Grassley met Ruth Corwin, and details of their courtship, are gone from memory 75 years later, but it is likely that the friendship of the Heitland and Nicholas clans was instrumental. What is known is that Louis and Ruth married on June 8, 1918, most likely at Ruth's parents' Cedar Falls home. Of Ruth Corwin Grassley's independence, Bunny Grassley Wiegmann noted years later, "When I got married, my mother said to me, 'Don't have *obey* in your marriage ceremony because I didn't. I did not raise you to obey any man.'"

Louis shipped out for the U.S. Army and World War I just six weeks later. Ruth, with her new last name, returned to Ackley to teach, a rarity considering teachers were expected to be single young women in those days. However, she gave up that career about one year later when Louis came home from the fighting in France.

They farmed for several years just west of Cedar Falls on a plot of land along Jepsen Road. Ruth showed a strong-willed, civic-minded streak as she became one of the first four women in Iowa, and perhaps the nation, to vote in a special election shortly after the 19th Amendment was ratified, according to the August 20, 1920, edition of the *Sunday Times Tribune* of Waterloo.

Her first pregnancy was a difficult one, and she stayed with her parents in their home at Sixth and Iowa Streets in Cedar Falls for the final month. There were grave doubts that mother or baby would survive, but on January 9, 1923, a daughter, Genevieve, was born. "When I was born, my grandmother said, 'Isn't she such a sweet honey bunny?' It just stuck," Bunny Wiegmann explained 71 years later.

By 1926, the family was living on a rented farmstead a few miles north of New Hartford, a typical small town with a couple of churches, a school, a grocery, a tavern, a few stores, and a grain elevator that sits along the railroad tracks on the south side of town. On November 28, 1926, Louis A. Grassley, Jr. was born. He was nicknamed "Bud."

In March 1927, the Grassleys bought their own plot of rich, black land and home four miles northeast of New Hartford. "They were paying on it during the Depression. I would say that was the only real debt they had. They never bought anything unless they could pay for it. Dad would go to a sale to buy horses and my mother would get so nervous because he had made up his mind he was going to spend probably $100 back in those days,

$50 each for a team of horses, and if they'd go for $55 he wouldn't buy them. I remember Mother said, 'Louis, it's getting into March; we've got to get them.'"

The white, two-story farmhouse near New Hartford with no electricity or indoor plumbing was the birthplace of their third child. Dr. Dyre Pelletier, with Ruth's mother assisting, delivered the boy at 10:30 p.m. on September 17, 1933. "Bud and I went to bed. He was in one room upstairs, I was in the other, and we never knew about it 'til the next morning Dad told us we had a baby brother. He said, 'What would you like to name him?' See, he already knew. He said, 'What about Charles Ernest?' We didn't care."

She added playfully, "We had our own lives. Bud was big for his age, seven, and I was almost 11. Then we had this brat around. He was kind of a cute kid. Mother thought he was the greatest."

Louis Grassley had chosen the name of his younger brother, Charles, the only other offspring from his father's marriage to Bertha. The baby's middle name was the first name of Ruth's sister's husband. Two more Grassley children were born after Chuck—Lois on May 10, 1937, and Eugene on December 11, 1940.

Bunny Wiegmann recalled a good life when reflecting on the little white farmhouse during the 1930s. "That house wasn't very old; the original one had burned down. Mother had really nice furniture, nice drapes. Mother taught school, you know, and used that money to buy furniture. She instilled in us to have a nice home. She said, 'Have it while your kids are growing up so they know they can take care of it.'"

During this period, Louis Grassley remained in contact with the Heitland family. The Grassleys traveled to Ackley in the summer, with the men going off to visit in the great big summer kitchen away from the house, and the women and children going indoors. Wiegmann remembered thinking the Heitlands "had it all" with their big farm. "They were really like Dad's family. He was always close to his mother, but never had the money to go back to Michigan City that much. He only went out a couple times, and Grandma only came here twice."

Wiegmann wondered years later how romance ever did blossom between her folks. "Dad wasn't a very affectionate person. I mean, he never showed it. I suppose they met because she was a school teacher, and he thought he was getting a pretty good catch."

Once a year or so, Louis would pull out an old suitcase filled with souvenirs from his service in Europe. "It was always kind of intriguing to Bud and me. I don't think he talked to Chuck about it. He always wrote home about being in Paris and Notre Dame and stuff. In 1972, the New Hartford Women's Club had a trip to England and France, and I said, 'Why not go, Mom?' Well, she didn't want to go alone, she said, even though she knew the women in the club. So, Ed and I went with her. When she saw Notre Dame, she said, 'What I really wanted to do, I've done now.' I suppose Dad writing home about that really impressed her."

Even in the midst of the Depression, the family scratched out a good living, if for no other reason than the parents' penny-pinching talents. Louis refused to use a corn-shelling machine like many of his neighbors, Wiegmann said, "because it might crack a shell." In 1936, Louis Grassley traded in his old Model T Ford and paid cash for a brand new Chevrolet. He drove to Michigan City that year to see his mother; she died two years later without seeing him again.

Throughout this era, Ruth and the children attended the First Baptist Church in New Hartford. "I never thought he was a religious man. We got our religious upbringing from my mother. I mean, she was strong," Wiegmann said. "Dad would take us to Sunday school, but he'd go down to the garage and I had the idea that dads didn't go to Sunday school when I was a little girl. But he would always take us in, and she saw to it that we were in there for Sunday school and he probably would go in for the Christmas program. My mother, that's where Chuck got his upbringing, that he knew it was important that we go to church and that we were Christians. I won't say we didn't miss because in the country the roads would be so darned muddy. There were lots of times we didn't go to Sunday school because of those conditions. But we always had Bible stories at home. I look back now and see how some people always had devotions and all that. We never had that, but we just knew that there was a Supreme Being."

Ruth Grassley's strict Baptist background dictated that there was never a drop of liquor in her house. Louis Grassley spent some time down at the tavern in New Hartford, "but Dad never drank a drop," Wiegmann insisted. "He was the shuffleboard scorekeeper. Nobody kept score as good as Louis did because he was fair."

When the first government programs came around, Louis and Ruth Grassley passed. "They didn't believe in government subsidizing you, and I remember when I went to school that next spring, the kids were all talking about their dads got this amount and that amount and they said to me, 'How much did your folks get?' I said they didn't get anything. And they said, 'Oh, they had to; they never told you.'"

Bunny went home, rattled off the names of the children whose parents had received government checks and asked her mother how much their family received. Her mother replied, "Your Dad and I talked that over and decided we weren't going to go into that because we didn't want the government telling us what to do."

However, Louis Grassley did try to encourage his neighbors, to no avail, to sign up for rural electrification. "So they went and bought their own electric plant, and we had the battery down in the basement. Every week you had to run that motor, and my dad, he had no patience if it didn't start right away. I remember [the repairman] said to my mother, 'Ruth, there's no use of calling me out here. Now let me show you how to do it.' So my mother took care of that because Dad would go down there and he had probably flooded it or something." When the rest of the neighbors finally decided to connect to the power grid, Louis Grassley still had his 32-watt Delco battery. In true fashion, he made certain he had run the batteries dry before getting rid of them.

Ruth Grassley was instrumental in starting the local library and volunteered there part-time for four years. She also served as president of the New Hartford PTA for two years. "She thought that was long enough, but they said they missed her because she always had a program, always had a one-act play to bring out what you should learn in school," Wiegmann recalled.

She was president of the American Legion Auxiliary for a few years, and also made time to throw parties on such occasions as the retirement of the local physician and mail carrier. For the doctor's party, Wiegmann said, "She took our living room carpet [to the town hall] because she wanted the place to look nice."

As if raising a family, volunteering for civic projects, and helping out with the farming business weren't enough, Mrs. Grassley also ran her own upholstery business out of their home, which had its beginnings in the Depression. "Our furniture wore out. It was tapestry, and she found out she could turn it and the

24

underside was just as pretty as new," Wiegmann said. "She did it so cheap. I'd say to her, 'Why don't you charge a little more? You'll make just as much and you won't be so busy.' She said, 'Yeah, but I won't be pleasing as many people.' In fact, the day Dad died, we couldn't hardly get his body out because she had so many people's davenports there, and she had to call them to come get them."

When her mother died in May 1974, two New Hartford women told Wiegmann of the respect that Ruth Grassley commanded. "They said, 'You know, when Mrs. Grassley spoke, we all sat up and listened because she didn't say anything unless she knew that it was important.' That's the first time in my whole life that I ever thought that my mother was maybe really somebody. I guess we were raised to be humble. I never ever thought that my folks were anything more than farmers."

Nor would her younger brother's lofty public position ever change her view of him. "I've just never seen him as anything but plain old Chuck," said Wiegmann, who watched her brother in the early years while Ruth helped her husband milk the cows and pick corn by hand. Even as a youngster, Grassley was "really a serious person," his sister recalled. "There's really not much to tell you that was funny about him. When he was about three years old, he spent an awful lot of time underneath the cookstove in the kitchen, playing with the cats. And he used to train these cats. Then he'd have them riding on his tricycle, and he could have them hanging by one leg on the handlebar, and my mother would say, 'You know, he's real smart because you can't train cats.' Those cats, I don't know if they were afraid of him or what, but he had them so trained. And my mother would always say if anybody came, 'You've got to remember he's awfully smart because he can train those cats.'"

As the young Grassley grew, he soon developed his own, strong-headed way of doing things. "You can't *believe* how particular Chuck is. But he gets that from my dad. My dad was so fussy. We were never allowed to help him with the separator—separating cream and the milk, you know—because we weren't able to move that pail quick enough so a drop wouldn't hit the [floor]. Because in the summer it would draw flies.

"Chuck had this little farm—this little barn and silo and all that—set up in the corner of the living room. This was when he was about eight. Gene, who was like one year or so, he'd always want to play with that, and Chuck didn't want him messing it up. Then my sister was in between, and Chuck wrote up a contract, and Lois could write her name so she had to sign it, and Gene could only make an X because he was only a little kid. They signed that contract that they could share his toys, but they couldn't mess up anything. It had to be correct, just like it was, so how much was there to play with?" Wiegmann laughed.

"We got home from school about a quarter to four. Mother said the minute they could see the top of that bus coming up over the hill, Gene would go in there and mess up that barn, and my mother would have to go in there and get it all straightened out because the first place that Chuck would come was there to see that that was all right. That kind of proves what kind of perfectionist he was. If you ever want to know how my dad looked, look at Chuck. Except Dad had curly black hair, and Chuck usually has a little wave in his hair. But he's got more of my mother's personality than my dad's because my dad is more like me. We have no patience, and my mother always kind of had the patience of Job."

The result: a rare bird, indeed; a perfectionist with patience. Despite his own perfectionist streak, Louis Grassley saw to it that his offspring had plenty of chores to do around the farm. No matter how much work he did, Charles grew up, not out, and became a loose-limbed, gawky kid. That's when a magazine ad introduced him to the Charles Atlas bodybuilding course. "He would have been about 14, and I remember one morning I was home—I'd already moved to Pennsylvania but I was back visiting for a couple months—and we kept hollering for him to come down because the bus would be coming. He didn't come down, and he didn't come down. Then he came down," Wiegmann chuckled, hunched over to imitate the pained youngster. "He'd been [bodybuilding]!"

When Chuck came home from school that day, he was still stooped and aching. "We never had any more [bodybuilding]," Wiegmann laughed again. "Another thing, when he was around 14 or 15, he built a two-acre golf course. I tell you that thing was manicured! And all the neighbor kids could come and play, but he had to supervise them. It seemed like he always wanted to do what was impossible. He expects an awful lot of himself. Both my mom and dad expected a lot of us. [Years later], when someone asked me how Chuck could really stand alone and go against Bush on Desert Storm, I said it wouldn't have been hard for him because we stood alone a lot in school if it was the way we believed."

Grassley had, however, an intense aversion to the unpleasant reality of death, which brought immeasurable sorrow to his family between 1950 and 1960. He was 17, just home from the state boys' basketball tournament in Iowa City, when he was told that his mother's mother had died while he was gone. Wiegmann recalled, "We were all up to my folks and he said, 'If you're going to talk about Grandma, then you leave. I'm not going to talk about it.' And my mother said, 'We *are* going to talk about it, Chuck, and if anybody's going to leave, you are.' She wasn't driving him out, but she was going to make it plain to him we were going to talk about it. Then he wasn't going to go to the funeral, so my husband went and talked to his good friends and said, 'You can sit with the mourners, but see that Chuck gets there.' And those two fellows in particular told Chuck, 'We're going to the funeral, and it would be terrible if you weren't there.'"

Tragedy struck again just after noon on August 6, 1955, when Charles' older brother, Louis A. "Bud" Grassley, Jr. was killed instantly when the car he was riding in collided with a semitrailer three miles southwest of New Hartford. The World War II veteran left behind a wife, Margaret, and three young children. Chuck, who had been married a year, again resisted going to the funeral home. "He never came over at night at the viewing. And Bud was so popular, oh was he popular! And everyone would say, 'Where's Chuck?' Well, we couldn't say he wasn't coming,'" Wiegmann said.

She recalled Grassley's young wife, Barbara, urging him to attend. "She said, 'How the heck is it going to look if I come to the funeral and you don't?' So he came, and three people he worked with at Rath [Packing Company] went through, and that's when he broke down. He said, if they cared enough to come he should be there, too. Well, five years later, my dad died, and we went through the same thing with Chuck. He died at home, very, very suddenly. . . . My mother said to him, 'Chuck, men do cry.' It's just like a crack in the record to me. 'Chuck, men do cry.'"

Repelled as he was by death, the young Grassley was just as strongly drawn to politics. When Grassley was in fifth grade, he recalled, he had an answer to the age-old question, What do you want to be when you grow up? "I'd say, 'a politician.' I don't even mean I had my eyes on running for office. The only thing I can relate it to is our family. My folks were never politicians. My mother was a schoolteacher back when you only had to go to a couple of summer schools at Iowa State Teachers College to be a teacher. Well, she taught in a rural school, and so I always figured my mother was well-educated. And I thought my dad, even though he wasn't well-educated, sure had a lot of opinions because he always read the paper. Anyway, my folks were always talking about what I'd say were public issues.

"It seemed to me in my home we were always talking about government. Probably government was doing something wrong. My dad used to think how bad it was that John L. Lewis could strike in wartime, that they ought to shoot him because it was so unpatriotic to strike. And he thought it was awful when Roosevelt didn't let Patton get to Berlin before Russia. See, this was World War II stuff, but this is about the time I was in fifth grade. So I wanted to be a politician, but why, I can't tell you. From that point on it's just sort of been that I just studied a lot about government."

The first family proclamation about presidential politics that stuck in Grassley's mind decades later was the day after Franklin Roosevelt's election to an unprecedented third term. "His name was there in the paper and my brother commented on it, and I remember my folks thinking he shouldn't have run for a third term," said Grassley, who had, by then, followed a bit of that 1944 campaign between FDR and Thomas Dewey.

Grassley seemed well on his way toward a political career by the time he reached New Hartford High School. He told his baseball coach, Robert Formanek, that he was going to run for a seat in the Iowa Legislature just as soon as he turned 21. It was during high school that he met Erma Plaehn, who later became one of his professors at Iowa State Teachers College, later renamed the University of Northern Iowa, in Cedar Falls. "She came around to our high school recruiting students. I don't think professors do that any more, but I told her I was interested in majoring in political science, and she remembered when I finally went to [ISTC]. Even though she was a Democrat, she encouraged me to study politics and to run for office."

New Hartford High was also where Grassley cut his first political deal. He had been class president in his freshman and junior years and treasurer as a sophomore. To follow in his brother's footsteps, he wanted desperately to serve as senior class president. Eva Kay Norton stood in his way. "Yeah, I did cut a deal with Eva Kay and Gladys Grandon. We sat at the restaurant in

New Hartford. It's a tavern now but it was called the Home Cafe, and we decided how she would back me for president if I'd back her for some office. So, I didn't have any competition."

Another classmate, Jack Hovelson, remembers Grassley had his sights set higher than the Statehouse. Hovelson, who went on to become a reporter for the *Waterloo Courier* and the *Des Moines Register*, recalled, "A bunch of us guys were sitting around talking about what we were going to do when we grew up. I would've been in tenth grade, and he would have been in ninth grade. One guy said he wanted to farm. I said I wanted to play newspapers. Someone said something else. And Chuck said, 'You guys will laugh at me, but I want to be President.' He was right. We laughed at him. But, he's in a pretty select group. The son of a gun has gotten a lot farther than anyone supposed."

Grassley scoffed at the memory. "I tell him that's a figment of his imagination. I never remember that."

Hovelson retorted, "He keeps saying I made it up, but I didn't. He said it."

Grassley and Hovelson got along well, though they weren't close chums. Hovelson was a year ahead of Grassley, and he had something the younger boy dearly wanted. "He was a first baseman, and I was a first baseman, and I had to wait until I was a senior to play, to get him out of there. I always tell him the reason he was able to play is because he was the son of the principal," Grassley laughed.

Hovelson had heard that joke before. According to him, he was the starter because he was better, though not necessarily a Stan Musial in the making. "Chuck was never a great athlete, never did play basketball [the school's only other sport]. He was kind of gangly, not the most coordinated kid, but he worked hard at it, and he tried. I taught him how to play first base, so when I graduated, he got to play one year."

On one occasion, Hovelson was delivering newspapers, and Grassley offered to help. Hovelson said he'd heard Grassley could name all the presidents in order and challenged Grassley to do it. "He didn't think I could, but I did," Grassley said proudly. Hovelson noted that Ruth Grassley was the great influence on her son in his early years. "Chuck and his mother go together—hard working, no drinking. She's the one that drilled the presidents thing into him, tutored him, got him interested in those things. Chuck was all business. He studied. He was just different. He wasn't a sissy, but he was serious about studying."

All the while, the desire to enter politics grew stronger still, though Grassley was unsure exactly what motivated him beyond the vague idea of public service. "You don't know what you think when you're 17 years old. For all I know, it could have been the color of it, because at that age I can't say that I was motivated by this law to pass or that law to pass. I don't ever feel in my own mind it was a desire for power. I never associated necessarily being somebody or being a powerful individual with being in office."

Chuck Grassley left New Hartford High School as valedictorian of the tiny Class of 1951 and headed for political science studies at the Iowa State Teachers College, enamored that back-to-back state representatives had hailed from his little hometown. "We had a guy named H. A. Moore elected in '44. He served for eight years. Then he retired and Wayne Ballhagen was elected. Here I was in high school with all these state representatives from New Hartford, so if they could be in the state legislature, maybe I thought I could be."

# W. W. Ballhagen, J. W. Lynes, and the Iowa Legislature

An aspiring young politician from small-town Iowa couldn't have asked for better role models than H. A. Moore and Wayne Ballhagen.

Moore, born in 1882, had deep Iowa roots as the son of early pioneers in Wright County. Educated at the Iowa State Teachers College, he taught school in Black Hawk County and was superintendent in Dike and Black Hawk County. He was a Mason, Rotarian, and Methodist Church trustee. The distinguished, bespectacled fellow served four terms in the Iowa House before retiring.

A New Hartford native, Ballhagen had owned and operated the local general store for 13 years and operated a farm for 10 years when he was elected to his first term in 1952. Though 31 years younger than Moore, he had his own distinguished look about him. Both he and his predecessor wore their Farm Bureau memberships like political badges of honor; Grassley would later carry on that tradition.

Winning election into the Legislature wasn't as easy as Moore and Ballhagen had made it look to a hometown high school boy. Getting past Ballhagen in the Republican primary was the first hurdle for the gangly, 22-year-old Grassley. The incumbent, who also faced a challenge from Gertrude Stockdale of Aplington, proved to be an insurmountable obstacle in 1956.

Stockdale had lost to Ballhagen in 1952, when the seat was vacated by Moore, and was defeated in a 1954 rematch. She was ready to give it a third try at the urging of her friend, state Sen. J. Kendall "Buster" Lynes, a Republican who "did not like his House counterpart," Grassley recalled. If Lynes had encouraged Stockdale, it seems logical that he must have especially disliked Ballhagen's legislative style, because a former colleague recalled that the traditionalist Lynes didn't fancy the idea of female lawmakers.

By Grassley's own account, he did not run the type of leave-nothing-to-chance campaign that would become his political trademark in the 1980s and 1990s. "I didn't campaign in her corner of the county, around Aplington, and she carried real heavily there, and I came in third. I made a mistake by not going down there. I maybe wouldn't have gotten any votes away from her, but I would have gotten votes away from him. I ignored it because she was so strong there," he said.

There weren't many issues in the race—typical for those days, he recalled—but his main selling point was completely out of character with his "just plain ol' Chuck" image in later years. "Oddly enough, I was espousing this business that I'd studied political science and had a master's degree in political science at UNI, which I don't think is a very smart way to run a campaign, and I wouldn't do it today," he said in May 1994.

"But it was really about the only thing I had. I had an office job at Rath's that was outside the county, so you didn't want to talk about that much. So here I was, this New Hartford boy that was trying to make good, and he'd gone to college and gotten a master's degree and wanted to tell you how to run your government." He added with a laugh, "It was kind of an elitist sort of thing to do."

His strength, though, was in the retail end of politicking; he had taken his two weeks of vacation and spent them going door to door. The others did not.

On Election Day, June 4, 1956, Grassley beat Ballhagen by better than 3-to-1 in their hometown. But it wasn't enough. The final tally: Ballhagen–1,124, Grassley–1,043, Stockdale–842.[1] It would be 24 hours before Grassley learned he had come so close. The Grassleys didn't have a telephone, and he went to work in Waterloo the next day not knowing, and not especially worried, about the election. "I stayed home. I don't know why, if I didn't think I had a chance to win or maybe I didn't know people gathered at the courthouse. That kind of shows a little bit of stupidity about the system, doesn't it? When I got off work, the Waterloo paper was out and somebody said, 'You almost did it. You ought to really feel proud of yourself.'" Grassley laughed loudly, delighted with the image he saw in his mind, and savored the words. "You almost did it," he repeated.

His sister Bunny Wiegmann noted, "He only lost by so few that a lot of people wanted him to run as an independent. He said, 'No, I won't. I lost, and I lost.'"

But Grassley had caught the eye of Buster Lynes, who complimented the young, defeated candidate at the party's state convention. "You did pretty doggone good. Now don't give up," Grassley remembers Lynes telling him.

Life went on for Charles Grassley. He worked at Rath until February 1957, when he quit to go to the University of Iowa to earn a doctorate. He shared the basement of 707 River Street in Iowa City with several other students, paying $17 a month for rent and commuting home on Friday afternoons and back on Monday mornings for one year. In the meantime, he moved his family to another farmhouse owned by Cedar Falls Bank & Trust president John Kyhl.

"If there's ever key events in your life, I remember that I came back from the University of Iowa on the Wednesday before Thanksgiving of '57, before I was going to run in the spring of '58, and I knew I just had to go over and see Buster Lynes," Grassley said.

He set out that evening for Lynes' rural Plainfield dairy farm without directions and drove around the area until he was ready to give up. "All of a sudden I saw this moustache—he had a moustache, you know—peer out the curtains, looking at this car going down the road. I saw him so I went back. If I had gone home, I maybe wouldn't have ever gone back."

The two men visited for several hours, with Lynes dispensing advice and Grassley absorbing it like a sponge. "He never did say, 'I'll help you,' but he said, 'These are the things you need to do. You need to go over and talk to Gomer Evans, the newspaper man at Clarksville, because he's a key person. You need to go talk to Clyde Fruden. You need to talk to this guy and that guy. Go do it before you ever announce.' Over the next several months, I went around and saw all those people, then I took the spring semester off from the University of Iowa to be home, at least, to campaign."

In a 1958 primary rematch with Ballhagen, Grassley did not campaign door-to-door. Instead, he got a list of 1956 voters and wrote to them. "And, I kind of rode, as I look back on it now, on the laurels of the '56 campaign, but in the meantime then I had Buster Lynes' help. He still didn't like the guy that was in, or maybe he considered him a threat, so I'm pretty sure without ever telling me that Buster kind of passed the word around that Grassley's all right."

Aside from the letter-writing campaign, Grassley insisted that he "sat around a lot," most likely because he felt certain his second run at Ballhagen was destined to succeed. "I went to the courthouse and just as I was getting up there, Ballhagen was walking out and said, 'It looks like you beat me,'" remembered Grassley, who won the June 4 primary by 200 votes.

He returned to the University of Iowa for summer classes and came back home in the fall to campaign. The general election was a breeze. Grassley defeated one of his cousins, Travis C. Moffitt, a Shell Rock Democrat, 3,021 to 1,690.[2]

The representative-elect had earned 42 hours toward his Ph.D., but would not return to take his comprehensives or write his dissertation, "Reorganization of the Administrative Branch of the State Government of Iowa."

Grassley's most vivid recollection of his first day in the House as a 25-year-old freshman was that "I was the youngest member and that everybody wanted to take pictures of the youngest member. I look back on them and how ugly I was."

He had a got-the-world-by-the-tail confidence of a recent graduate student who felt like he knew all there was to know about government. The mood was bolstered by some friendships he had developed through Buster Lynes and Clarence Christophel, a 48-year-old Republican who operated a 240-acre livestock farm three miles west of Waverly on Highway 3. Christophel had the right credentials—Wartburg College graduate, Farm Bureau member, Chamber of Commerce, Lions Club—and he had a legislative lineage. His father had served in the House during the 41st and 42nd General Assemblies and the Senate in the 43rd and 44th.

In the 1959 session, Grassley offered an amendment to strike from the Iowa Constitution references to the secretary of state, treasurer, attorney general, auditor, and secretary of agriculture, so all of the offices would become appointive rather than elective. "This is the political scientist, the egghead, you know. It really got all the conservative Republicans mad at me," Grassley said later. "I had a lot more to learn, but I think I thought I was in the middle of it. As I look back, I see that I wasn't as aggressive as you have to be to be a successful legislator. I don't really think I knew how to legislate, even though I had studied all this and wanted to do it."

Enter Buster Lynes again.

When Grassley won election to the Third Congressional District years later, he became identified with the legendary staunch fiscal conservative he succeeded, H. R. Gross of Waterloo. But Grassley's real political mentor was Lynes, who was, by all accounts, a big bull of a man with a reputation for getting things done. The *Cedar Rapids Gazette*, at the time of his death, noted that when people first saw "this big, gruff fellow with the cereal bowl haircut and the Charlie

Chaplin moustache, you wondered whether he had just stepped out of a modern comic strip or was one of the original Keystone Cops. But if you stayed around a while—and it didn't take long—you soon discovered he was no blundering bull in a political china shop. You learned, rather, that he was one of the shrewdest, sharpest, most skillful floor parliamentarians and backstage string-pullers ever to grace the hallowed halls of the Iowa senate."[3]

Lynes had been Senate president *pro tempore* in 1959, and was majority leader in 1961, when the General Assembly only convened every other year. His brother, William, was a state representative who rose to Speaker of the House.

Attempting to make a newcomer understand his love for Iowa, Buster Lynes once pointed toward the Statehouse and said the building represented the state. "It is big, solid and isn't going to change very fast, but it will always be there steady as a rock," he said.[4]

Lynes might as well have been describing himself.

"He was a shrewd cookie," remembers Robert Rigler, a former Republican state senator from New Hampton. "Buster was pretty gruff, had no time for female legislators and no need to have open meetings or that nonsense, as he called it. No new ideas, hell, the place ran well the way he ran it, he thought."

During one debate, a Republican senator from Davenport named Jack Schroeder rose to ask Lynes to explain a particular piece of legislation. "Buster said, 'I don't have to, I've got the votes.' That's the way he usually operated," Rigler recalled with a fond chuckle. "He was honorable, tough, not an eloquent orator, but he didn't have to be because he had the votes."

Around northern Bremer and southern Chickasaw counties, the road between Highway 63 and Lynes' hometown of Plainfield was known as "Buster's Boulevard" because he was the man who had the clout to get it paved.

Rigler ran for the Iowa Senate in 1954 with the goal of getting another road paved, the one that ran past the famed Little Brown Church near Nashua, and would later become Highway 346. Rigler's effort to hard-surface the road was a window into Buster Lynes' hard-nosed legislative style.

Once elected, Rigler, who later served as the chairman of the Iowa Transportation Commission, approached Lynes about the best way to get the project funded. Lynes advised Rigler to get himself on the Senate Appropriations Committee and then the three-man subcommittee that handled highway spending. Lynes also had his contacts with the Iowa Highway Commission in Ames. "Buster knew how to do it because he'd done it before," Rigler said. It looked like his road project was wired for success. Then came the nomination of Luke Caffrey of rural Cresco to the Highway Commission. In those days, road proponents were divided into two camps: the asphalt men and the concrete men. The concrete lobby tended to contribute to Republicans; the asphalt to Democrats.

Lynes, opposed to the Caffrey nomination, closed the Senate chamber for debate. "Kicked everyone out, had guards at the doors, and we had a written ballot. I voted for confirmation," Rigler recalled. "How the hell Buster knew I don't know, but he came over and told me, 'Rigler, if you want your Little Brown Church road paved, you'd better vote against Caffrey or we'll never forget it.' That's the way Buster played, pretty hard ball." Fortunately for Rigler, the GOP floor leader, state Senator Duane Dewel of Algona, intervened. "He said to Buster, 'You can't pick on these young freshman senators.' But I took Buster's advice, got myself on the Appropriations Committee, worked a couple years with the Highway Commission, and we got it done."

Lynes, Rigler recalled, was also a "real tooter" for Grassley.

"Chuck was in the House, of course. He was about the same then, a big country boy, naive as hell. Not nearly as naive as the image he projected, but he was pretty damned naive," Rigler said. "He was considered Buster's boy. We used to snicker when Grassley came over to talk to Buster, figured Buster was giving Chuck his marching orders." But, that was only so much insider teasing. "Chuck had good common sense, had a good mind. Buster got him off to a good start, but Chuck grew as a legislator. He was never a stooge for Buster; there were a few guys who were, but he had a mind of his own," Rigler recalled. "He stayed pretty conservative, but he stayed his own man. Like any successful politician, his time in the Legislature was a good learning experience. He never did become a dynamic leader, but he always knew what was going on."

C. Joseph Coleman, a Clare Democrat who served in the Iowa Senate from 1957 to 1991, described Lynes' leadership style succinctly: "heavy-handed."

Imitating Lynes' deep, gruff voice, Coleman said, "'What do you want to argue with me for? I've got the votes.' Senator George O'Malley used to call him Papa Bear. Buster was a spokesman for the Farm Bureau, and the Farm Bureau wielded a lot of power in the Legislature at that time."

Only 10 of the Senate's 50 members were Democrats, but Coleman said they played a pivotal role because the Lynes-led rural conservatives and GOP moderates were split just about down the middle in the late 1950s. "The Republicans had to court the Democrats to get their ideas across," Coleman recalled. "I got along very well with Buster Lynes even though I was a Democrat, and he was a Republican and a Republican leader. He just seemed to take a liking to me. He knew if I thought his proposals were fair and reasonable I would ride in there and support him."

Coleman recalled one occasion in which the blustery Lynes was none too happy with his young protégé. "Buster came back over from the House and said, 'I'd like to pour some lead in his boots.' I don't remember exactly what it was about, but I think Buster thought Grassley was his representative, and he was going to do whatever Buster said in the House. He thought he was going to control Grassley, and Grassley had different ideas."

Grassley recollected only one run-in with Lynes, but couldn't remember the bone of contention. "I remember I was on a certain side of the fence, and he came over to the House to tell me I was wrong. The Farm Bureau used to keep records of people's votes, and I remember one year I had a voting record of 20 out of 20 votes. They said we were 'the guys with 20–20 vision,' so at least on those issues Buster and I didn't disagree. So I can't remember what issue Buster would have felt that strong about."

What he did remember 35 years later were the lessons learned from Lynes. "He taught me to be tough and honest and gave me the admonition that alcohol and politics don't mix. You're more in control of yourself, more alert the next day."

With inspirational teachers it is often easy to overlook the contributions of the student. While Buster Lynes undoubtedly was a crafty politician and parliamentarian willing to share his knowledge, Grassley proved an eager, able, and determined student of the art and science of Iowa politics and government.

Buster Lynes was 59 when he died of a heart attack in his sleep at his farm home on May 5, 1962. He had served 22 years in the Iowa Senate. Gertrude Stockdale drove down from Aplington to break the news to Grassley, who was at his mother's telephoneless home. "This guy was just a hunk of a man, 250 pounds, all muscle, you never figured he was going to die," Grassley said.

"I felt bad. My mother knew I felt bad. He was probably the only politician who died that I cried at his funeral."

Grassley, his name already on the primary ballot for his third House term, sought to succeed his dear friend and political mentor, but he ran into an ambush at the special nominating convention in Waverly. "I just found out how many enemies I had," Grassley lamented years later. He was defeated 23–6 under rules that had been adopted to force his supporters within the Butler County delegation to vote as a bloc under instructions from leadership. Lynes' brother, Bill, was responsible for all six Grassley votes from neighboring Bremer County. Vernon Kyhl of Parkersburg, John Kyhl's nephew, got the other five Bremer County votes, and won everything in Butler and Franklin counties.

It boiled down to one issue. "I was against liquor by the drink, and he was for liquor by the drink," Grassley said. "I would have won on the issue in the primary, but the country club Republicans controlled the convention. The guy that steamrolled the convention was Herman Faber, so I couldn't get the votes.

"See, liquor by the drink was going to be the salvation of the economy in Iowa, just like gambling today," Grassley, a teetotaler, said in 1994. "I suppose the argument was people would drink more, that you'd collect revenue on what they were clandestinely drinking in the key clubs, then you'd have more control. And I still remember the argument: if you opened a bottle you didn't have to finish it." Grassley easily won his third term in November 1962, beating Garner 3,017 to 1,672.[5] Harold Hughes, a Democratic truck driver and reformed alcoholic, won the governorship in part because he favored liquor by the drink.

Two House Republican colleagues, Floyd P. Edgington, Sr. of Franklin County and Henry W. Busch of Waverly, became Grassley's new sounding boards in 1963. Edgington, born in early 1899, had been a livestock farmer since 1920 and a hybrid corn seed grower since 1938. He was serving his sixth House term. Busch, who had served 15 months overseas with the 103rd Infantry Division during World War II, was serving his first term. Grassley also whiled away some evenings visiting with a state senator from Worth County named Leo Elthon. He had been lieutenant governor on November 21, 1954, when Governor William Beardsley was killed in a traffic accident north of Des Moines. Elthon served the final two months of Beardsley's term. "I felt he was my tie to past legislative history," Grassley observed.

He had other contacts. After backing the wrong candidate for Speaker of the House in 1959, he was on the winning side in 1961 with Henry C. Nelson, a Winnebago County farm manager and real estate broker, and later with Robert Naden, a Webster City electronic scoreboard maker.

On the recommendation of Clarence Christophel, Grassley took a room at the Brown Hotel during the 1959 and 1961 sessions. As always, there was a practical consideration. "I had a chance to get someone to share the rent," Grassley declared. That someone was state Rep. Fred M. Jarvis, an Alta Republican who was almost 61 when he won his second term in 1958 by just 73 votes. An Iowa Department of Agriculture employee from 1939 to 1953, he had been a grain and livestock farmer since 1954, sold real estate, and worked at a car dealership in Schaller.

"They were dredging Storm Lake at the time. It was only 18 inches deep because of siltation, and his sole goal was to get $50,000 to keep the dredge going. He played poker every night with key legislators to keep in touch and keep them satisfied. He had to keep in touch with the Appropriations chairman," Grassley said. "I never thought much of gambling."

Grassley adjusted surprisingly well to life without Buster in the 1963 session. "I didn't think that would be possible, but I kind of had to then start standing on my own."

He did it by continuing to speak out against liquor by the drink. What he won was passage of the state's implied consent law, which states that any drunk driving suspect refusing to submit to a blood alcohol test automatically loses his or her license.

"I sponsored that in '61, but didn't get it passed. With Dave Stanley's help, I got it on the liquor by the drink bill in '63. It had all the liquor by the drink people mad, but I use that [today] to prove I was able to legislate when I didn't have Buster around and I had to do it on my own," Grassley recounted.

The local "country club Republicans" may not have been pleased with his opposition to liquor by the drink, but no one challenged Grassley in the 1964 primary. He had time to actively campaign for the party's presidential nominee, Barry Goldwater.

It would have been just another worry-free general election for Grassley, in his district with a 3-to-1 Republican advantage, had it not been for Goldwater's ill-fated campaign against Lyndon Johnson. "I was teaching an adult education course at Denver High School the night of the Goldwater debacle, and as I was driving over to the courthouse later that night, I was hearing all these reports about all these legislators that lost. The thought came to me, it didn't seem possible, but I began to think I could lose."

Grassley defeated Travis Moffitt's wife, Beverly, 3,884 to 2,498, but Democrats were swept into control of the Iowa House by a 101–23 margin.

Francis Messerly, a Finchford Republican and Grassley friend serving his first Senate term, recalled, "It was no fun. The Democrats controlled every office in the Statehouse and both the House and Senate. The opposition's responsibility is to keep the majority honest, and I worked hard at that. I read all the damned bills and tried to amend them to make some sense. [Grassley] was good at that, too. The little guy had a lot of intestinal fortitude at that time. He wasn't afraid to speak out."

Grassley's involvement in abolishing capital punishment, which started in 1963, continued during the 1965 session. "I went back through all the executions in Iowa. The executions were carried out, except in one instance, on the governor's predilection to commute or not to commute based on his personal [view of capital punishment]. So it wasn't really the judge or jury that was deciding you should hang, it was the governor. So I used the statement on the floor of the House, I don't know if it was ever quoted in the papers, but I said, 'We're either going to hang them all or none of 'em. Since we aren't going to hang 'em all, we shouldn't hang any of 'em.' So I kind of argued it on the unfairness of it, the checkered use of it."

After the 1966 elections, the balance of power was restored for Republicans as their House numbers swelled to 90. Grassley was just beginning to feel that his presence was making a difference, but he remained, by his own estimation, an "awful poor speech giver."

"I didn't give so many speeches. Quite frankly, I think it was a lack of ideas. I remember when I really felt like I was an effective legislator. You'd speak occasionally and there'd always be a buzz when you speak. Then later on in my legislative career when you stand up to speak it was quiet. People'd listen to what you were saying. That would have been about the last six years."

At the Martin Hotel on the northwest corner of Third and Locust, where he'd been staying during each session since 1963, Grassley found a new friend in LaVerne Schroeder, a McClelland Republican, who entered the House in 1967. "We kind of had the same ideas, straightforward on stuff," Schroeder recalled.

In Schroeder's eyes, Grassley had a simple philosophy: "Just document your material and be straightforward. He gave everybody the benefit of the doubt as far as trust. He felt anyone who got elected to the House or Senate had to have integrity and be straightforward and honest. We probably had a few people who probably weren't straightforward and honest and tried to take advantage of Chuck, but they didn't prevail."

Grassley was, Schroeder remembered, all business all the time. "There'd be several new legislators stop over for an hour or two some nights" to seek Grassley's counsel. "We weren't in the crowd that went out drinking. Sometimes you were viewed as an outsider, and that didn't matter to us."

During the 1960s, Grassley often ate dinner at a Chinese restaurant, King Ying Low, at 223 Fourth Street. "It was close and cheap," Grassley said. "I ate their pork loin with dressing. I didn't eat the Chinese stuff; I'm an American."

He also found his way down to the Bishop's Buffet near the *Des Moines Register* building at Eighth and Locust, and the Bolton and Hay restaurant within walking distance of the Brown and Martin hotels. "I suppose there were a lot of greasy spoons I ate at, too."

In the early '70s, he'd eat now and then at the Latin King which, at Hubbell and University, was fairly close to the Capitol. Grassley and a few colleagues would go late in the evening when they planned on returning to the Statehouse to work even later. Walking distance was important to Grassley because he didn't have his own car in Des Moines very often, if at all, until his last few sessions.

"If I wandered too far I had to have someone give me a ride because I wasn't going to pay for a taxi," Grassley said.

In the early years, Grassley hitched a ride to the Capitol with Christophel or drove Lynes' car while the Senator slept. Between 1963 and 1971, Grassley rode along with Messerly. Messerly lived just inside Black Hawk County about four miles from Grassley's farm. Grassley chipped in for gasoline. Messerly recalled how they ran out of fuel more than once between Des Moines and home and coasted into the nearest farmhouse to borrow enough to get them back on their way. "He used to say, 'Why didn't you fill the tank?' And I said, 'Hell, you only gave me three dollars a week!'" Messerly said.

In 1973, Grassley drove his own vehicle to and from Des Moines, a 1972 Chevrolet pickup truck. In true Grassley style, the vehicle is still in the family, registered in his son Robin's name and still running, more than two decades later.

He had given serious thought in 1967 to a bid for lieutenant governor, laying the ground work and making contacts that fall and into early spring 1968. "I thought there was a real good chance to do it. All of a sudden out of the clear blue sky comes a guy by the name of Roger Jepsen. Just two years in the state Senate, and he's going to run for lieutenant governor," Grassley said. "So I got cold feet, and I just made up my mind since he was going to appeal to conservatives and me with rural support, I wouldn't have much of a chance. So I just gave up."

By 1969, Grassley was chairman of the House Education Committee, which had been the Schools Committee in past years. He would become chairman of the Appropriations Education Subcommittee in 1971. "It used to be we'd only have the university presidents [appear before the subcommittee]. I got vice presidents and deans in there, and everybody was nervous. The presidents were nervous some dean would tell me something they didn't want us to know."

Lobbyist F. Richard Thornton said Grassley was still "a little bit country, but very perceptive, very thorough. They always wanted him on the conference committees. He was an educational whiz."

"Charlie," as Thornton and others from that period in Grassley's life knew him, was "always in it for the 'everyman.' He never had an agenda, he just did what was right. He always took time in the off-year to stay in touch with things and get ready for the next year. You never caught him off-guard, could never trick or trap him. He was always thinking about an hour ahead of you, and he had the capacity to retain just about everything he was involved in."

Arthur Small, an Iowa City Democrat serving his first term as a state representative, recalled the mood during the 1969 session when Grassley and other Republicans cut spending for the universities. "There's no question there was sort of a general climate of opinion in the air amongst legislators that they were turned off by the behavior of some students who were protesting the [Vietnam] war, and they were certainly not going to reward them."

Messerly said, "I was chairman of the Senate Appropriations Committee when I noticed at the universities they were burning draft cards and holding parades saying, 'Hell no, we won't go.' I became quite upset and used my position to make it clear that the people of Iowa owned those universities and were paying 76 percent of the cost of those students going there, and we expected those students to show some respect for this country."

Grassley felt the same way, according to Messerly. "He and I, when we'd ride, we'd discuss these things. We went to the university a number of times to get them to calm things down and recognize their obligation to democracy. I made a lot of speeches down in Iowa City, also met with the Board of Regents, and so did Chuck. We met with the law enforcement people down there, too. We were quite upset about it. I had a son who was a Marine serving in Vietnam, and that didn't calm my nerves any. I think we did, through our efforts, muster some public support for our position, and the public came to the conclusion that at least there were people against [the protests]."

At the second year of the 1970 to 1971 session, reapportionment was especially cruel to Grassley. Incumbents' districts are often drawn so that they do not face another incumbent or, so that they at least represent most of any new district that is reshaped by the 10-year census and shifting population. Instead, he was thrown in with Luvern Kehe, a Waverly Republican and construction company president who had the benefit of already representing the new district's population base. Grassley thought, "How can I compete against a big town like Waverly?"

With the primary delayed until August by a protracted redistricting battle, he had plenty of time to think. "Barbara said, 'Well, you ought to go down fighting.' And I talked to some other friends that had always supported me, and they kind of said the same thing, that I might as well try it. I did, and I did OK. I got 900 votes to 150 for him in Butler County, and I carried his county. I even carried Waverly."

For the first time since 1958, Grassley had been forced to put together a real campaign. He recruited comanagers, state Jaycees president Bill Schuldt, and attorney Gene Shepard from the heart of Kehe territory. Kehe, Grassley concluded, was "a good legislator from my standpoint, a conservative person. He was kind of hardnosed, but he just didn't work very hard [in the primary campaign]."

Grassley aggressively pursued public forums and raised what was considered a great deal of money for a campaign that year—$1,800. "I spent about $1,000, but still that was more than I'd spent in all my other races put together. I would say quite candidly I called on a lot of my friends in the lobby in Des Moines to get money. It was before PACs—they probably got their individuals to give it to me—but it was a sort of a thing I just very blatantly went to people that I worked with and had a philosophy like theirs and said, 'Well, I helped you, now I need some help.'"

The general election in the Republican-dominated district was much easier for Grassley, who rolled over Tim Youngblood, a Waverly Democrat and Wartburg College senior. Grassley returned to Des Moines with more clout, becoming Appropriations Committee chairman in 1973 just as a young Leland Republican and Drake University law student named Terry Branstad began his first House term. The two men already knew each other from a meeting at the University of Iowa. Branstad, an undergraduate, was at his first College Republicans meeting when he met Grassley, the group's guest speaker.

By 1973, Branstad said, "I was on Chuck's team. He was the Appropriations Committee chairman and we got together at Bishop's Buffet in downtown Des Moines. He had a whole group of conservative Republicans and Democrats, people like Adrian Brinck from West Point and Dutch Wyckoff from Vinton, Kenny Miller from Independence. Then he had all these people like Vern Harvey. And he had the subcommittee chairs on Appropriations give us presentations so we'd support it. He put together a whole team of people that supported him on holding the line on spending."

As is the case in politics, not everyone was "on the team." In fact, Grassley didn't have the cooperation of some members in his own party. "I always say the first money I really saved the taxpayers was in 1973 when I was chairman of the Appropriations Committee and Governor Ray recommended appropriating $220 million to the State Board of Regents. We passed a bill through the House for $195 million. Art Neu got the bill through the Senate at $220 million instead of at $230 million. We went to conference, and I got that bill out of committee for $205 million, so I figured I saved the taxpayers $15 million. Usually in those days, for the Board of Regents it wasn't whether you were going to get the governor's recommendation; it was how much more. They were that powerful. The Appropriations subcommittee was usually made up of people from Black Hawk, Story, and Johnson [the three university counties]. When I got to be chairman of the

Appropriations Committee [who appointed subcommittee members], I made up my mind we were not going to have anybody from those three counties on there, so we didn't."

That budget skirmish wouldn't be the last one, and friction developed between Grassley and third-term Republican Gov. Robert Ray. The Senate did Ray's budget bidding. "Even though we had a Republican House and Senate, as much as we cut the budget, the Senate would increase it," Branstad laughed.

Grassley also joined in a lawsuit against Ray over his use of the governor's line-item veto authority. In the end, Grassley considers the implied consent law his greatest accomplishment in the Iowa Legislature.

While he remains proud of fiscal accomplishments, such as maintaining the state's rainy day fund and saving $15 million tax dollars by refusing to rubber-stamp the Regents budget, he also takes pride in other reforms, such as a 1969 bill that put the responsibility on local districts to see that all children, particularly those with developmental disabilities, were adequately educated.

When he was House Appropriations Committee chairman, he worked to form area education agencies (AEAs) at the suggestion of Helen Henderson, a former Waterloo woman who started the Iowa Association of Retarded Children, which later became the Association for Retarded Citizens.

He felt motivated by the antiquated county school system and its shortcomings in educating children with handicaps. "I was not necessarily a pioneer in accepting all the things she and her organization thought government should do. It was a combination of need and leadership responsibility that led me to it," Grassley recalled.

The original scheme was to develop a kindergarten through grade 14 concept with the community colleges as a service organization for special education, some nonclassroom services, and "enhancer courses" for high school students. He coaxed the idea through the House, despite support from only several community colleges. The AEAs, though, became stand-alone entities later, bothering the bureaucracy-averse Grassley.

He collaborated with House Speaker Maurice Baringer, Senator George O'Malley, and the president of the state employees union, Ed Moses, who worked at the old Iowa Highway Commission, to draft and enact the Merit Employment System legislation that would replace the old patronage system. And Grassley noted his subcommittee work that set up the Iowa Law Enforcement Academy.

Even as he listed these accomplishments, Grassley discounted his role. "Even if I hadn't helped, the AEAs would have eventually been created; if I hadn't gotten implied consent, eventually it would have been passed; and the Supreme Court said we had to have a better-trained police force. These things would have happened anyway."

Twenty years after he left the Iowa House, some of Grassley's actions are still fresh in his memory. During a May 1994 interview with a Maquoketa radio reporter, Grassley was asked about the death penalty issue in the GOP primary between Governor Terry Branstad and his challenger, Representative Fred Grandy. "I support the reinstitution of the death penalty, and I suppose I'm one of the reasons Iowa doesn't have the death penalty today," Grassley said, sounding as if he were in the confessional, "because in the 1960s I suppose I was soft-hearted or something. I not only voted to do away with the death penalty, I spoke for doing away with the death penalty as a member of the House of Representatives. I look back now and say that that was one of the mistakes I made in my career in politics, thinking the death penalty should be done away with."

It wasn't the only mistake Grassley believes he made; he also regrets voting to allow no-fault divorces. "It's a way of avoiding individual responsibility. That's what is wrong with American society today."

The '60s and early '70s were an era when Iowa lawmakers had little of the support staff and bipartisan Legislative Fiscal Bureau and Legislative Service Bureau expertise. "Maybe you could get Legislative Research to write a bill, but you wrote most bills, did your own research, wrote your own speeches, and wrote your own amendments. If you accomplished anything, you knew *you* did it," Grassley said, almost wistful. "You didn't accomplish it with a bunch of staff. Now, Congress doesn't accomplish anything without staff."

However nostalgic he may have been for the ways of the Iowa House, it was the United States House of Representatives that became his focus by mid-1973.

# College, Work, and Family

Charles Grassley built up a family of his own at a young age.

Still living at home to save money, Grassley was a history student at Iowa State Teachers College in Cedar Falls by day and a billing department employee at Rath Packing Company by night. In American Government class, Grassley struck up a friendship with a big, gregarious football player named Bob Molinaro, who later became a successful Waterloo trucking executive. "I obviously liked the kid," Molinaro said. "He told me right off, 'I'm going to be a politician.' There was no doubt in his mind what he wanted to do. He regarded it as an honorable profession, and I think he still does."

Molinaro described Grassley as "just a young kid, rawboned, honest. . . . You could see the honesty in him, and the sparkle. You talked to him, and God, it took him five minutes to say anything. You just kind of liked the farmer attitude in him. We'd go out at noon, almost every noon. We'd go to mostly drive-ins. We had a lunch deal," Molinaro laughed. "I'd buy the hamburgers, and Chuck would eat them."

Like Grassley, Molinaro was working nights. He was dispatcher for the then-fledgling Warren Transport Company. Grassley would join him, and the two would spend hours talking about politics and government. "Chuck loved to talk about politics. Loved it."

One night, a bruised and battered young man walked into Molinaro's office. It was Grassley, beaten by a couple of campus bullies after he had suggested they should take back something offensive they'd said several young women he didn't even know. "He was defending the young ladies' honor," Molinaro smiled. "Those guys did a number on him, really bad. Both eyes were black, his face was all puffed up, he couldn't talk. He came to solicit my aid to go find those guys. We went out and drove around, but we never did find them. And I don't think Chuck wanted to find them! He was not a fighter."

Molinaro was also there when Grassley took another drubbing—at the polls. He ran for class president and finished third in the four-candidate field. Grassley's explanation: "I was working at Rath, didn't live on campus, and didn't have time to campaign. And I didn't run a very smart campaign, to be perfectly honest. But mostly, I suppose, it was not being around enough."

Molinaro worked for that campaign and marveled at his friend's gumption. He also arranged a date for one of his cousins and Grassley. "They went out a few times. He was very shy, very, very shy. I just had to have the whole thing arranged."

Grassley, a tall, rail-thin young man with black wavy hair and blue eyes, had remained active in his church and vigilant against the evils of alcohol as preached by Ruth Grassley and the Baptist doctrine. "It's pretty hard, biblically, to say in black-and-white it's wrong, to drink, but most evangelical churches have had some kind of their own positions," he said 40 years later. "It used to be pasted in the front of the hymnal, and of the things you believed as a Baptist, one was to not drink. It's not there now."

He also had the lasting impression of being in New Hartford with his mother on Wednesday nights, open-air movie night in the empty lot next to where the library now stands. He could remember her pointing out a drunk creating a nuisance after being kicked out of the tavern. "She said, 'They take your money, and when you get drunk they don't want anything to do with you, and they throw you out.'"

One conclusion advanced, more implicitly than explicitly by those who disagree with Grassley's political philosophy, is that he is a naive, stuck-in-the-Fifties, Ozzie Nelson family man who understands nothing of real families or modern society because of his sheltered, straightlaced upbringing. Such inaccurate assumptions, though somewhat understandable, fail to scratch the surface of Charles Grassley. Yet, he does not argue against those suggestions because he possesses a rare trait among public officials: he refuses to hold up every detail of his family life to public poking and prodding for his own political gain.

Grassley met his future wife in December 1953 in, of all places, a bar in the Russell Lamson Building in Waterloo. He had not suddenly rebelled, but was merely following a cousin and a friend, who had met a couple of local "girls" a few days earlier. The young women wouldn't agree to a second date unless the young men found a date for their friend, Barbara Ann Speicher. Grassley recalled, "It was all a group event, but it was within a few days I called her on the phone. So, there was something there, I don't know what it was, but it was not love at first sight. From our early dating, I doubt I dated anyone else. I think she continued in those early months to date other people, to my chagrin."

The location of their first meeting, though an amusing anecdote, is not the main point. Barbara, who had come to Waterloo as a secretary at Rath Packing Company, was, in 1990s vernacular, the head of a single-parent household. She had married right after high school, given birth to a son, and divorced. Her parents looked after the child during the week while she worked.

Those experiences, though quite personal and never flaunted before the electorate for political expedience, demonstrate that Grassley has an intimate connection with this generation's wave of "non-traditional families" (and give his publicly aired concerns about divorce a level of authority) that his liberal critics have neither recognized nor appreciated.

Grassley drove a blue '52 Chevy coupe between college, work, and the family farm near New Hartford. Because of his second-shift job in the billing department at Rath, they only dated on Wednesday and Sunday evenings. "We'd go to movies and stuff like that, but he was busy. We never did much," said Barbara, who by then was working at the Continental Bread Company. "We were kind of sticks in the mud, and still are."

If their temperaments were the same, so, too, were their early years.

She was born on October 21, 1932, at her grandparents' home in Sumner, a small town in Bremer County. Her birth had hardly been routine; the umbilical cord was wrapped around her neck and stopped her breathing. Fortunately, she was in the able hands of Dr. W. L. Whitmire, who delivered her and restored her breathing.

Barbara's father, Earl Speicher, descended from the Pennsylvania Dutch. He was a plumber at the time of his marriage in 1931 to Verla Haag, of German lineage. He had an eighth-grade education. She had attended a junior college in Minneapolis. (A remarkable similarity to Grassley's own parents.)

The family moved to the first of several farms in the Fredericksburg area when Barbara, the oldest of five children, was in second grade. She received her elementary school education in several one-room rural schools. Eventually the family moved to a farm just south of Lawler, and Barbara graduated as Chickasaw County's eighth-grade valedictorian. She was closer to the high school in Lawler, but her mother believed she would have more opportunities in New Hampton. From 1946 until her 1950 graduation, Barbara spent week nights in a boardinghouse for school girls. "I didn't do too much in extracurricular, like basketball. I was very uncoordinated. Still am," she laughed in

August 1994. "But they had things like history club. I did that. Latin club. The school newspaper. I worked on that. The *Annual* staff." She had also taken the business course that led to her secretarial job at Rath.

Four decades later, neither Barbara nor Charles Grassley can recall the details of his marriage proposal, except to say that they had talked it over. Barbara quit her job at Continental, began attending morning classes at Iowa State Teachers College, and worked afternoons at a local mortgage company.

They were married August 22, 1954, in the Little Brown Church in the Vale near Nashua. Barbara had misjudged the travel time involved and was late for her own wedding. The best man was delayed by a flat tire.

She would wait a long time to receive a diamond engagement ring. "We were very poor when we got married and just got our wedding bands," she said. "When we were married 30 years, I got a diamond. He ordered it from a friend in the jewelry business and had it sent to the house. I opened it because I didn't know what it was. He was so disappointed, but he didn't tell me the package was coming and don't open it. I couldn't believe it! It was worth waiting for."

After a honeymoon to South Dakota's Black Hills, they settled into a house owned by his grandmother and aunt at 724 State Street in Cedar Falls. Grassley adopted Barbara's son, Lee, and cared for the boy as his own from the start.

Her family always called Barbara's husband "Grassley" out of practicality rather than aloofness or animosity; the names "Charles" and "Chuck" were already taken by her younger brother.

The Grassleys attended First Baptist Church because it was just a few blocks away. Barbara's family had belonged to the Church of the Brethren, one of the historic peace churches, but she was comfortable among the Baptists. During her four years of high school, Barbara went to the Baptist Church for one hour during the week instead of study hall and received one-eighth of a credit for her effort.

Grassley worked the second shift at Rath from 1951 until he graduated in March 1956 with a master's degree in history from Iowa State Teachers College. Then he worked days until February 1957, when he started at the University of Iowa.

Bob Ostrem, Grassley's supervisor, recalled that his employee occasionally had a hard time juggling the responsibilities of work, study, and family. "I don't know if you could do it, but I sure couldn't," Ostrem marveled. Still, Grassley was more than competent in his nightly duty of tallying the price of individual packages of meat destined for shipping to various parts of the country. "He could handle his own, and he did. It makes it so much easier on the supervisor if you don't have to worry about whether [an employee] knows anything or not. You just tell him what you want."

The job was repetitious, but a Rath job at the sprawling factory on the banks of the Cedar River was considered choice employment in the Waterloo area. Even then, Ostrem said, co-workers were aware that Grassley's life revolved around politics. "I don't know what did it, but we knew he was a Republican, too. And some of those guys he worked with just loved to tease him about it."

They lived in Cedar Falls until March 1956, when, to establish residency for his first run for the Iowa House, they rented a farm with no running water less than a mile west of where he was born and his folks lived. "I carried water and heated it on a kerosene stove. It was not wonderful," Barbara understated. "That house was absolutely the coldest!"

The family had grown with the arrival of a daughter, Wendy. Like Lee in 1952 and three siblings who followed her, Wendy was born at Schoitz Hospital in Waterloo. "Wendy was due on March 1 but wasn't born until the 10th, and we were moving on the 15th. When she was born, there was the *worst* blizzard. It took us like two hours to get [to the hospital], and there wasn't anybody else on the road. At the time, New Hartford was in the district [basketball] finals, and we stayed in the parking lot—I don't know how far apart the pains were—and we listened to the last five minutes of the game."

In January 1957, the family moved several miles west of New Hartford to the farmhouse owned by John Kyhl. To Barbara's tremendous relief, running water was a "standard feature."

Grassley, studying in the doctoral program at the University of Iowa, lived in Iowa City during the week and commuted back and forth on weekends for more than a year. Just as he began to put down political roots in Butler County in 1958, Grassley started farming a small piece of the family property. His father wanted to plow up a pasture and told his son that he could raise crops on eight acres if he would remove a fence.

Grassley farmed the same small plot the following year. Concluding that continuing the family's dairy operation was too much work for his already busy schedule, he bought newborn calves and started raising veal. Later, he raised beef cattle.

When his father died in February 1960, Grassley started renting the 80 acres from his mother. He was also working at Universal Hoist in Cedar Falls. The job began in August 1959, but he was laid off in September 1960. He continued to farm the 80 acres until 1965, then more than doubled his operation by purchasing 120 acres.

The family moved into New Hartford in March 1961, and he began a 10-year stint on the assembly line at Waterloo Register Company, where owner Ed Kelly showed a remarkably progressive accommodation to his employee's schedule as a citizen-lawmaker.

In 1964, Grassley had the chance to buy an acreage near his folks' farmstead. The small, old, two-story house was warmed by a gas space heater and the land's price was a bit on the high side. Grassley sought advice from people he respected and paced the floor at night before deciding to buy. Barbara never regretted the decision. "We moved out there just to have a big garden and can [foods] and all those kinds of things. He would buy calves and we would feed them and sell them to people he would work with."

Life was pretty routine for the children, though they didn't see much of their father, what with his work in the fields, factory, and Legislature. "With five children in a farmhouse that size, we had a pretty chaotic place some times. That's probably why one of Father's favorite sayings was, 'This is not a gymnasium,'" recalled Wendy Grassley Speckerman.

The youngsters were drilled on the importance of schoolwork, but there was time to plop down in front of the black-and-white TV or play board games. They also had their chores—mowing the lawn, helping in the garden, or canning foods. Robin, who took up farming as a profession, was helping in the fields by the time he was 12 years old. Grassley wasn't around to see the kids' day-to-day activities, though he usually made it to the boys' Friday night sports events at New Hartford High School.

Speckerman noted that she and her siblings began to relate more to their father as they reached adulthood. "I don't know quite where along the way, whether it was me or whether it was Dad. I think a lot has to do with him being a grandfather, and he's felt a lot more comfortable with his grandchildren and that helps him be more comfortable with his children. And maybe he sees that maybe he didn't spend as much time with us as he should have."

Barbara Grassley echoed those sentiments. "I think the fact he has worn so well, I guess you'd say, with the people of Iowa is because he does work. He gives of himself so much. In the earlier years, it was at the expense of his family. There were a lot of times he wasn't there, but I always was. I think now, and I don't know if he's ever said it, that's one of the things he regrets because I'll tell you, he spends a lot more time with the grandchildren than he did with the children."

After his election to Congress in 1974, with its larger paycheck and greater demands, farming became a way to unwind and keep in spiritual and practical touch with Iowa.

As he spent more and more time in politics, Grassley relied on advice from his wife and sister to size up the people who sought him out. "Bunny can spot a phony a long way off or somebody who's out after him," one friend said. "I've heard her tell Chuck, 'Don't be telling me that, I used to change your diapers.' So, he doesn't push her around, and he doesn't push Barbara around. When it comes to evaluating people, whether it's staff, constituents, or PAC people, Barbara's got her feet on the ground and doesn't pull any punches in telling him what she thinks. Don't underestimate Barbara. She's a smart one, and she'll fool you with her broad range of knowledge. Even when Chuck was in the Legislature and she had her hands full with the kids and all that kind of stuff, she nevertheless knew what was going on."

Barbara decided to complete her college education in the early 1980s, and earned a bachelor's degree from the University of Northern Iowa shortly before her 51st birthday. Even that decision came with a trade-off. "I was thinking about all the neat stuff I was going to be missing out here [in Washington] with the new Republican administration, but I had thought about completing college before, and I never could [because of family obligations]," she said. "I never would have finished out here."

Hired by a Washington lobbying firm, RBC Associates, after college, Barbara Grassley is as straightforward about her feelings as her politician husband. The result, manifested in a spirited argument about the best way to negotiate a Washington road detour, for instance, is something that friends who have shaken the initial shock fondly refer to as "The Chuck and Barbara Show." It is a cathartic give-and-take that ends as quickly as it begins, leaving them emotionally unencumbered as they move on to the next subject.

Mike Schreuers noted that Barbara also provides yet another anchor for her down-to-earth husband were he to let the trappings of the U.S. Senate go to his head. "I remember a conversation with Barbara, and she was talking about how the staff and everybody fawns over these guys and how their heads get out of size. And she said, 'I've got a two-by-four at home, and if he can't get through the door because of the size of his head, I'll bring it down to size.' That's probably part of Chuck's genuineness."

# "The Inflation Fighter"

Grassley's victory in the 1972 primary against Luvern Kehe, with the help of supporters from the "big town of Waverly," seemed to lay to rest Grassley's political inferiority complex that had reared its ugly head in 1968 when Roger Jepsen managed to scare him from the lieutenant governor's race.

Grassley admitted later, "If I'd gone from the easy races I had in the '60s and '70 to go run for Congress, I wouldn't have known how to campaign. So the '72 race, the primary, was a blessing in disguise."

With Kehe vanquished, thoughts of the congressional seat started to creep into Grassley's head even as he campaigned in the fall against his general election opponent. "I was in a parade in Waverly, and Bob Case was in that parade, too. Not as a candidate, but presumably representing H. R. Gross. The point is, he was in the parade and I remember how he called me over to tell me how good I was doing and what a good legislator I was. It was just like, 'you're such a good legislator, just stay there.'"

Grassley added, "We thought in '72 when H. R. Gross opened up a district office for the first time in Waterloo, the first district office he ever had, so that Case could come there, that was it. But he didn't really announce he wasn't going to run until the first week in January [1974]."

Grassley had always had Congress on his mind, according to Bunny Wiegmann, but "he never would have run against H. R. Gross." The former WHO Radio personality was, in Grassley's words, "almost like a god with some of his constituents." Gross, in fact, shared the airwaves for a while with another famous broadcaster-turned-politician, Ronald "Dutch" Reagan. He remained at the Des Moines station when Reagan went off to Hollywood, and was elected to Congress in 1948. He made his reputation as one of the stingiest members ever to serve in the House of Representatives. He also delivered scathing attacks on his opponents and was a parliamentary wizard.

Grassley met Gross for the first time during the 1958 general election as GOP candidates teamed up for a "campaign blitz" of Butler County. "My mother went to this banquet with me in Allison, and she sat across from H. R. Gross and just stared at him. Afterwards, we were going home and I said, 'Why did you stare at him like that?' and she says, 'I always knew him from the radio and this powerful voice, and I just couldn't visualize this little man being H. R. Gross.'"

Chuck and Barbara Grassley invited H. R. and Hazel Gross and Mr. and Mrs. Buster Lynes to their place shortly into Grassley's second legislative term. And, while the young lawmaker had a great deal of respect for Gross, he did not pattern himself after the Congressman in those early years.

It was a different story in 1974. Grassley campaigned as the next generation of the H. R. Gross philosophy. "Once you got elected, you sure felt the need to emulate him. You just had so much respect, he was a tremendously respected guy."

After backing out of the lieutenant governor's race in 1968, Grassley didn't think there were many avenues for advancement for several years. His old pal William Harbor of Henderson was running for lieutenant governor against Art Neu of Carroll in 1972. But by August 1973, as Grassley and a delegation of state legislators visited Washington, the signals were getting stronger that Gross was a lame duck.

Staying at the Quality Inn on New Jersey Avenue, N.W., at the foot of the Capitol, Grassley told fellow representatives Del Stromer of Garner and Andrew Varley of Stuart that he was going to run for Congress. "Andy said to Del, 'You know, I think he's half serious about it.'" The group visited Gross, and thoughts of succession passed through Grassley's mind, but the Iowa delegation was still reeling from Sen. Harold Hughes' surprise announcement that he would not seek another term. Grassley returned home, and if he was going to run for Congress in the 18-county Third District, he sure didn't show it. He didn't begin his campaign in earnest until Gross' formal retirement announcement on January 7, 1974.

State Sen. Charlene Conklin of Waterloo announced her candidacy the next day and was joined in short order by Case, Grassley, Cedar Falls lawyer Barton Schwieger, and Waverly businessman John Williams. State Rep. Stephen Rapp of Waterloo, former Federal Communications Commissioner Nicholas Johnson, Mason City chiropractor Ron Masters, and University of Northern Iowa professor Jim Skaine entered the Democratic primary.

Pete Conroy, who owned a Mason City real estate agency, was one of Grassley's first supporters. "Pete had run against H. R. Gross in the '54 primary," Grassley said. "I don't know why he backed me but, actually, he visited the Legislature one time in 1973 and encouraged me to run."

Yet Grassley would not dish up any tired pretenses about a "ground swell of support" that forced him to submit to the will of the people. "Listen, I ran for Congress because I wanted to run for Congress."

Before too long, Dean Kleckner, a Rudd farmer who was vice president of the Iowa Farm Bureau Federation, called together a group of farm leaders at the White Bear Restaurant in Parkersburg. Grassley recalled, "He said, 'We've got a friend of ours that wants to be in Congress, and I think we ought to get behind him.' I don't remember him being one of those begging me to run for Congress, but he just sort of took charge of that meeting." Kleckner, fellow Farm Bureau leader Bob Furleigh and Chuck Gerk of Clear Lake, along with Conroy, took charge of the all-volunteer campaign, too. Other farmers, like Graydon "Hunk" Anderson of rural Greene, also pitched in.

Gerk, who sold insulation and carpet across northeast Iowa, had made his presence known at Governor's Days in Clear Lake the previous July. "He'd say it loud so everybody would hear, 'Everywhere I go, they're just talking about Chuck Grassley for Congress!'" Grassley said with a laugh. "The guy was just making it up, but over the next year, he'd just keep saying, 'Everywhere I go, they just want Chuck Grassley.'"

Grassley hadn't contacted Furleigh until January to remind him of his previous support. Furleigh, already volunteering for Case, switched sides.

Grassley also got a big assist from his sister, Bunny, and her husband, Ed Wiegmann. She noted that former state GOP chairman and Waterloo trucking company owner Jack Warren, a Case supporter, had told Grassley not to waste his time in Black Hawk County. "Ed said, 'If we're in this election to win, we're going to do all 18 counties.' So, Ed and I took Black Hawk County. Of course, Ed wasn't afraid to campaign, he was a salesman. People said they didn't know if Ed was running or Chuck was. He thrived on it."

Bob Molinaro, who was Warren's son-in-law, and another Waterloo businessman, Verner Nelson, also boosted Grassley's stature in Black Hawk County with weeks of hard work that culminated in a two-shift, Sunday-before-the-primary brunch that brought in 750 people.

The campaign was, by all accounts, a fun affair as more and more volunteers came forward. One, Mo Stewart, allowed the basement of her Dike home to serve as the campaign's main headquarters until Election Day. Conroy said, "We held straw polls all the time and, of course, the old story is you never hold a straw poll unless you know who's going to win. Anyway, Chuck Walk, the editor at the *Globe Gazette*, said, 'Would you guys stop sending me results every time you have a family reunion!'"

Still, spring 1974 was a depressing time for many Republicans. The Watergate break-in and cover-up conspiracy sent Richard Nixon's presidency into its death throes. Grassley was faced by a rapid-fire chain of events that would have destroyed most candidates.

On May 3, in the legislative session's final hours, Grassley was hobbled by a pain in his left knee. "He said, 'I did something to it at the factory or on the farm. It'll go away,'" recalled lobbyist F. Richard Thornton, who had recommended a visit to his father, surgeon F. Eberly Thornton of Des Moines. "It wasn't getting any better, so I thought better safe than sorry. I said, 'Let's go to lunch.' And I took him to Dad's office." X-rays revealed a tumor, and Dr. Thornton made hasty arrangements for the legislator to check into the University of Iowa Hospitals.

The pain Grassley was feeling was caused by his knee sliding off the side of his femur as the bone deteriorated. He was admitted to the hospital in Iowa City on Sunday, May 5, and after several days for lab tests, surgery was set for Wednesday, May 8. The primary election was just 27 days away. The most immediate fear, though, was that his leg would be lost. If a biopsy turned up cancer, doctors were prepared to amputate the leg. The biopsy proved benign, but the ensuing surgery was difficult and the recovery was slow and especially painful.

Barbara Grassley recalled, "The doctors told me, you know, it was really very bad, and they explained to me they had taken this tumor out. It was a parasite and they scraped it until they got to good bone, and that there was a hole the size of a man's fist, and they said, 'He really, really shouldn't be running. Can he go back to the Legislature and try next time?'"

Grassley had already given up his safe legislative seat; there was no turning back. Barbara said, "I think when he walked into that hospital he thought the campaign was lost."

Grassley spent almost two weeks in the hospital. He would spend months on crutches.

Jim Gritzner, a reporter-producer for KWWL-TV in Waterloo who had gotten to know and like Grassley while covering the Legislature, went to lengths to keep the ailing lawmaker in the news. Barbara Grassley said, "That Tuesday was when Jim was doing a special on all the candidates. He went down to the hospital, dressed Chuck up in a coat and tie, took him into a room in the hospital that had books in it so they had a background, so nobody ever knew. But he did tell people it was in the hospital."

During those two weeks, Grassley spent all his time campaigning on the telephone. "This lady's son was in the next bed," Barbara said, "and she said, 'I can't even call my son. [Grassley] is always on the phone.'"

Ed Wiegmann saw to it that his route always took him through Iowa City. Furleigh and Conroy got a shock when they visited. "Chuck has light-sensitive eyes, and when he sleeps, he has the sheet pulled over his head. Well, Bob said, 'My God! We're too late!'" Conroy howled.

On the home front, the hired man's financial difficulties and unseasonable rains were making it hard to get Grassley's crops planted. But on the campaign trail, friends and supporters picked up the slack for their hospitalized candidate. Farm Bureau members threw their machine into a higher gear. Barbara Grassley, state Rep. Henry Wulff of Waterloo, and Iowa Falls attorney David Hanson became surrogate speakers. Hanson was the lawyer for a group of lawmakers, including Grassley, who sued Governor Ray over his abuse of line-item veto authority. He won the case 9–0 in the Iowa Supreme Court. Grassley later nominated Hanson for the Circuit Court of Appeals. He always took pains to describe Hanson as an outstanding judge, but he also felt a deep sense of gratitude for past loyalty.

Grassley was released from the hospital on Saturday, May 18. His sister and wife loaded him into the car, and he made an appearance at an Ackley fundraiser that night. He spoke the following day at the barbers' convention at the Rodeway Inn in Waterloo. Ed Wiegmann rented a stretcher to carry his brother-in-law into the event; Grassley refused. He walked up a flight of stairs and stood on his own, despite excruciating pain.

As the campaign progressed, Grassley got to be, in his sister's words, "just like a jack rabbit on those crutches. The doctor never took the cast off. He just changed it because of the activity."

Then Grassley's mother died on May 27, Memorial Day. Fred Garbes, a neighbor who kept hogs on the Grassley farm, discovered Ruth Grassley around noon. After calling paramedics, he contacted Bunny Wiegmann. "Mom always gave the Memorial Day address at the New Hartford Cemetery. I'd talked to her that morning, and she said, 'I've got to get ready to go.' At 12:30, Fred called and said Mom had a serious heart attack and wanted to know where I should have them take her. I told him Sartori [Memorial Hospital in Cedar Falls]."

Chuck Grassley was on his way to Mason City with his brother, Gene, behind the wheel. They were late, and Gene was speeding. "He said, 'Now we're going to get slowed again, the red lights are on,'" Wiegmann said. "The Highway Patrol told them to go back to Cedar Falls. They said later they wished they'd been picked up for speeding instead. [Hospital personnel] knew Mother was dead for more than two hours before Chuck and Gene came. My best friend was a nurse, and she kept coming out and saying, 'Have Chuck and Gene arrived?' When they came, we never saw (the nurse) again; the doctors came."

Ruth Grassley had been resuscitated in the emergency room with electric shock. She saw Wiegmann's nurse friend and said, "I spoke at the cemetery this morning." Those were her final words, and a truly extraordinary woman was dead at age 76.

Wiegmann said, "Chuck had announced his candidacy on February 12, Lincoln's Birthday, and my mother started calling the next day. I said, 'Mother, I wouldn't start so early because it's a long way 'til election time,' and she said, 'I've got a lot of people to call.' She called five people every day, including Sundays, to support Chuck and get them to sign the nomination paper, too. If she got a good response, she called 10. She died on Monday and on Sunday, she had said, 'I got all my calling done.' The day she died she was addressing cards for the farmers in Buchanan County. She had them half done."

Chuck Grassley mourned Tuesday and Wednesday, but did not go to the funeral home on Wednesday night until after it was closed to the public.

Thursday night, hours after his mother's funeral, Grassley appeared at a debate in Marshalltown. On Primary Day, he was worried by the light turnout—32,217 Republicans—especially as farmers took advantage of good weather to work their fields. "I guess what didn't materialize in the rural areas did materialize in the urban areas. I mean, who would have thought I'd ever carry Black Hawk County the way I did?"

He received 2,943 votes in the district's most populous county, compared to 2,488 for Case. His 13,506 votes accounted for 41.9 percent of the total and averted a district nominating convention, where he would have likely lost to Case, who had ended up with 9,076 votes and 28.1 percent. Conklin finished third (6,087), followed by Schwieger (2,126), and Williams (1,422).[1]

A victory celebration in Schreuers' office was attended by only seven or eight people. "We had to wait for Chuck to leave to pop the champagne," Schreuers laughed. "I don't even think he knew there *was* champagne."

Warren recalled, "Bob Case felt bad that H. R. Gross didn't really come out strong for him. Bob was a good man. When we needed anything for the party from Washington, Bob got it. That's where I think he got misled. He figured he hid his gold with the party people, but he forgot when you have more than one good person running, the party stays neutral."

Gritzner observed, "If you were hiring someone to be your congressman, you'd hire Bob. But Chuck was the most electable."

The youthful Rapp came out of the Democratic primary with a 42-vote edge over Johnson. His 35.8 percent, compared to Johnson's 35.6 percent, just squeaked over the threshold to avoid a convention, but U.S. District Judge Edward McManus ordered a rerun of the Democratic primary in Tama County because a polling place had not been set up at the Meskwaki Settlement. When all was said and done on July 3, Rapp remained as the Democratic nominee, but he had lost one month of precious time that Grassley spent campaigning across the entire district.[2]

The vanquished candidates spent heavily, and several felt it in their own pocketbooks. Conklin, the mother of five and the first Republican woman to serve in the Iowa House and Senate, contributed $23,030 of her campaign's $38,439. Case was second, with $26,878 in expenditures. Williams financed his campaign almost entirely with loans from the State Bank of Waverly, which were secured with a $24,332 mortgage on his parents' home. Almost a year later, he still owed $20,000. Schwieger's effort cost $7,986. Johnson had spent $42,075, compared to Skaine's $11,488.[3]

After the primary election, Jack Warren jumped aboard the Grassley bandwagon, and would prove to be a great fundraiser and organizer. Grassley had no paid staff during the primary and did his own scheduling. He recalled that he had also done his own fundraising, collecting $16,000 and spending about $13,000 in the primary. "Finally, I guess somebody in Washington said, 'If Grassley doesn't hire any staff, we aren't going to give him any money.' So, we got Clete Uhlenhopp to come out from Gross' staff."

Around that time, Terry Branstad brokered a deal in which his friend, Drake University Law School classmate John Maxwell, would apply his political skills to the Grassley effort. Maxwell was supposed to be the youth coordinator; it wasn't long before he was practically running the show.

Grassley's chances of winning were still heavily discounted by the Republican National Committee and the Republican Congressional Campaign Committee. "They saw a young, aggressive, articulate opponent in Steve Rapp. They had, in a typical Washingtonian attitude, mischaracterized Grassley's rural mannerisms with a lack of intelligence," Maxwell said. "That could not have been farther from the truth, but we really had no help out of the congressional committee or the RNC. They'd actually told people there would be four [Republican] Iowa congressmen elected before Grassley."

One prominent Republican who came through for Grassley was Secretary of Agriculture Earl Butz, a feisty curmudgeon who would be forced out of the Ford Administration in 1976 after telling a crude, racist joke.

Grassley had known Rapp from casual House conversations and had even shared a ride to a candidates' forum during the primary. "Rapp, you know, really knew how to campaign. He could run his own campaign. I liked him as a fellow legislator; I didn't like him as an opponent, although I didn't dislike him as an individual. He was smart, you know."

Rapp was also eloquent. He had won the Veterans of Foreign Wars national speech contest over 350,000 other contestants to earn a Harvard scholarship, and was smart enough to draw Grassley into as many debates as possible over the course of the fall campaign. "My gosh, I don't know how many debates I had with him," Grassley said, "but I look back now and that was another crazy thing to do. I'll bet I had 10 debates with him and half of them were on television, and he'd just eat you up and spit you out."

After a July debate on KWWL-TV, a frustrated Jack Warren told Rapp, "We're going to beat you. I don't know how we're going to beat you, but we're going to beat you."

Grassley did score some points with voters during the debate. "I always kept referring to him as the 'young, Harvard-educated attorney,' and [Rapp] said in those three adjectives you could spit out the most negative connotations about somebody."

Still on crutches, Grassley kept his focus on the retail side of politics—winning votes one at a time—as he crisscrossed the district in search of hands to shake. "He probably made the most of the sympathy vote during that time," Schreuers said, "but it did not stop him."

Rapp had broken his leg during what was supposed to be a touch football game in the midst of the 1973 legislative session. During the 1974 campaign, he said, "I thought, 'What bad luck!' I'd be walking the parades, shaking hands along the side, and Grassley would come along dragging that cast and people would cheer. It was an advantage to him."

Adding self-inflicted insult to injury upon his return to the Legislature from a hospital stay that resulted from the broken leg, Rapp inserted in the House Journal that he would have supported a $2,500 raise of legislators' $5,500 salary. Republicans found the Rapp notation and turned it into fodder for an H. R. Gross blast at the young Democrat. In a television commercial, Gross asked voters, "When was the last time you had a 45-percent pay raise? Steve Rapp supported one just five months after becoming a state legislator."

An August poll showed Grassley trailing Rapp by one point. By October, the order was reversed, but still too breathtakingly close for comfort.

"I've never been in a race where I felt so much like each minute of every day may have counted to be the difference," Maxwell said. "We didn't have to tell Chuck to work harder. He called headquarters at eight o'clock one Sunday night and was mad because he'd just finished what he was supposed to be doing and there wasn't anything else on the schedule. People were calling us saying, 'This guy looks haggard.' We told him, 'You've got to get some rest. People say you look tired,' and he said, 'Gosh, I think people would *want* to see me looking tired. That means I'm working hard. They want somebody that works hard.'"

Grassley ran the entire campaign, including the primary, for less than $110,000 by exercising the family's trademark stinginess with a little help from his sister. An employee of F. W. Woolworth's, she borrowed the store's heavy-duty stapler so the campaign wouldn't have to pay for more than the staples. Conroy recalled Grassley stopping at Nichols & Green, a Mason City store, after he'd worn out his shoes going door to door. "Chuck's a little better now, but, geez, to get into that wallet, to actually come up with the money out of that pocket, was tough for him! The guy brings out these shoes and Chuck tries them on. Good shoes, and the guy says they're the latest style but they're comfortable. Chuck says, 'How much are they?' and the guy told him. Chuck said, 'Have you got some that aren't necessarily in style?' He bought that pair of shoes, but he had them for years. I said, 'What you ought to do is bronze those babies!'"

In one of those truly rare contests in which the outcome could turn on any and every statement, Rapp got himself into trouble by proposing, in Mason City, to end what he called the investment tax credit "loophole." Maxwell said, "This may have been more important than any other thing. Every farmer knew what the investment tax credit was. If you went out and bought a tractor for $50,000 and financed the whole thing or the bulk of it, when you got to the bottom line you could take a credit of $5,000 off your tax bill. It was a very major, major factor that everybody in the small towns knew about. The farmers and dealers lived on it. Chuck hit him on it, and Rapp denied it. But one of the young volunteers Furleigh had there had a tape recorder."

Rapp reversed his position, but the toothpaste was already out of the tube. "The statement really gave us leverage," Maxwell said, "that Chuck Grassley was not only one of them but Rapp posed a serious threat to something that was very important to their livelihood."

Meanwhile, the Grassley campaign worked on two fronts—selling its man as an experienced legislator, voice of the farmer, and natural heir to the H. R. Gross legacy, and playing up his years at Rath and Waterloo Register, while portraying the 25-year-old Rapp as too inexperienced, too young, and immature.

In particular, Rapp got sandbagged for merely playing along with a common legislative practical joke on a fellow freshman named Terry Branstad. "When Terry got to the Legislature, Highway 9 ran through his district and the big issue up there was doing something about old, narrow, curbed Highway 9," Maxwell chuckled. Branstad quickly developed the reputation that he couldn't stand up to debate without mentioning Highway 9, no matter what the issue. When the highway appropriations bill came to a vote, someone introduced an amendment that said "no funds may be used for the maintenance, repair or improvement of Highway 9."

The ever-serious Branstad went berserk as the amendment passed overwhelmingly on a record roll call. Everyone had their laugh, someone immediately moved for reconsideration, and it was repealed on a voice vote. Rapp had gone along with the joke; Grassley had not.

"We put together a newspaper ad that said Steve Rapp voted to cut off funds for Highway 9, and reproduced the roll call vote out of the [House Journal]," Maxwell said. "Local people contributed money and we ran that ad in every weekly along that highway, there were about a half-dozen of them, a week before the election."

Rapp was furious when he learned of the tactic, and tried to set the record straight by telling people that it was all a joke and lawmakers had just been having fun. Maxwell said with relish, "Of course, he walked right into it. We said, 'What are we telling you? The guy's so immature he's down in Des Moines making us jokes when it costs $25,000 a day to run the Legislature.'"

Though not bitter years later, Rapp reflected, "It was dirty pool."

Even considering the legislative pay raise ad, scorched-earth commercials aimed at the opposition weren't the driving force that they would become in future races.

Early in the campaign, Gritzner had introduced Grassley to Mike Schreuers, then a partner in Carnaby Square, a small, two-year-old advertising and television production company in Waterloo. Grassley became the firm's first political client and large ad account. "While Chuck had spent 16 years in the Legislature, he had been known as watchdog of the treasury. He carried all those conservative credentials that, at that time, Third District Republicans looked for, but yet was seen as unpolished and probably a bit of a country bumpkin," Schreuers said. "We were billing him as 'the inflation fighter.'"

"For the most part, telling the positives of Chuck probably would have won most elections," Schreuers said, "but he wasn't opposed to doing the contrast stuff that needed to be done. Because in politics you have to define your opponent as well as define yourself. Sometimes, it's even more important to do that." Some negative spots went out over radio airwaves, but political TV advertising's simplistic infancy translated to flowery spots of Rapp's volunteers cleaning up a creek and Grassley's Lincolnesque life.

On Election Day, the candidate went to Woolworth's and ate dinner with his sister. Wiegmann said, "He said, 'It's up to the Lord now. We're going to win.' I said, 'I have not been praying for you to win. I've been praying for the Lord to send the people to the polls because all the people told us they'd vote for you. If they all go, you'll win.'"

H. R. Gross had lost Black Hawk County by 2,000 votes and still survived Lyndon Johnson's 1964 landslide. Grassley's strategists calculated he could only afford to lose by that same margin. When the results came in, Rapp had scored a 3,902-vote victory in the county and a 10,000-vote lead overall. Grassley and his supporters believed all was lost. "But where we were praying for a 2-to-1 margin in Butler and Grundy counties, we had a 3-to-1 margin. In fact, those two counties alone offset the Black Hawk loss," Maxwell said.

Indeed, something miraculous did happen that day—snow. Just enough in the morning to stop farmers across north-central Iowa from harvesting their crops. "It was like God had laid His hand over the Third District," Maxwell said.

Grassley was in New Hartford, watching the results coming in. "All I could think is, what do you say when you lose? I've never said anything when I've lost. Jack Warren told me to come on down to Waterloo because the rural areas were coming in, and it looked like I was going to win. But I didn't want to go down there if I was going to lose."

He did not have to give a concession speech, but barely.

Grassley received 77,659 votes, 50.87 percent of the total, to Rapp's 75,005 votes. The Congressman-elect carried 11 of the district's 18 counties, with his strongest showing coming in his home county of Butler, 3,802 to 1,594. His narrow victory in the district that hadn't elected a Democrat since Franklin Roosevelt's 1932 landslide made him the only Republican in Iowa's eight-man congressional delegation.[4] Rapp's misstep on the investment tax credit was certainly a factor. Grassley's experience, age, and his Farm Bureau network helped, too.

In the first congressional elections after the landmark U.S. Supreme Court decision known as *Roe v. Wade* declared women had a constitutional right to legal abortions, another issue made a difference. "The pro-lifers did a great job [for Grassley]," Maxwell said.

Rapp acknowledged that Catholic priests in some parishes—Stacyville, in one instance—spoke out on the issue by noting Grassley favored a constitutional ban on abortion. "The effect of that was to turn my race around completely in that area. [George] McGovern carried that precinct 2-to-1 over Nixon, and I lost it."

Grassley later said, "If you only win by eight-tenths of a percent, and you're the only Republican in the state to win, you don't really know what you did right that made a difference." But he did know one thing. "If it hadn't been for John Maxwell, I don't think we ever would have won."

Mike Schreuers believed Grassley would have "creamed" Rapp had the race not been in 1974. But in a perverse way, that Watergate year also defined the uniqueness that is Chuck Grassley. "We're all products of our times, and I guess what the people wanted in '74 was some degree of integrity. That has to be the reason Chuck Grassley won in '74," Schreuers said. "He brought hard work, integrity, and something of values that they could relate to to the table. I think if anything, Steve was so young that he probably got knocked for ambition, and some of his values probably weren't quite as developed yet."

Shortly after the election, Grassley called his staff together. "He said, these were pretty much his exact words, 'We're the only Republicans that won and in order to get back, we're going to have to take care of people the way the Democrats do. Our motto is going to be,'" Maxwell broke out in gentle laughter, "'We're here to clip their toenails.' He said, 'If that's what the constituents want us to do for them, then that's what we're going to do.'"

# Mr. Grassley Goes to Washington

Barbara Grassley says of her husband every now and then, "You can take the boy out of the country, but you can't take the country out of the boy." Yet, taking the boy out of the country would prove to make him downright cranky at times. His first trip to Washington after his election to Congress left him in a state of small-town, slack-jawed wonderment that anything worked inside the Beltway.

Maxwell chuckled, "He called back to the headquarters, we were all around, and he's just down in the dumps. He says, 'I knew it was bad, but I didn't know it was *this* bad. Why, they've got people on the automatic elevators they're paying just to punch the buttons for you. They've got people out here they're paying to direct traffic where there is no traffic. It's awful.'"

Awful or not, here he was. And he was going to grin and bear it. He came back at the start of the 94th Congress in the front passenger seat of his new Administrative Assistant Pete Conroy's '66 Dodge with clothes, blankets, dishes, and other household supplies piled high in the back seat. The shoe-string operation did not stop with the travel arrangements. Conroy recalled, "I had the car; he paid the rent. And I always said, 'Chuck, you got the best part of the deal' because [the landlord] was only charging, maybe, two hundred bucks a month."

Conroy was worldly enough to know that tongues wag in Washington. Insiders try to dig up dirty little details about incoming members of Congress and their top staffers. "They start checking you out real fast and, of course, one of the connections is whether you're gay or not, no question about it. Chuck and I were living together in his apartment, and I could read the signs, of course. We'd get invited out. All those guys had heard Grassley was straight, but they couldn't believe it because he's a savvy politician and he's living with his A.A. Little did they know it was to save a lot of money," Conroy laughed.

Mike Schreuers visited the place once, and recalled the common bathroom at the end of the hallway. "I don't know how many other rooms had to share the bathroom, but I thought, 'This guy is for real. He *doesn't* like to spend money.'"

The compact, fun-loving, unconventional Conroy and the loose-limbed, straight-arrow Grassley must have been Washington,

D.C.'s answer to the old TV sit-com "The Odd Couple," with Conroy playing the part of the brash, free-spirited Oscar Madison and Grassley as the perpetually perfect Felix Unger.

Those different styles were accentuated one day when the duty of leading Capitol tours for the visiting home folks fell on Conroy, a real showman who admitted to breaking the monotony by "maybe extending a little bit."

"I'd point out bullet holes where the British had burned down the Capitol," he explained. He got caught by the boss. Imitating Grassley's most concerned voice, Conroy mimicked, "Now, Pete, you don't know *that*." Conroy replied in defense, "Who says they aren't? There are dents right there in the walls. This is where the smoke stains were."

Grassley had one glaring shortcoming in image-conscious Washington. He had not changed his opinion that clothes were a superficial measure of the man. Memories of his style in the Iowa Legislature lingered for years. As one former colleague noted, "I could always tell what day it was by looking over at Chuck. If he was wearing the blue suit, it was Monday, Wednesday, or Friday. If it was the brown suit, it was Tuesday or Thursday."

He admitted years later that he wouldn't have known if his socks had matched his suit in those days, and wouldn't have cared, anyway. However, he experienced a fashion epiphany on the night of the annual Washington Press Club dinner in early 1975. Conroy noted that the Congressman was not going to attend because the required attire of the night was a tuxedo. The aide rounded up formal wear for his boss. "He caught a glimpse of himself in the mirror, and you could sort of see he was thinking, 'Hey, this doesn't look bad at all!' It wasn't anything vain. It was just at that point, he sort of realized that clothes do make a difference."

The transformation was not complete, by any means. Conroy actually plotted with Bunny Wiegmann, Barbara, and a Cedar Falls clothing store, The Stag Shop, to upgrade the Congressman's wardrobe. "I forget who put me on to The Stag, but I called them from Washington and said, 'When he comes in there this weekend, grab him, and don't take no for an answer. Put some good clothes on him.' From then on, he just began to accept it. He wears clothes well, you know; he's tall and lean."

Grassley's "particular" streak—a Felix Unger-esque insistence that everything be in its proper place—would leave Conroy breathless on one occasion when the landlord decided to paint the apartment during a congressional recess. Grassley came back and found his belongings weren't in the exact spots they had been when he left. "He said, 'Who's been touching my things? No one is supposed to touch my things!' He was just smoking. He never does anything overt or screams or yells, but he was just absolutely right at the end. When he's like that he'll usually get up and walk someplace."

Grassley was hardly the Roommate from Hell, but he did not exhibit the same inhibition about touching Conroy's property. He did it in a roundabout manner. Conroy recalled an incident one late night when he was in bed and Grassley came in from the office. "I heard him walking to the refrigerator, saw the light come on, and he was standing there, looking at my ice cream. Finally, he says, 'Hmmm, I wonder whose ice cream this is.' Hell, he never bought groceries anyway, so it sure as hell wasn't his!" Conroy laughed. "I said, 'Go ahead, Chuck, and take it.'"

Grassley didn't need to wait for someone to tell him to stand up and oppose an automatic cost-of-living increase that would increase congressional salaries from $42,500 to $46,000. He soon learned, as if he hadn't already known, that first-term representatives have almost no clout, and minority party members like him had even less. Still, Conroy observed, "The congressional pay raise fight defined him."

While galvanizing his image back home, Grassley's activism on the issue didn't win any popularity contests among House members. That may have further lessened his already minimal desire to argue with Democrats. "First of all, he was too smart to be political," Conroy said. "Where the hell are you going to go? The Republican Party was at its nadir. You really had to watch yourself, and you didn't have any power."

Far from home, family, and the familiar faces and surroundings of the Iowa General Assembly, Grassley was lonely and blue at times. "Let me tell you this: the House is very impersonal," he recalled later, "and you don't really know the guy you might be sitting next to."

But he did make friends on both sides of the aisle, with the Agriculture Committee and its largely Midwestern membership as a foundation. He also struck up a friendship through the House Committee on Aging where the venerable Florida Democrat Claude Pepper was chairman and Grassley was ranking member. "Talk about who he was close to! He was a real fan of Chuck

Grassley," Conroy exclaimed. "Philosophically, they were apart on a lot of things, but nobody worked harder and [he] was in a lot of ways like Chuck Grassley. He was a farm kid from north Florida. If you ever looked at Claude Peppers's hands, huge hands. He never traveled with a coterie of staff. He'd get up to give a speech and you may have heard his jokes before, but he always had a good beginning, a good middle, and a good close."

Meanwhile, home-state Democrats frequented Grassley's office. "Emil Husak, a good friend of Chuck's, was in there a lot," Conroy said. "The only problem we had was with Bob Ray. Bob Ray didn't set foot in Chuck's office. Chuck nailed him, sued him [over the line-item veto]. It wasn't really a problem but he just cut Chuck off, didn't come see him. Now, that eventually tempered. Bob Ray was too smart to let it go forever."

Grassley even hit it off with Bella Abzug, an outspoken New York Democrat with a penchant for outlandish hats and liberal stances. About 9:30 one night after work, Conroy and Grassley were walking into the Tune Inn for a late dinner when Abzug pulled up in a cab. They joined in a lively dinner discussion in the friendly, landmark pub at Pennsylvania Avenue, S.E., and Third Avenue. "The bartender was still telling people three or four years afterward, you should have been here when Grassley and Abzug went at it," Conroy said. "She had two hamburger steak dinners. Chuck's too much of a gentleman to say anything about it, but, boy, it didn't pass me. She knocked off that first one, and handed the plate back to the waitress and said, 'Fill it up again.'"

Grassley, while not presuming to take over his precedessor's role as a shrewd parliamentarian, did not ignore the lessons of Gross' popularity back home. The new Congressman continued mailing a newsletter to constituents. "I never heard him hold H. R. up as somebody he tried to emulate," Conroy said. "I think he learned a lot and respected H. R. for knowing his district, and certainly nobody knew that Third District any better than H. R. But I don't think he knew it as well as Chuck did, either, because Chuck was back there more often."

The first employee Grassley hired after Conroy was Yvonne Goodman, who had worked for Gross in 1949. Goodman had a remarkable institutional memory and an uncanny skill for getting the job done quietly and effectively. Conroy recalled an occasion in which Goodman led him to some much-needed, scarce office equipment deep inside the tunnels below the Capitol complex.

Conroy, incredulous, wondered aloud how Goodman knew. "Mister Conroy," she said, prim and proper, "in Washington, you don't tell all you know."

Grassley kept two other former Gross employees: Clete Uhlenhopp in Washington and Tom Penaluna in Waterloo. Uhlenhopp and Penaluna departed within a year—the former for another congressional staff, the latter for the private sector—but Goodman remains on Grassley's staff today.

Grassley worked long hours and tried to absorb as much as he could about his colleagues and the issues. "When he signed constituent letters in the early days he'd do that over in the House, listening to what these other guys were saying. The House was almost always deserted, too, but he was there signing his mail," Conroy recalled.

From his seat on the House Banking and Currency Committee, Grassley launched a high-profile campaign against a federal bailout of New York City. Appearing on a network television program with a colleague from New York, Grassley proved to be knowledgeable and articulate about New York City's suspect financial practices. "They figured they were going to have Chuck for lunch, but it didn't work that way," Conroy said with pride. "That was the first time he was really on a national show, and you could see right away the [host] had respect for him. It helped and yet it hurt. Sometimes they wouldn't have Chuck on because he wouldn't come across as a right-wing crazy, which is what they wanted."

Even before Grassley's first day, Steve Rapp was preparing himself for the next election. Having worked as special counsel to the Iowa House Democratic Caucus from January to July 1975, Rapp returned to the Waterloo law firm of Lindeman & Yagla.[1] He worked to pay off his $7,500 campaign debt and replenish his coffers. He made his formal announcement on February 1, 1976, criticizing Grassley for failing to win funds to extend what was then known as Highway 520 into the Third District from eastern Iowa.[2] Rapp avoided a rerun of the bruising 1974 primary, and enjoyed the limelight with appearances by presidential nominee Jimmy Carter in August and vice presidential candidate Walter Mondale in Cedar Falls in September.[3]

Grassley, however, was riding a crest of popularity from his relentless constituent service work—the "clip-their-toenails" philosophy—and voters' getting to know him. His fight against the pay raise put him in good stead with fiscally conservative Third District voters. He made certain they knew about it, too, by hand-delivering checks to Treasury Secretary William Simon in October 1975 and again in September 1976.[4] A week later, he announced he would accept the raise if reelected. He had only refused this raise because it was "improper" for members to accept a raise approved in the same term.[5]

As he prepared for his own reelection campaign, Grassley was courted by Ronald Reagan, who was locked in a tight contest with President Gerald Ford to win Iowa's eight delegates to the Republican National Convention. "If Chuck would have gone for Reagan, Iowa would have been stronger for Reagan. It could have made all the difference in the world," Conroy said. "Reagan could have beaten Carter. But we'll never know."

Grassley knew he didn't need any distractions in what was expected to be a tough challenge from Rapp. He was, after all, at or near the top of many liberal groups' target lists. By September, however, one poll showed him ahead 62–18 percent. "We broke with a spot that showed two Democrats, Jack and Karen Pearson from Waterloo, saying, 'I'm going to vote for the man not the party,'" Schreuers said. "The hate mail and the hate phone calls they got were incredible, but it really just knocked Steve out of it right from the beginning. When you can relate what people feel in a simplified manner, then all sorts of other possibilities click into place."

Rapp offered detailed plans for tax reform, government reorganization, and congressional reform that would limit members to six terms and reduce the power held by committee chairs. He proposed stopping "at least some of the exploitation of average citizens by oil companies, gas companies, and utilities" and called Grassley "the Inflation Fueler" for voting 11 times to "increase the price of oil and everything that comes from it." He tried to drive a wedge between Gross supporters and Grassley, saying Grassley's unsolicited mass mailings were something "H. R. Gross never did." But Rapp could not work up a head of steam. Grassley, in the position to call the shots, managed to keep him in neutral by agreeing to only two debates near Election Day.[6]

Rapp accused Grassley of misusing his free mailing privileges to solicit campaign funds and filed a complaint with the Commission on Congressional Mailing Standards of the U.S. House of Representatives. A Cedar Falls man claimed he had received a fundraising card mailed by Grassley at public expense with two Grassley newsletters.

Maxwell said the mailing could not have happened that way because congressional mailings came out of Washington and campaign mailings from Dike.[7] A week before the election, the commission, headed by Rep. Morris Udall, an Arizona Democrat, cleared Grassley. Rapp insisted he had no apologies to make. (Years later, Rapp called the incident his biggest regret of the campaign.)

Despite the attacks, Grassley was a lighter, happier man, and the press took notice: "A smile comes easily—a far cry from 1974 when Grassley suggested at one meeting he considered it almost sacrilegious to smile 'in these troubled times.' The usually somber, 'no-nonsense' candidate even has a few jokes in his repertoire."[8]

Foremost, he had put some welcome distance between himself and the May 1974 operation that saved his leg, and he had time to soothe the emotional pain of his mother's death. But, Maxwell added, "The pressure was off of him. This is a guy that worked. Hard. Committed himself beyond the limits of what most people would ever dream of, and he succeeded. Trying to be head of a big family while working two full-time jobs. Trying to build a farm while either serving in the Legislature when it was paying virtually nothing, or when they weren't in session, he was punching a time clock at a factory. He was burning the candle at both ends."

On the issues, he supported a constitutional amendment to prohibit abortion, a shift from 1974 when he favored an amendment to permit individual states to decide. He described his original stand as "the cop-out amendment."

He was known as much for what he opposed as for what he supported—standing against a comprehensive national health care system, food stamps for strikers "unless because of their low salaries they were entitled to food stamps before they went on strike," and repeal of the Taft-Hartley Act that permitted states to have right-to-work laws.[9] He also criticized Democrats on the grounds "they give you the feeling they believe somehow government can replace Christ."

Grassley carried all 18 counties, eliminating Rapp as a threat to his future job security. However, he also rekindled the flames of an old animosity.

Herman Faber, the Parkersburg insurance agent who had opposed Grassley in 1962 and helped him 12 years later, felt cheated as the campaign and its spending ended. Faber insisted that he had an agreement with Grassley to run the campaign through the primary for $3,000, including expenses. He contended he spent $5,000 out of pocket. A month after the general election, he was still waiting for his money. "I told Grassley, 'It's about pay day.' He said, 'Well, Herman, I can't pay you. The election laws have changed.' He just deliberately beat me out of it. It was a drop in the bucket compared to what the campaign had left over. Grassley is the biggest crook in Washington as far as I'm concerned," Faber said 18 years later.

Grassley's campaigning against congressional pay raises continued in his second term, but he failed to block a second increase, which boosted salaries from $44,600 to $57,500, as colleagues voted down his amendment 241–181.[10] He did prevail over the Federal Highway Administration officials, who withdrew their proposed requirements for states to convert road mileage signs into metric measurements. He was amenable to voluntary conversion, but noted that Iowa alone would have had to spend at least $1.8 million to meet the requirement.[11]

He also took up the cause of small towns, which were shortshrifted in the census. It was more than a matter of pride; federal funds are frequently allocated on a per capita basis. "He'd hear about those issues out there at those listening posts he held," Conroy said. "He had the [Congressional Budget Office] look into it, and it turned out they weren't getting their fair share. When you look at the big budget deals, $10,000 or $15,000 isn't much, but it means the swimming pool is open or shut in a place like Eagle Grove."

He adopted a higher profile on issues for the elderly, calling mandatory retirement "one of the cruelest forms of discrimination still present in our society." He also called for eliminating outside income on Social Security limits as inflation soared. Claude Pepper issued a press release lauding Grassley as "a formidable ally in the cause of the nation's 23 million elderly."[12]

Grassley may have wished for a mandatory retirement age for candidates in 1978 when no credible challengers came forward, but the presence of 72-year-old retired Marshall County farmer John Knudson forced the incumbent to go to the expense and effort of putting together a campaign organization. A Republican legislator in the late 1930s, Knudson was now a "give 'em hell" Democrat in the Harry Truman spirit. He feistily vowed to stand up to the military establishment: "I'd just tell the admirals and generals to go to hell." He complained that too many government decisions were made in "the board rooms of big labor and big business." And while Knudson was sympathetic to the needs of farmers, he said some reminded him of "the coon dog sitting on a cactus. He'd rather sit there and howl than get up and do something." He even had a run-in with the United Auto Workers. When the UAW's Iowa political action director Chuck Gifford said Knudson couldn't win, the candidate spit back, "You ought to be sure your brain is in gear before you turn on the switch."

By September, Knudson had raised only $3,800 compared to Grassley's $107,000 reelection fund. Even that did not dissuade him. "I don't care how much he spends," Knudson said. "He's got a poor product to sell." Knudson handed out literature like the report card that claimed Grassley had failed in two straight terms of Congress. "Send this Gross impersonation his flunk notice November 7 and vote for John Knudson, the Grade A candidate."[13]

Voters tuned him out.

On November 7, 1978, Grassley scored 74.9 percent of the vote (103,659 to 34,800) en route to his third House term in the 18-county Third District. Maxwell's research indicated the margin was "a record in terms of any Iowa incumbent or challenger facing an opposition party member on the ballot."

During the course of the campaign, Grassley had aired commercials on Des Moines television stations, even though only one or two Third District counties were solidly in the market. "We were beginning to set the stage," Schreuers said. The time had come to make the move political pros referred to as "up or out."

# David Takes on Goliath

The seeds of Grassley's 1980 campaign for the U.S. Senate were sown in the midst of the 1976 campaign when a second, more comfortable victory over Steve Rapp was certain. Ironically, the farmer-candidate himself was not involved. The subject was broached as Grassley's top political operatives shared dinner one September night at Waterloo's Sunnyside Country Club.

Arthur Finkelstein, a consultant provided to Grassley as an in-kind contribution from the National Conservative Political Action Committee (NCPAC), noted that polling results showed Grassley had a depth of public support indicative of a long-time congressman instead of a first-termer topping opposition "hit lists." Forecasting Grassley would be easily reelected, Finkelstein inquired about what lay ahead.

"Jack Warren sort of led the conversation from there," Maxwell said. "I can't remember if he even mentioned [Grassley running for] governor, but Bob Ray was 'governor for life' then, so I doubt it. I recall him saying, 'Who's up next in the Senate?' I said Clark would be in '78. Jack kind of said, 'No, that's too soon. He won't be ready yet. What about Culver?' I said, 'That'd be 1980.' So he said, 'Yeah, let's think about that. Culver in '80. Grassley would be in six years. Culver wouldn't be that strong. That makes sense. That's what he should go for next.'"

Finkelstein was leaving town the next day, but he sat Maxwell down at the Cedar Falls Holiday Inn. "Finkelstein says, 'If he's serious about running for the Senate down the road, here are some things he should be doing to position himself,'" Maxwell recalled.

Maxwell would not have dared approach Grassley about a Senate race four years away with the reelection campaign still in full swing. But over the next two months, he expanded on Finkelstein's suggestions. "I worked up a 'political decision memo' for Grassley, which I gave to him after the election." He concluded that Grassley had two choices: throttle back and settle into a long-term, safe seat à la H. R. Gross, or adopt a more aggressive approach to position himself for higher office. "I said, 'Obviously, it's your choice, but let me know which way you want to go.' The memo had a place to check off, and he checked off 'prepare for statewide.'"

Grassley quickly decided he didn't want to challenge Clark. "There was maybe a period of time I did," Grassley said, "but I thought it would be easier to run against Culver than Clark for the simple reason that Culver was liberal and proud of it. He stuck to his positions, and I saw Clark as someone more pragmatic and unpredictable. And I think Clark was a little more personable to me. Whether it was sincere or not, I used to pick up a lot of compliments he used to say to third parties. At least, I considered them complimentary."

Conroy said the same forces were at work in Grassley's nonstarter race against Clark and a 1990 consideration of a gubernatorial run. "He's thought about that, but it comes down to things just don't fall into shape. When he made up his mind to run against Culver a lot of people said, 'Chuck, what are you doing? You've got a safe seat.' It was a tough decision, but he made it, as far as I can see, like all his decisions. He made it all by himself," Maxwell recalled.

"Chuck will never indicate it because I don't know that I've ever heard him say anything about any politician, that includes Kennedy or any of the other guys. But I think knowing Jepsen from the Legislature and some of the flaws that turned up, and knowing Jepsen didn't have a great background in Iowa politics but beat Clark, I think made up Chuck's mind: 'I'm going after Culver.' Plus, Culver was 'get-able,' but it wasn't as obvious, at least in my book. I thought it was going to be one hell of a tough race when he made the decision."

That should have left Culver squarely in the road ahead, but there was no direct route for getting into that Senate campaign. Grassley thought about running for lieutenant governor instead of a third House term. Maxwell said, "Grassley felt if he ran for lieutenant governor, he'd be a statewide officeholder. He'd be midterm [running against Culver], so he didn't have to risk anything, and all he wanted to be was lieutenant governor anyway. So if he lost, he'd still have the job he wanted. He made up his mind he wasn't happy in the House, and he'd rather be back home than be in the House. And he'd rather be in the Senate than be back home. He wasn't risking anything because it wasn't a risk for him not to be in the House anymore. [The late legislator and Wellsburg businessman Harold] 'Grumpy' Fischer told him he could come sell insurance with him and two years later he probably would have run for something. He was serious. I had to talk him out of it in '78. I had to convince him, no, he'd have more credibility and all being a congressman. You can raise money better."

Grassley also chose not to run because one of his conservative legislative pals had jumped in the race. Branstad was running for lieutenant governor because he didn't think he could unseat state Sen. Berl Priebe, an Algona Democrat. Later, Grassley insisted that he could not recall wanting to seek the lieutenant governorship in 1978, but added, "If John said I did, I did."

Bunny Wiegmann had not wanted her brother to challenge Culver because of the emotional toll on the family. She thought the 1974 campaign was a living hell and didn't want to relive the experience. "I said, 'Oh, Chuck, you can always get elected to Congress, I'm sure, because they didn't even run anybody good against you. Just stay where you're at.' And he said, 'If I'd listened to you, I'd still be on the farm.' And I said, 'No, that's not it. You just don't know what it does to us.' And he said, 'Well, what do you think it does to me?'"

Others did not have as much emotional investment. Bob Bradsell, a public affairs producer for Iowa Public Broadcasting Network since 1970, had gotten a pretty good look at Grassley during production of "Iowa Press" and another program, "100 Days." Maxwell and Jim Gritzner, who knew Bradsell through his own reporting days, made the initial overtures to bring Bradsell on board as Grassley's press secretary in 1977.

"Then Chuck Grassley called me at home one night and talked to me at some length," Bradsell said. "At the time I think he was probably interested in the fact I had some credibility with the press. First impressions of Grassley are quite often inaccurate, and journalists often walk away with first impressions as all they've got. So, he had a need for somebody who could represent him in depth, and that was of interest to me."

Bradsell moved to Washington in the summer of 1977 and was brought up to speed early on about the Senate strategy. "I wouldn't be at all surprised if the motivation to go with a guy like me was that my statewide abilities fit neatly into that plan," he said.

Bradsell moved off the House staff late in the 1978 campaign to go to the Third District and get some practice as a political spokesman. He returned to his official duties and waited for the start of the Senate campaign. "We had consciously discussed the '80 campaign prior to Election Night because one of the things we did was convince Chuck and Barbara to get on an airplane and fly to Des Moines . . . and appear at the big bash there, due to the obvious opportunity for press exposure," Bradsell recalled. "Grassley was prominently featured on the front page of the *Des Moines Register* the next day, so it was a good thing to do. He flew all around the Third District the next day to thank voters, so there was a conscious effort at that point to charge into 1980."

Right after the 1978 election, the rumor mill began to churn out Maxwell's name as heir-apparent to Grassley's Third District throne. Over the course of a few weeks, political columnists at the *Register, Cedar Rapids Gazette,* and *Waterloo Courier* dished out speculation. Maxwell laughed, "I've never, ever had any interest in running for office. Ever. But I suppose the thing they saw was Clark worked for Culver and Case worked for Gross."

Grassley mentioned the story to Maxwell the first time it appeared, only to hear an unequivocal denial from his aide. The scene was replayed a week later, the third time he took Maxwell to lunch in the House Dining Room. Maxwell, laughing, slipped into his best Grassley drawl to recount the story. "'I see in the paper again you're running for Congress. I just want to tell you that you can forget it.' 'Forget it?' I said, 'I never thought of it in the first place.' He said, 'Well, I keep reading it in the paper. I've got to tell you I'm relying on you to [oversee] this campaign. I don't think I can win if you're not running it, and if you're running for Congress you can't be running my campaign. So, if you're not running my campaign, I'm not running for the Senate, so there's no vacancy. So you can forget it.' It was classic Grassley."

Bradsell became the day-to-day director of the Senate campaign when no one else stepped forward, and he volunteered, as much out of frustration as anything, to take a crack at it.

As the race neared, a Jack Bender cartoon in the September 20, 1979, edition of the *Waterloo Courier* showed a tiny Charles Grassley, who had tied together a giant's shoelaces. On that giant's pant leg was one word: CULVER. That David vs. Goliath analogy seems all the more appropriate because of a strengthening undercurrent that began to shape the race. The religious right, still a small force in American politics, was about to make itself felt in the second Senate race in Iowa in just two years.

Another player whose talents were yet to be fully appreciated or despised, depending on one's party affiliation, would sign on with Grassley. Roger Ailes, the Madison Avenue ad man who had worked for Richard Nixon's 1972 campaign, became

Grassley's media consultant. He went on to fame as Ronald Reagan's ad guru and president of the CNBC television network. Ailes exhibited a masterful touch, first in a tough primary against wealthy Des Moines businessman Tom Stoner, and again in the general election. Grassley's advertising consultant Mike Schreuers said, "I don't think the business of political consulting was quite what it would be, and he was seen as something of a dark outsider. People want to get their hands into Iowa because that's where the presidential bids start. So if they're handling a race in Iowa, chances are they're going to handle a presidential bid."

Ailes was fearless as a strategist and in everyday life. "We were shooting a spot with a young lady, and we wanted the background to be Waterloo and so, for one reason or another, it was shot right out in front of Pat's Tavern to show the Civic Center or something like that," Schreuers recalled. "But there were some bikers there, and they were drunk and they were starting to give us some problems. I thought Ailes was going to take on the whole bunch alone. I went to find a phone to call the cops. I said, 'Something bad is going to happen.'"

The confrontation was defused, but it wouldn't be the last. Ailes would also clash with Wendell Harms, a staunch conservative in Grassley's organization. One intimate recalled, "There was a terrible quarrel between Wendell and Roger Ailes. Roger finally said, 'I will never be in another meeting with Wendell Harms.' Wendell was kind of a hothead and he controlled the money and, of course, Ailes also spoke his mind candidly. [Before the start of one debate], Ailes left when he saw Wendell was there."

Nor did Jack Warren have much time for the ultraconservatives. "I kicked the hell out of 'em. Chuck did give me the authority." He chuckled, "Leroy Corey was one of my best workers when I was county chair. He got organized and did a pretty good job, but when you let him go, oh God! Right wing! Leroy Corey, Branstad, and Chuck were all right-wing, ultraconservatives, but Chuck came around beautifully. He understood there was a lot more people than just those guys, the right-wingers. I said to myself, 'Doggone it, at least he's got some brains. He can move according to the people he's representing.'"

Others, however, questioned the recollection. They described Corey as an integral part of the campaign operation.

Warren also said he told Grassley that he hated to see abortion included in the GOP platform or the campaign debate because the issue "hasn't got anything to do with running government." Grassley said he was pro-life, and "we shouldn't be killing babies."

Warren replied, "All right, say you are because of your church or whatever. Then, don't talk about it any more. A lot of candidates sidestepped it, but Chuck didn't. He said how he felt, moved on, and came through like a veteran."

Stoner, a moderate who had managed two Bob Ray gubernatorial campaigns and was elected state GOP chairman in 1975, jumped into the race first by officially forming his election committee in early May 1979. Stoner's friends were worried that Rep. Jim Leach, a Ripon Society stalwart from Davenport, would also make a move. He did not.

At his formal announcement on June 11, 1979, Stoner vowed to campaign on four major issues—inflation, energy, agriculture, and the combination of national defense and foreign policy.[1] His strategy was to emphasize his moderate stripes and depict Grassley and Culver as "failing to reflect the mainstream views of Iowans." He cited their support of loan guarantees for troubled Chrysler and the creation of a U.S. Department of Energy.[2]

When Grassley got into the race with his utilitarian slogan "Grassley Works," he concentrated his fire on Culver, his energy on organizational work, and gave only passing notice to Stoner. "I'm proud of my record, and most Iowa Republicans are proud of it. In fact, Tom Stoner was, until he became a candidate." Noting that Stoner had criticized nine of his approximately 4,000 votes, Grassley declared he had a "99.8 percent approval rating" from his opponent.[3]

But Bradsell showed no such reluctance in needling his counterpart, Jerry Mursener. The clash of the managers, both former newsmen, began to get ink in newspapers across the state. As one insider observed, "The two just hated each other, and it drew away from the campaign. I mean, they were just publicly going at it, and it wasn't serving either candidate."

Bradsell, who moved on to become a campaign consultant in New Jersey, said the story was half accurate. "There was some professional tension, much as professional athletes might know and toy with each other from time to time. But the relationship developed into a great interest with the press community. And I think it got in the way a bit because the two managers were overshadowing the candidates. I tried to tame it, but Jerry would goad me into things, and I'd do the same with him. . . . But Jerry and I remained friendly."

The Governor, logically partial to his former campaign manager over his former legislative nemesis, had nevertheless remained out of the primary until Bradsell irritated him. After Ray had criticized Grassley on the issue of foreign trade, Bradsell was quoted in the *Waterloo Courier* as saying, "This little game of pretending neutrality is a little silly." Ray apparently agreed and immediately "cleared the air" by endorsing Stoner. Grassley, on the other hand, gladly accepted the counterbalancing aid and endorsement of Lt. Gov. Terry Branstad.

In early May, Stoner committed a major misstep by trying to capitalize on pockets of paranoia about the Trilateral Commission. Conservatives charged that the international organization of political and business leaders was a sinister force that was throwing America into an economic crisis to create a one-world government. The smoking gun was a $150 contribution to Grassley from the Chase Manhattan Political Action Committee. Chase Manhattan was headed by David Rockefeller, who was also an influential Trilateralist. Other Trilats included President Carter and Vice President Mondale.

Stoner's camp was hit by a wave of defections, and the press had a field day. Bob Case called the accusation, based on the flimsiest evidence, "one of the most incredible blunders in politics." Always striving for balance, Case also wrote, "On the other hand, Grassley cannot really claim to be the simon pure candidate who never, ever would have an unkind word to say about his opponent. For example, Grassley is trying to make a big deal out of Stoner's wealth, claiming Stoner's campaign is 'an attempt to purchase a seat in the U.S. Senate.'"[4]

It was not a complaint Grassley would articulate about one of the men seeking to succeed him, Cooper Evans, who had invested $137,200 of his own money in the Third District GOP primary by March 31, and who, were he running in all six Iowa districts, would have spent a pro-rated $823,200. But Grassley had enough money problems of his own that he didn't need to pick another fight.

Ed Wiegmann and Bob Molinaro applied their persuasive powers to the more reticent big-money Republicans, persuading many to sign $1,000 notes for the campaign. If Grassley won the primary, the notes were repaid. If not, they were out a bundle. Wiegmann was so enthusiastic about his brother-in-law's career, Warren said, that he was "even going so far as to say Chuck was going to be President of the United States someday."

Meanwhile, Grassley counterpunched Stoner by unveiling an agricultural policy that claimed farmers would not be in desperate shape had the federal government not interfered. He subtly stoked the prairie fire of resentment against the Trilateral Commission by noting, "The agricultural policies of the current administration, whether by neglect or design, are posing the greatest threat to the family farm in years." He said farmers needed price protection and an immediate flow of cash to stay in business.[5]

Grassley directly addressed the Trilateral Commission connection charge in Cedar Rapids a week before the election, saying it was so ridiculous that people started questioning Stoner's judgment. While abhorring negative campaigns, he said he had "never faced an opponent as desperate as Tom Stoner appears to be." Grassley accused Stoner of running a "mud-slinging campaign" and "trying to buy a seat in the Senate." The Congressman, professing to be running a "pay-as-you-go" campaign, said Republicans "ought to consider the massive debt Stoner is accumulating, which would be carried into the general election campaign, plus the fact his wealth would be used against him by John Culver."[6]

In Waterloo, Stoner, who personally opposed abortion but thought the government should not be involved, said he would "refuse contributions from the ultraconservative, New Right coalitions," which he described as a "disturbing and disrupting influence on the political process and the Republican Party." He put Leroy Corey's Committee for Another Responsible Senator in that category.[7] Corey said he would support Stoner if the former party chairman won the GOP primary, but worked against that outcome. A few days before the primary, Corey's PAC sponsored appearances in Waterloo, Cedar Rapids, and Des Moines by Major General John Singlaub, who had been relieved of his command in Korea by President Carter for speaking out against troop withdrawals. Ostensibly in town "to expose John Culver's anti-defense voting record," the wiry, crew-cut Singlaub allowed that he feared Stoner was a liberal and said Iowans should support Grassley because of his "100 percent pro-defense voting record."[8]

The Sunday morning before the election, the Iowa Pro-life Action Council supported Grassley with a flier distributed in church parking lots. The three-color brochure featured a picture of an 18-week-old, thumb-sucking fetus. Urging Iowans to

"Vote Chuck Grassley" on Tuesday, it read, "If you don't, he [the fetus] may never have the chance to vote."

Robert Ray said the leaflet was unfair and might backfire because "the people of the state of Iowa have a sense of fair play." When Grassley was asked why he hadn't stopped the brochure, according to the Associated Press, he bristled, "I guess because I've been busy campaigning."[9]

In the end, Grassley's well-honed organization prevailed. He rolled up 65.5 percent of the statewide vote, losing only nine of the 99 counties, while receiving an astounding 87 percent of the vote in Black Hawk County. Grassley built his success on his solid Third District base and a replication of the Farm Bureau's phone-tree rural network. But, Bradsell concluded, "Stoner was looked on as a politician, in almost the classic sense of the word. He was polished. He was citified. All the things Chuck Grassley was not. I don't think the average voter was out looking for a slick politician in 1980."

Stoner had spent $1.22 million in a losing cause, including $885,000 of his own money. Grassley emerged with a $65,327 debt and began the most denunciative campaign of his career, with the New Right leading the charge.

The strategy was a political necessity. While Grassley found himself as the cover story of *The Review of the News*, a 50-cent publication of the John Birch Society, Culver was riding a wave of stature-enhancing good press from *New Yorker* writer Elizabeth Drew's flattering new book, *Senator*. Clearly, the six-foot-four, 250-pound Culver had to be cut down to size.

Culver, a 47-year-old, first-term senator who had served five House terms, was a star fullback at Harvard, and had roomed with Edward M. Kennedy. His formal announcement declared the race would hinge on "the judgment of the people of our state as to which candidate possesses those qualities needed to respond to the current problems we face today as well as the unknown future demands." He touted his record of energy and soil conservation programs, leadership in "responsible and successful fights to control unnecessary spending and cut the burden of regulations and red tape," authorship of anti child-pornography laws, funding for infrastructure repairs so "our children will go to school over safer bridges," and sponsorship of clean water laws and flood control projects.

A former U.S. Marine with six years on the Senate Armed Services Committee, Culver made it his business "to understand our nation's defense needs and what is being done and not done to meet them." His stated philosophy did not sound different from that articulated by Grassley in future years: "We should buy only what we need and get what we pay for and that means ready, reliable weapons, not gold-plated gadgets that cost too much and never work right," Culver said as the campaign began.

Culver had made it clear that he had no intention of backing away from his record.[10] That was exactly what Grassley had anticipated and his strategists and the New Right had hoped to hear. They unleashed an unrelenting, vicious barrage which included a NCPAC fundraising letter mailed to 35,000 people nationally to finance the media air war against Culver. "When Teddy Kennedy hurried back to the Kennedy compound at Hyannis Port after the death of Mary Jo Kopechne, he called together a group of Kennedy 'Camelot' backers to help him concoct his fallacy-ridden story of the events of that fateful night. [One was] an obscure Iowa congressman named John Culver, now Sen. Culver," the letter read.[11]

There was also a Christian rally attended by 600 people in Marshalltown on September 2, in which a plan to replace Culver with the "godly, right-minded Chuck Grassley" was outlined. Two speakers at the Christian Voice Moral Government Fund event said the "sleeping giant" of fundamentalist, evangelical Christians had the strength to spell the difference in the contests. Lay Christian leader Gary Jarmin from Pacific Grove, California, accused Culver of being "part of the crowd which legalized the killing of babies, provided rights for homosexuals, made the streets safe for criminals and rapists and who kicked God out of our schools. God loves John Culver, and so do we. He deserves our prayers, but not our votes."[12] (An odd statement coming from someone ineligible to vote in Iowa.)

And the John Birch Society charged that Culver was a big spender, soft on communism and weak against the "monstrous crime of child pornography." (The attack was a deliberate misdirection play aimed at his strength as the author of a law to crack down on purveyors of kiddie porn.)[13]

Grassley said he would have been troubled by the attacks had he launched them. Instead, he was bothered by suggestions that he should have denounced the denunciations of Culver. "Maybe I even did sometimes and found out indirectly the groups resented it," Grassley said. "Even if I had renounced it, they would have kept doing it, and people would have thought it wasn't a sincere renunciation."

He was pragmatic, noting that if he talked about the independent expenditure groups, Culver would have more opportunities to do the same. "We would have been talking about something we couldn't do anything about, and it would have detracted from the campaign. The independent expenditure campaigns' goal was to keep him off track, and his goal by talking about it was to keep me off track so you just weren't focusing on the campaign," Grassley explained.

Culver had his own independent supporters, too, in groups like the National Council of Senior Citizens, environmental groups, and organized labor that joined the Senator in assailing Grassley and the New Right. "To me," Grassley said later, "everything I heard about the New Right was the 'old right' I'd been a part of for 20 years. It was just the plain old conservative movement. It wasn't new; somebody just put a new label on it. I'm not sure I agreed with everything of the New Right, but there sure was an effort to link me to it, to say I'd taken on a new aura of political ideology that I hadn't."

Grassley got in some hard licks, too. Besides accusing the Senator of "getting rich" in office, he claimed Culver "probably represents the views of Jane Fonda more than any other senator." Culver was bringing the United States to "a position of military weakness," and as a result, America was no longer second to none, as Culver insisted.

Culver, he said, was "the biggest spender in the United States Senate, even a bigger spender than Ted Kennedy. . . . The times have changed. John has not." Grassley also charged that Culver was among those Democrats who "do not want to wrestle with tough economic problems. They live for the next election, not the next generation."[14]

With the benefit of hindsight, Grassley said, "If I had to reflect on that, he himself was probably pretty armed services oriented, but he was a leader in that area at a time when the entire liberal movement in Washington was dramatically directing resources for defense into social programs and we, at that point in the debate, had what was called a 'hollow army.' I would've been smart enough to say to myself the analogy of the hollow army, and when you get enough of our troops on food stamps, there's something wrong. The Jane Fonda symbolism, I probably picked that up, and it was probably used by other Republicans." That attack, he said, would have come late in the campaign, when Culver's emphasis on his military service was cutting into Grassley's base of support. "People viewed him as more pro-military than me."

Grassley had registered for the draft as a 17-year-old when the Korean War entered its eighth month, but received a college deferment, then a family exemption well beyond the end of the fighting. He never served in the military. "Besides that, Culver looked tougher than I did, and he was on the Armed Services Committee." Grassley's campaign ran TV ads showing Culver's face on a spinning weather vane, saying one thing in Iowa and voting another way in Washington. "We said we needed a strong military, and he didn't vote that way," Grassley recalled later.

Even an independent candidate took a swipe at Culver—literally. Garry DeYoung of Hull charged the stage at a University of Northern Iowa rally for Culver and grappled with moderator Lyle Alberts. As Culver moved in to assist Alberts, DeYoung swung at him. That proved to be a mistake. Culver, employing his football skills, pushed DeYoung across the stage and bulldogged the big man to the floor. No one was injured and no charges were filed, but the incident was just one more indignation heaped upon the proud, honorable Culver.[15]

Culver campaign manager Brent Appel, the Iowa Democratic Party's press secretary in 1978 when he and the Senator met, offered his perspective on the election that was pivotal in Grassley's career.

Culver had known early on what was looming on the horizon, according to Appel. The Senator and his brain trust, which included pollster Peter Hart, knew the right wing was very strong within the Republican Party of Iowa and growing stronger; they had expected Grassley to emerge from the primary. Culver and his advisers also recognized the force and fury of the New Right, which was energized by Jepsen's 1978 upset victory.

"We expected heavy expenditures; there were. We expected the New Right to do the dirty work; they did," Appel explained. "Did we expect New Right groups to be as venomous as they were? We did, and they were. I don't think we were caught in any way unaware or surprised in that respect. In general, independent expenditure groups commit character assassination, and then the actual candidate says, 'Well, that isn't me talking; it's just independent groups.' But in fact, they're part and parcel of an attack. It's clear that the Grassley campaign was aware of them and set their message to be consistent with what was going on out there. The word 'independent' has funny connotations. There are different reports, different officers, different boxes, sure, but even though you have presumably independent campaigns, they can still work together hand in glove with others just by being aware of what's being done on radio by someone else, what their message is, and seeing where their expenditures are. At a minimum, that's what happened. I thought the overall message was rather well-orchestrated."

Culver tried to blunt the attack with a head-on challenge, telling Iowans the New Right had selected him as a target and "this target is fighting back." Speaking to the Iowa Postal Workers Union convention in Waterloo on June 7, he lashed out at the New Right and questioned Grassley's pledge to balance the budget while increasing military spending by $10 billion.

Culver said the current year's $150 billion defense budget already was a $20 billion increase, the biggest increase in the post-World War II era. The Soviet Union, he argued, was more frightened of U.S. economic vitality than exotic weapons that bled America's finances. He described the New Right as a "kind of national religious political action committee" that opposed government, labor, poor people, and civil rights, and favored big business, big military, big oil companies, big corporate profits, and big tax cuts for persons with incomes in the upper tax brackets "regardless of what hardship any of these policies may bring to the majority of the people."

Calling the New Right "a new virus, born of hate, orchestrated by opportunism" that should not be "confused with the true conservatives of the past," Culver noted that Grassley would not disavow the actions of NCPAC or LeRoy Corey.

Citing the Christian Voice's zero rating of him on moral issues in 1979, Culver boomed, "Apparently these people waste no Christian concern on such matters as food stamps for the poor, social security for the elderly, equal rights for all Americans, including minorities, equitable tax policy for middle and low income citizens, health care, and international policies to preserve peace."[16]

Over the summer, he distinguished himself from Grassley on the B-1 bomber, oil windfall profits tax, the economy, Social

Security, rail transportation, and trade with China. Challenging Grassley to prove the charge that Culver was a "big spender," the Senator said, "John Culver has saved you a lot more money than Chuck Grassley. It is not enough just to talk about saving money. Action is what counts."

He held up as proof his successful 1977 fight against the B-1 that saved $30 billion. He charged Grassley had voted against the bomber at least five times between 1975 and 1977, but "now that the climate has changed and it's politically popular, Mr. Grassley has flip-flopped, and at a current cost of $60 billion." Still, trying to emphasize his own politically popular commitment to a strong defense, Culver said he could support a bomber that could penetrate Soviet air defenses, but not the B-1, which, he argued, would be obsolete before it was in full production. He also noted that in the previous five years, he had voted for $552 billion for defense, just $2 billion less than Grassley.

He assailed Grassley's support for a balanced budget amendment as one of several "simplistic, quick-fix solutions that ignore the complexity" of budgetary and economic problems. He charged that Grassley had failed to support a measure to keep Social Security solvent, which, if it had prevailed, would have resulted in benefit cuts for Iowa's 486,000 recipients the next year. Grassley's vote, as only one of 96 members of Congress opposed to improved trade with China, was "a classic example of his New Right associations taking priority over Iowa interests," said Culver, who noted that China held enormous consumer potential for U.S. farm products.[17]

He also criticized Grassley's refusal to take a stand on the state Equal Rights Amendment (ERA) on the ballot. "If he's too nervous to take a stand on a matter of fundamental justice here at home, he has no right to serve in the Senate. You vote 'yes' or 'no' in the Senate, not 'maybe.'" Culver chided his challenger for saying he'd simultaneously cut taxes, balance the budget and increase defense spending. "It's an insult to our intelligence for him to try to convince Iowans that can be accomplished. We're going to get you on this, Chuck, before the campaign is over."[18]

Grassley explained years later, "If he said that today, he'd be absolutely right. We could have had a balanced budget in two or three years just by freezing the budget. It wasn't the Reagan tax cut that caused the deficit. We had more revenue year after year after year. Cutting taxes is absolutely essential, as long as you cut the involvement of government, the spending. Even if you don't, there's some economic good of cutting taxes. And I stand guilty of supporting the Reagan defense build-up. We couldn't have continued the way we were under Carter and kept our international standing and prevented nuclear war. But within three or four years, I led the charge to end the Reagan defense build-up."

Grassley proved adept at bobbing and weaving away from the hard blows, as when Culver hammered away at votes against elderly heating assistance, a home insulation program for the poor and old, and 1977 Social Security revenues increase. "The congressman's campaign may claim he is a friend of Iowa's senior citizens, but the record is what counts, and the congressman's record clearly shows that he has not effectively represented senior citizens' interests."[19]

Grassley had a not-so-secret weapon, Pete Conroy noted. "Claude Pepper was a real fan of Chuck Grassley, and that's how we drove Culver's people nuts. We broke out [dozens] of quotes from Claude Pepper complimenting Chuck. So, what could Culver's people say? Besides that, Chuck was the ranking member on Aging."

During a debate before the Iowa Daily Press Association on September 6, 1980, in Des Moines, Grassley was awkward and uncomfortable; Culver, rhetorically speaking, mopped the stage with him.

Grassley adamantly refused to state his position on the ERA, saying he has the same right to "the secrecy of the ballot box" as any other citizen. When a panelist tried to press him to answer whether he identified with the rising conservative forces in the Republican Party, Grassley dodged, "I think it's a battle between John Culver and Chuck Grassley."[20]

Grassley would claim that he was not trying to have his cake and eat it too by voting in the state Legislature to ratify an Equal Rights Amendment to the U.S. Constitution and voting no in Congress to extend the ratification period when the issue failed to pass 38 states by the seven-year deadline. "Seven years was the tradition. I stayed out for two reasons. It is their choice but, more importantly, it's a state issue. Both sides, they just want to use you or detract from the campaign so you spend all your time talking about a state issue you had nothing to do with but as one vote out of 1.2 million, and you're off the things you ought to be talking about."

Grassley also admitted years later that he was intimidated. "My gosh, he's six-foot-four and 250 pounds! And it was not only his physique, but how he handled himself. I had never seen an exhibition of his temper, but he had that independent candidate down on the floor at UNI."

In a debate two weeks later at the National Cattle Congress and televised by the Iowa Public Broadcasting Network (IPBN), Culver ridiculed Grassley's support for the Kemp-Roth income tax cut. The incumbent said he supported a $12 billion Democratic jobs program to curb unemployment instead of a tax cut that would cause a $60 billion deficit. Grassley replied that if one of the panelists were out of a job, it would be a recession; if he were out of a job, it would be a depression; but if "John Culver was out of a job, it would be a recovery."

Culver jabbed at Grassley again about the ERA, scoffing at his previous explanation that federal officials should not dictate to voters. "I'm not dictating to Iowans how to vote on the ERA," Culver asserted. "I just feel that as an elected official it is my responsibility to let the people know where I stand on the issues. I think you owe it to us to tell us where you stand on the state ERA. It's a matter of fundamental justice."

Grassley said his actions spoke louder than words, noting that three of his top five salaried employees were women while Culver's top paid five were all men.[21] Grassley's campaign would recall that the counterattack really knocked Culver off balance. But Grassley actually had a more potent weapon. Schreuers later observed, "Roger Ailes is not a great campaign spot maker, although he had people who could do that, but when it comes to preparing candidates there's no one better. I can remember doing the open and close at Bob Bradsell's place prior to the [IPBN debate]. Roger simplified. He brought it to the point of compelling relevance. 'This is what people in Iowa want to hear.' He was just great at that."

Several Grassley associates also recalled Ailes' attention to detail. During the second debate, Ailes took a moment before the candidates arrived to tend to the water. Schreuers recalls that Ailes poured a glass of water for Grassley so the candidate wouldn't have to do it later and risk a minor disaster. But he may have done even more. Culver's pitcher was perched precariously on the edge of his podium shelf. As he approached moments before the debate started, the pitcher of cold water tumbled, splashing his pants. Democrats said later that they heard second-hand reports of Grassley's people gloating that the pitcher was rigged to spill.

Set-up or just the victim of sheer bad luck, Culver was rattled by the unexpected bath, and his performance showed it. "From that point on, the guy was shook," Schreuers said. "You could see it was a turning point. It was really incredible because he was Mr. Confidence, if not Mr. Arrogance, beforehand."

Appel agreed, "I don't think the salaries thing was much of a deal. The water thing, however, did unnerve him a bit. What role Grassley or Ailes or anyone else had in it, I don't know, but I think the water did leave the Senator in an awkward position. Instead of getting calm at the start, he was looking at his pants."

Grassley also heard the story, but his version had Ailes filling Culver's glass so full that the Senator couldn't take a drink without risking a spill on himself.

"Farmers were saying to me later, 'Did you see Culver sweat? Chuck really had him sweating,'" Conroy said. But Appel concluded, "If someone said that second debate was a big turning point in the campaign, I guess I wouldn't agree. It wasn't perceived that way in our campaign."

Long before Ted Kennedy made the refrain popular against George Bush in the 1988 campaign, Grassley was asking "Where was John Culver?" Grassley pointed out that in six years in Congress, he had returned to Iowa 158 times, conducted 152 listening posts, and worked 788 days in the state in addition to 1,262 in Washington, while not missing a single vote in five of the six years. Culver had missed 500 votes, Grassley said, and he "likes to travel a lot but not necessarily back home to Iowa." During 16 years in office, Culver had been to "nearly 50 countries and all at taxpayer expense. But how many times has he come to Iowa? How many Iowa communities has he come to?"

The Congressman challenged Culver to "let us know where he's been the past six years. Only by knowing this can the people of Iowa compare the records and decide if they want another six years of a senator from Washington sent to Iowa or a senator from Iowa sent to Washington."[22] Culver also found himself responding to charges from Grassley that he was "getting rich" in office on money paid to him by so-called special interest groups.[23]

When Culver described himself as not a liberal but "a progressive in the best tradition of Iowa," Grassley fired back, "A progressive is a liberal running scared."[24]

On October 26, the Iowa Pro-life Action Council distributed 300,000 leaflets "friend to friend and neighbor to neighbor" in church parking lots across the state. Grassley was endorsed because of his opposition to public funding of abortions and his support for a constitutional amendment to prohibit abortions.[25] Culver battled down to the wire, arguing that Grassley was a man so out of touch with Iowans and the political mainstream that "he has voted consistently out of step, some 612 times, from every other Iowa member of the congressional delegation—Republican or Democrat."[26]

Civil rights activist and Georgia legislator Julian Bond also toured the state for Culver and other Democratic hopefuls, charging that Grassley was "a Scrooge in Washington and a Santa Claus at home. He votes against programs to benefit you in Washington, then he comes home, hands out the goodies he voted against and tries to make you believe he's doing you some great favor." He lambasted Grassley's financial supporters as "a group of neofascist religious storm troopers."[27]

Grassley, after coming on stronger in the second debate, was confident in the third and final debate in Des Moines on October 31, which he believed was a draw. "I overheard [Culver] telling [Harold] Hughes the polls were starting to look bad. That would've been the Friday before the election, and that was kind of a confirmation through their source of what we were getting through our tracking."

The bottom fell out of the Culver campaign over the final weekend. Swirling rumors about the imminent release of U.S. hostages in Iran, the much-anticipated "October surprise," forced President Carter into a Sunday press conference to issue a denial. Appel said, "All that didn't play well with voters. It reminded them of weakness in foreign policy. Not that we were dependent on that, but it was not helpful. Indeed, other campaign managers told me they felt a down draft that last weekend, too."

Another component was in Culver's control. "We eased back on some negative ads toward the end," said Appel, a Des Moines attorney, "and I don't think that was wise in retrospect. It was designed to end with a flourish, end upbeat. If I had any call to make over again, it would be that one. The rationale would be we'd had a lot of 'negative' up for six weeks; there'd been a lot out there and the thought was to ease up. Seeing the results, we should have piled up the negatives."

Those results had Grassley posting victory by a large margin: 683,014 to 581,545. His campaign had spent $2,557,043, including $737,000 in the primary. Culver's campaign spent $1,940,402.

However, the Democrat's campaign raised enough money

that it was not necessarily a factor in the election outcome. "Toward the end, in fact, I had more money than I thought I would," Appel said, "and ended up throwing it into radio because we'd bought up on TV. If I'd had more money I could have put it to good use, but I don't regard it as a factor."

Luke Roth, Grassley's organization director, was immediately convinced the Senator-elect was in office for the long haul. "I knew if we could get him elected the first time, from then on it wouldn't be a problem because people would get to know him and people would get to like him. I knew we were electing somebody for 24 years."

Just as he had in early 1975, Grassley replayed the role of outsider as he advanced to the Senate. For, although he had been in Washington for six years, he was, for the most part, unknown to his new colleagues. Conroy noticed that Grassley started to show more polish during the Senate race. "I'd say it was the line of demarcation. There was more television time. That really started giving him more exposure statewide and, to some extent, nationally. After all, Reagan was running, and they'd been together in the campaign. Not that the House wasn't big time, but it was certainly more parochial than the Senate."

Still, Grassley had a long way to go. Conroy recalled the morning that the Senator-elect, still living in the cramped old farmhouse northeast of New Hartford, received a call from Strom Thurmond, who would become chairman of the Senate Judiciary Committee as the Republicans swept into power. Thurmond urged Grassley to take the committee as one of his assignments, but Grassley was having trouble hearing over the household's morning din. "He said, 'Wait a minute, Senator,' and yelled, 'Would you guys shut up! I'm on the phone!'"

Thurmond might have been taken aback, but others had more ominous concerns. Grassley was being judged by the company that his campaign kept—the religious right, the vitriolic New Right, the John Birch Society, right-to-life and right-to-work organizations—and the presumption that he was Roger Jepsen's protégé. "His advance billing was that he was this right-wing, didactic, not overly pleasant guy," Senator Joseph Biden said, "because . . . he was touted as one of the products of NCPAC and the right-to-life movement." It was in that climate that Capitol Hill regulars began to refer to Jepsen and his junior colleague as "Tweedledum and Tweedledumber."

# Goodbye, Tweedledumber

> *"Early impressions are hard to eradicate from the mind. When once wool has been dyed purple, who can restore it to its previous whiteness?"*
>
> —Saint Jerome (342-420 A.D.)

Saint Jerome never spent any time on Capitol Hill, but his words fit the early days of Charles Grassley's move from the House to the Senate. The House was a place where a member could get lost in the woodwork, if he or she chose, yet hold the job almost forever thanks to the institution's potent "incumbency protection" features.

The Senate was different. By virtue of his election, Grassley had chosen to participate in a less forgiving arena, where it was tough to undo inaccurate impressions created by opponents. He carried the same mark shared by virtually all of the Republican newcomers who had helped the party win majority status for the first time since 1954. "New Right" had become dirty words in many Washington circles, where Democratic and liberal sore losers congregated. Along with the company he had kept during the 1980 election, Grassley's mannerisms made it easy to dismiss him as a slow-talking, dumb-as-dirt political Neanderthal. He was deemed by many as somehow not worthy of inclusion in the World's Most Exclusive Club, a one-term mistake who would go away if ignored long enough.

Grassley, determined to not fade away, worked at building rapport. "He's very good with his colleague relationships," said Sen. David Pryor, an Arkansas Democrat. "I got a little note in the last day or so congratulating me on something. He didn't have to do that, but he does."

On the Special Committee on Aging, Grassley became friends with Chairman Thomas Eagleton, the Missouri Democrat who was forced out as George McGovern's running mate in 1972 after reports he had been treated for depression. Eagleton even got an autographed picture of the great St. Louis Cardinals' first baseman Stan Musial, a Grassley idol from his days on the New Hartford High School diamond. "We never had any problems," Conroy said. "That was a hell of a committee. [Dan] Quayle was on it. Chuck Percy. John Warner. Bill Cohen. It just worked. Key guys respected Chuck, and I give a lot of credit to Eagleton."

The butt of jokes in Capitol corridors and cloakrooms—Name the state that has a senator dumber than Roger Jepsen. Answer: Iowa—and an easy target for the media and liberal special interests, Grassley could have been excused for allowing a bunker mentality to set in around his office. Instead, he ignored the liberals' taunts of "Tweedledum and Tweedledumber," a label stuck on him and Jepsen to portray them as two like-minded dim bulbs who shared outdated, discredited conservative ideas. He kept his focus on the people who had sent him to Washington because he knew impressions among the home folks were, ultimately, more important than what the Beltway crowd thought of him.

He cranked up his constituent service machinery, applying his principles of diligence on a statewide scale. Shortly after the bruising race against Culver, in fact, Grassley recounted to Maxwell that he had been in his hometown cafe years earlier and heard two people talking about the previous day's visit by one of the state's U.S. Senators. Grassley told Maxwell, "Someone said, 'It must be an election year. That's the only time we ever see him.' I'll be darned if anyone is ever going to say that about me." Maxwell added, "I think that may have been the reason for his 99 counties [tour] every year."

Such attention to detail built his reputation, brick by brick, in Washington. Some efforts, like his defense spending reform crusade and other breaks with the Reagan Administration, were high profile. Others were in the work-a-day world of legislating where he exhibited unexpected traits, such as tenacity in the battle to secure former Iowa Attorney General Evan Hultman's nomination as U.S. Attorney for northern Iowa, or a surprising philosophical stance in his willingness to help craft a compromise on reauthorization of the Voting Rights Act of 1965.

Other, more subtle events were effective in making an impression only on keen-eyed Capitol Hill denizens who began to see that Grassley was far shrewder than their initial, flawed reports indicated. The AWACS deal in October 1981 demonstrated Grassley's hallmark caution, always suggesting where he would come down, but never getting himself so far out that he couldn't recover and move in another direction.

At issue was Senate approval to sell $8.5 billion worth of sophisticated AWACS planes to Saudi Arabia.[1] The planes operated like a flying air traffic control tower and would allow their prospective owners to monitor anything and everything in the

Middle East air. Israel and its powerful lobby were understandably concerned about the deal, not only from a technical standpoint, but as a possible harbinger of shifting alliances. Opponents in the Senate and elsewhere argued that the AWACS tilted the uneasy balance of power in favor of the Arabs, leading to the potential for all-out war involving the United States and the Soviet Union if Israel was overwhelmed by an attack.

The AWACS deal also was the first major foreign policy test for the new Reagan administration, and both Republicans and Democrats wanted to set the tenor for the next four and perhaps eight years. Grassley, during a ten-day visit to Israel in August, had been told by one of that country's top intelligence officers that the AWACS would allow the Arabs to monitor tank movements. He and Jepsen announced their opposition to the sale, with Jepsen flatly declaring on October 20, 1981, "I'm going to vote against it, period."[2]

Pressure, particularly on freshman senators, was as intense as any ever experienced. Grassley signaled that he would only drop his opposition if Jepsen changed his mind. "It was the shrewdest political move I ever saw. Roger was suddenly worth two votes, and all the heat was off Grassley and on him," one of the Senator's aides recounted.

Administration officials did not give up completely, but their efforts hurt their cause more than it helped. When White House lobbyist Powell Allen Moore called Grassley to suggest that the Hultman nomination might be expedited in exchange for a yes vote, the Senator exploded.[3] Grassley requested a one-on-one meeting with the President. In the private quarters of the White House, Ronald Reagan and Charles Grassley talked for a half-hour on the afternoon of October 27. "I guess I just wanted to hear it from the horse's mouth," Grassley explained.

He also went to Andrews Air Force Base for a tour of an AWACS plane. When he asked about its ability to track tanks on the desert floor, he was told tanks didn't move fast enough to be picked up. "For the first time," he said, "I questioned the credibility of the Israeli argument, and I've been a strong supporter of Israel."

Others suggested Grassley more than questioned the Israeli argument; he was angry at being misled. Domestic politics also concerned him. "I was in my bedroom getting ready for work and it came over the radio, probably, how the Democrats were lining up against it almost to a person," Grassley said. "I thought, 'My gosh, if this thing is turning out to be an effort to embarrass the President and have international connotations to weaken our leadership, should I play along?' That intelligence officer plus this issue for political purposes by the Democrats began to make me question if I was on the right side."

Meanwhile, Jepsen had his own White House meeting. He never told Grassley how it went, and Grassley winced, "You didn't need to talk about it with Roger. You didn't *want* to talk about it with Roger."

The reason was explicitly spelled out on the front page of the October 27, 1981, *Des Moines Register* as an unnamed Reagan aide claimed, "We just beat his brains out." The source told reporter John Hyde, "We stood him up in front of an open grave and said he could jump in if he wanted to."

Jepsen told the *Waterloo Courier* that the *Register* story was an "absolute, total fabrication." He insisted that his 40-minute meeting with the President had been cordial, and "we honestly did talk about Iowa football for a long time." Whatever was discussed, Jepsen changed his vote "after prayerful and careful consideration" with his wife, Dee.[4] Jepsen asserted that his reversal on the issue had gone beyond the AWACS deal itself, and he had decided to "support the President." He added that he "couldn't stand the company I was with," a stab at liberal Democrats leading the opposition.[5]

Jepsen went from being a hero in the Jewish community—to whom he had promised his uncompromising support for Israel during a speech before its political action arm, the American Israel Public Affairs Committee [AIPAC]—to its most disdained target after AWACS. "It seemed to me like if it hadn't been for the story in the *Des Moines Register* . . . and he'd had good rationale for changing his mind, he probably could have survived it," Grassley said. "I think Roger being so adamant and my hearing the reaction . . . has taught me to be very cautious about issues I tackle generally and, very particularly, about AIPAC."

Grassley had picked his way through the political mine field unscathed, but not without criticism. Burlington's *Hawk Eye* editorialized that Grassley's explanation was "pure Charlie Brown, Casper Milquetoast to the core. He thought it was 'key' that both Iowa senators vote the same way. He thought it was bad that Democrats were using the issue to embarrass the President. [Grassley's vote] was based purely on narrow political grounds."[6]

Though Jepsen had made other missteps, and more were yet to come, the episode was the beginning of the political end for Jepsen. At the same time as the AWACS episode, Grassley was engaged on another front, defending the honor (and nomination) of his friend, Curly Hultman. The Waterloo lawyer was accused of abusing his power as U.S. Attorney for the Northern District of Iowa during the Nixon and Ford administrations, and participating in a conspiracy against John "Jack" Nard, a Pennsylvania contractor who was the target of three grand jury probes concerning the construction of Armour & Co. meatpacking plants in Sioux City and Pittsburgh.

Hultman's accuser before the Senate Judiciary Committee was none other than Nard, who had pleaded guilty in the 1960s to one felony count of tax evasion and had once been represented by Sen. Orrin Hatch, a Utah Republican. Hatch teamed with Sen. Dennis DeConcini, an Arizona Democrat, to lead the opposition to the Hultman nomination.[7] Grassley warned against "second-guessing" grand juries and courts that had cleared Hultman on three occasions. Judiciary chairman Strom Thurmond of South Carolina said the committee would limit its probe to contradictory statements Hultman made in December 1980, when he had appeared before the panel with only DeConcini present. Hultman's argument was that he had been called on short notice, with little time to prepare, and spoke to the best of his recollection.[8]

When the showdown came, Grassley went on the attack against Hatch and DeConcini in a marathon session that stretched almost eight hours. Neither of Grassley's adversaries remained at the hearing, though Nard's former attorney had served as committee chairman during much of it.[9] The campaign against Hultman dragged on for months, gaining new life with accusations that the Army Reserve major general had falsified his military medical records; but he finally won confirmation in May 1982. Grassley proved to Hatch and DeConcini that Iowa's junior senator was a force to be reckoned with.[10]

"The 'Tweedledum and Tweedledumber' talk didn't last long," said A. Arthur Davis, the former Iowa Democratic Party chairman. "You had this guy who sounded like a rube, looked like a rube, originally was thought of as not very bright, in fact kind of dumb. But then, if anything, I think he probably gained more than he should have. It turned out he wasn't dumb, in fact he's bright. Then, the pendulum swung. People said, 'Oh, he's astoundingly bright.' Whereas with Harkin, nobody ever thought he was dumb, and, in people's minds, he may not rise to the same heights of Grassley on how smart he is."

Converts to the Grassley club became numerous, particularly among defense spending reformers. Journalist Carl Cannon wrote, "By taking Ronald Reagan literally and looking for ways to stamp out waste, fraud and corruption in government, particularly in the Pentagon, Grassley has assailed the Reagan administration and its trillion-dollar military build-up while becoming a folk hero to many liberals and conservatives alike. 'I'll just say it this way: He's not a politician at all,' gushed Joe Berniece, an official with the non-profit Project on Military Procurement, a self-styled watchdog group. 'He's a statesman.'"[11]

The *National Journal*, based on a survey of senators, aides, administration officials, and political strategists, rated Grassley as the best politician in the 16-member Republican class of 1980.[12]

Others at least paid proper due.

Grassley, in the words of Pulitzer Prize-winning writer John McCormally of Burlington's *Hawk Eye*, would be "doing more for disarmament than the Catholic bishops or the Quaker peace marchers."[13] Chuck Gifford, a United Auto Workers official from Burlington, also took note of Grassley's conversion from bumbling reactionary to Iowa legend. "In this state, he is what Grant Wood was. It's that American Gothic image thing. If we had a Mount Rushmore in this goddamned state, there'd be one face on it. His. And I don't understand why."

Around the time of Hultman's confirmation, Grassley began to stand out from the GOP crowd in another realm, joining Democrats in championing the cause of Wayne Cryts, a Mexico, Missouri, farmer who was arrested after he took his grain from a bankrupt elevator. The Senator offered to serve part of Cryts' jail time or help with chores while the farmer was locked up. Cryts was out by the time Grassley went to Mexico, but the farmer-senator spent a weekend working on the farm to call attention to the way farmers' property was often forfeited when an elevator went bankrupt, but other people would not lose their property if, say, a warehouse went broke while their furniture was inside.

Grassley also undertook a masterful mission of political self-preservation that had all the earmarks of party teamwork and altruism when he jumped in with both feet to reelect his Third

District successor, Representative Cooper Evans, who, like Grassley, had narrowly won his first term and faced a rematch with a tough opponent.

Grassley knew by looking down the road to his own reelection that there was plenty of incentive to use his political network on Evans' behalf against Black Hawk County Supervisor Lynn Cutler. If Cutler unseated Evans and won again in 1984, she would be a two-term congresswoman operating from Grassley's political base and ambitious enough to strike out against him. He saw to it—through his organization, endorsement, and campaigning—that Cutler's political viability was terminated in 1982.

His opportunity to shine on the farm front arose the next year, as it often does, through the misfortune of others. The victims were the inhabitants of southern Iowa's hilly and loamy land, an area that had been too difficult for many farmers to scratch out a living on, even before the drought of 1983.

Jepsen and Grassley pressed for targeted federal relief, just like the drought aid that farmers in parts of Texas received in 1982, without success. But when dairy and wheat state senators, including Grassley friend Bob Dole of Kansas, authored new legislation to increase federal support for their industries and failed to provide relief for Iowa, Grassley applied a procedural "hold." The bill, expected to pass easily in November 1983, was going nowhere fast when the Senate went on holiday recess. Over the winter months, a test of wills evolved.

Every senator from a dairy or wheat state was upset with Grassley, but he wouldn't budge. Lacking a seat on the Agriculture Committee, he employed the "hold" as his leverage. Closed-door meetings that included Reagan's top numbers cruncher, Office of Management and Budget director David Stockman, failed to break the impasse.

Finally, Grassley and Jepsen were able to force their opponents back to the table, where an agreement was hammered out in March 1984. Southern Iowa's farmers received at least $310 million in direct emergency loans; the Farmers Home Administration doubled its operating loan limit to $200,000 and guaranteed loan to $400,000; 20 percent of the loans were earmarked for the neediest farmers; the maximum repayment period was doubled; and the application deadline was reopened. Farmers were also allowed to borrow against pre-drought property values, which were 60 percent higher.

The drought had provided an early, though largely unnoticed sign of a crisis in the making, said Ken Cunningham, who started working on Capitol Hill for Rep. Tom Tauke in 1979 and joined Grassley's staff early in the first term to handle transportation, agriculture, and other issues. "The Farm Credit System was telling farmers to borrow more than they wanted. Loan officers were getting paid on the volume of loans they were selling. We could see it in the Midwest before the rest of the nation could see it, but it was tough to get the attention of the administration, get the attention, frankly, of people in Congress and the Senate from other parts of the country because the problem seemed isolated to a handful of states in the Midwest."

Grassley contended a decade later that Iowa State University professor Neil Harl was the only person who really recognized that a farm crisis was coming down the pike, but no politicians believed him at that time. "I always say that was a big mistake, and I'll always listen to Neil Harl," Grassley said.

Cunningham was impressed, though, to find a senator willing to help constituents across the political spectrum. "We got a letter of request from a prominent Democratic, agricultural family in Iowa seeking Senator Grassley's help, and I didn't know what his policy would be in helping people who adamantly opposed him. He said, 'Ken, I was elected to help the people of Iowa, and we're going to help them.' Time and again I saw that, and I was very impressed by that."

Frequently, the culprit was the Farm Credit System, which was putting the squeeze on family farmers by, in Grassley's view, artificially lowering the value of borrowers' land and property to raise interest rates to keep itself afloat. Farms could not cash flow, and farmers by the thousands were going broke. Sheriffs' sales of land and equipment were commonplace throughout 1984 to 1986. Alcoholism, divorce, and mental health problems soared with the rural unemployment rate and despair. The most desperate farmers killed bankers, neighbors, law officers, and themselves.

Grassley put himself at odds with the administration. He also used his chairmanship of the Judiciary Subcommittee on Administrative Practices as a forum to delve into the Farm Credit System. Cunningham said, "The whole Farm Credit System was set up to be a cooperative. Then these guys making six-figure salaries in Omaha and other places were not treating the farmers like bosses, but cut their throats. We tried to get that out in the public, what these guys were making, and to make the system more accountable."

The day-to-day struggle against administration agricultural policies put Grassley in good standing with Midwest farmers who felt their plight was ignored by President Reagan and much of official Washington. Because of its animosity toward Reagan in particular and Republicans in general, the farm movement was, for the most part, highly partisan in favor of the Democrats. Yet Grassley enjoyed a peaceful coexistence. As the 1986 election neared, he was not as big a target as his Republican colleagues because his emphasis on the issue was not seen as an expedient political rebirth.

At a huge rally in Sioux City in February 1985, Grassley was the only Republican official to attend and speak. He talked about the trend that was pitting defense spending against farm interests, saying he was for "farms not arms." Cunningham had not heard the expression before, and wondered if Grassley had coined the expression that became a rallying cry for hard-pressed farmers. The possibility exists, but it is remote. Grassley, by his own admission and any stretch of the imagination, is not a phrase-turning politician. Credit of authorship certainly rests elsewhere.

At the end of 1985, talk show host John McLaughlin named Grassley "Politician of the Year" for his work on agriculture and defense spending issues. Grassley was also winning awards from agricultural commodity groups for his efforts. He was recognized as "Ethanol Man of the Year" for protectionist efforts to block imports of the corn-based fuel from Brazil that would have cost U.S. farmers an estimated $500 million a year in the mid-1980s.

Cunningham contended Iowa's economic well-being was the common thread running through the drought aid battle, credit relief for farmers, the fight against imports of subsidized Canadian pork and Brazilian ethanol, and other agricultural issues tackled by Grassley.

"So much of our economy is tied to agriculture. It used to be seven of 10 jobs, directly or indirectly, were tied to agriculture in Iowa. Now, it's six of 10. Many of these battles had the effect of helping our economy, but it's not always apparent, because when you're in a crisis, you always want it to be better, and what you really may be doing is fighting to keep it from getting worse," Cunningham explained. "Those closely involved—the cattle, soybean, corn, and

*Ruth and Louis Grassley with
unidentified man [middle].
(Courtesy Mrs. Ed Wiegmann)*

*A young Grassley on the farm. (Courtesy Mrs. Ed Wiegmann)*

*Practicing for junior high band.*
*(Courtesy Mrs. Ed Wiegmann)*

*With sister Lois. (Courtesy Mrs. Ed Wiegmann)*

*First day in the Iowa Legislature 1958.*

*At Republican social function with J. Kendall "Buster" Lynes [center with moustache]. (Courtesy J. W. "Bill" Lynes)*

*House of Representatives photo 1974. (Iowa Official Register)*

*Celebrating the 1980 Senate victory. (Grassley staff photo)*

*Barbara and Chuck Grassley during the Senator's Foreign Ambassadors Tour visiting California Junction, Iowa in August 1995. (Mary Jo Archibold)*

*Meeting with President Reagan (White House photo)*

*Bill signing in the Oval Office. (White House photo)*

*Iowa Republican delegation meets with Vice President Bush 1984 on Air Force Two. (White House photo)*

*White House meeting on AWACS 1981. (White House photo)*

*On the campaign trail 1992. (Grassley staff photo)*

pork associations—knew what Grassley was doing. They don't hand out those awards for somebody who just puts out slick press releases."

In 1986, in large measure due to Grassley's prodding, a new section of federal bankruptcy laws written specifically for farmers, Chapter 12, was enacted. Despite his publicized differences, Grassley did cooperate often with the administration. He supported the President at least 70 percent of the time, including aid to Nicaragua's *contras*.

He also worked on building his own network in Washington. After passage of the Older Americans Act, Grassley suggested that Conroy make a move over to the Federal Council on Aging in Health and Human Services in 1981. "I said, 'What? Are you trying to get rid of me?'" Conroy smiled. "Because we'd had some shoot-outs, sometimes it was money or something like that. But one of the things Chuck learned was if you can put a key staffer somewhere in the executive staff, it's good for you. Not only that, but you can affect the definitions and regulations and other kinds of things. It's just a smart move." Conroy became the council's director, and worked there until his retirement.

Tom Harkin, a Cumming Democrat who became Iowa's junior senator by upending Jepsen in 1984, found Grassley receptive to cooperation on issues important to Iowa, despite sharp political differences. "When it comes to issues, especially concerning Iowa, we work closely together. Our staffs have a good relationship. Ethanol. The flood [of 1993]. There are always agricultural issues. We work together on Farm Bill stuff. And whenever there are certain things cities need, we tend to work together on those."

Grassley has proved to be "one of the best politicians I've ever met," Harkin said. "He understands politics and the right buttons to push, what to say, when to move and when not to move. His politics are more one of 'don't get too far out in front on any issue, gauge carefully, find things that have a broad appeal and work your constituency, just work it well, keep in close contact with your constituency.' I think that's probably akin to his more conservative nature."

Bipartisanship did not always produce successful results. He teamed with Sens. Joe Biden, the Delaware Democrat, and Nancy Kassebaum, a Kansas Republican, in 1984 to propose a one-year budget freeze that would have cut $260 billion from annual deficits by fiscal year 1987, nearly double the $144 billion worked out by administration officials and Senate Republican leaders. Federal Reserve Board chairman Paul Volcker predicted the freeze would have lowered interest rates at least one percent. Hence, the so-called KGB approach was the strongest threat to the Reagan plan because of the "dramatic simplicity of its across-the-board impact."

"But that may have been its fatal flaw," *Washington Post* reporter Helen Dewar wrote, "as conservatives rebelled at the deep cuts it would have made in Reagan's military build-up, liberals balked at the constraints it would have put on major domestic benefit programs such as social security and many moderates shuddered at both results." It was defeated 65–33.[14]

Grassley would, however, earn respect from (and a victory over) one of his political heroes, Mr. Conservative himself, Sen. Barry Goldwater of Arizona. He came to Goldwater's attention "when he started to find fault with the military budget," the former Arizona senator wrote in June 1994.[15]

"Because that was my specialty in the Senate, I had to defend it," Goldwater recalled. "I will say this, he knew what he was talking about. He had done his homework, he was thorough, he was convincing, and I grew to be, more or less, a follower of his."

Grassley's endorsement in presidential politics also carried respect. "It means credibility and integrity. With Grassley, there's nobody with more integrity," said Senate Republican Leader Robert Dole, who won Grassley's backing in the 1988 caucus campaign and again for 1996.

With Grassley's help in 1988, Dole scored a big victory in the first-in-the-nation Iowa caucuses that almost knocked Vice President George Bush out of the contest. "I don't care if they're Democrats or Republicans," Dole said. "People know he's an honest person, pushing Congress to comply with all these laws they impose. Barbara and me and he and Elizabeth did a swing around the state after I announced. That was above and beyond the call of duty." Dole had concluded long before that politically, legislatively, and personally, Grassley was "the kind of guy you want to have around.

"I think he's one of my closest friends. We're from the same part of the country and have the same interests. There's not much time to socialize around this place, but we think alike, have the same priorities—senior citizens, agriculture, health care—so there's a lot of common interest," the feisty GOP leader said. "We both have a sense of humor. We're both pretty direct. You don't have to guess where we're coming from, and I think we both have a lot of common sense of the Midwest brand. We have a strong work ethic. How many times has he visited each county?"

If there is any weakness in Grassley, Dole offered mildly from his Capitol Hill office, it is "just like the rest of us, you get involved in so many things that you're not as focused as you should be sometimes. But he's generally somebody who gets an earlier start than most of us and he's here 'til the last dog is hung at night. On weekends, he's on the plane back to Iowa, so if you wanted somebody to be your full-time representative, you've got it in Grassley."

Even Orrin Hatch, with whom Grassley had clashed over Hultman's nomination, eventually showered his colleague with praise. "You'd have to call Chuck one of the leaders, without question, in agriculture. He's had an effect on almost every ag bill before the Senate. His personal actions are exemplary." Speaking from a position of firsthand knowledge, Hatch said Grassley was "known for his honest, blunt, straightforward manner." But he also praised the Iowan's "really infectious sense of humor."

"When he puts that Grassley smile on you, you can't get mad at him. He has a tremendous capacity to laugh at himself. Decent. Honorable. Very practical," Hatch said. "He is one of the few who really deserve the appellation of 'great senator.'"

# An Orange Chevette in the
# Pentagon Parking Lot

Charles Grassley wasn't looking for an argument with the Pentagon when he began his second full year in the United States Senate. "We started out in 1982 with an option to either push Reagan's FY83 budget or do an across-the-board freeze," explained Kris Kolesnik, Grassley's staff expert on budget-related issues. "The target was the 'humongous' $95 billion deficit that everyone was shocked about."

Remembering Grassley's campaign promise to maintain a strong military, the new staffer was a bit apprehensive about his task. "I presented him with the two options, and he said, 'Let's go with the freeze,'" Kolesnik recalled. "I said, 'That means we'd have to freeze defense.' He said, 'Would everything else be frozen?' and I said, 'Yeah.' He said, 'Well, then let's do it.'"

Grassley sought to enlist fellow conservatives to the cause, but some expressed fears that the MX missile or B-1 bomber would become casualties in any war on the deficit. "We tried to get them focused on the problem of the deficit and the fact that if you don't hit everybody the same way, nothing's going to get done," Kolesnik said. "We went through that year and couldn't get much support from Republicans for the concept, so the mission Grassley left me with at Christmas vacation was, 'You've got to look into the defense thing, and if we can freeze it, how? And if I can't, I want to know that, too.'"

Kolesnik soon concluded a freeze would work, but the issue was so complex that the easiest way to convey the point to Grassley was to have him call Secretary of Defense Caspar Weinberger and ask to speak to a cost analyst whose recent conclusions had been leaked to the *Boston Globe* and *Wall Street Journal*.

Chuck Spinney had charted the costs of 150 weapons programs to reach his conclusion that the Reagan Administration was "grotesquely underestimating" the cost of its massive build-up. "It wasn't the normal type of bullshit analysis done in this building," Spinney said years later. "I just carpet-bombed them. Someone said my presentation could have been shortened, after two or three examples you got the point. But my whole purpose was to make them numb."

Dr. Lawrence Korb, Weinberger's Assistant Secretary for Readiness, agreed with Spinney. "I always felt we were building up too quickly. In fact, yes, we needed to spend more on defense given what had happened after Vietnam . . . and that the Soviets were trying to sort of outspend us, but I didn't think we needed to do it as much as we did. In fact, before I went to the Pentagon I wrote that we needed a build-up not a binge, which is surprising to me that they even picked me. And, of course, [Jimmy] Carter on his way out had pushed the budget up sort of like, 'Here, you guys. You said it wasn't adequate. Top it.' Which we did. So, I always felt we were sowing the seeds of our own destruction."

The armed services could not absorb that much money, which was a doubling of procurement spending over five years. "So you take the problems already there and compound them," Korb explained. "People forget that other than Reagan's philosophy of 'we're going to spend [the Soviets] into oblivion,' most Republicans have been very careful about spending money on defense. What do we remember Eisenhower for? [His warning about] the military-industry complex. Jerry Ford fired Jim Schlesinger for bitching about low levels of defense spending. That has been the Republican tradition. Grassley is closer to that tradition than the Reagan philosophy. People used to say to me, 'Why are you complaining about the deficit?' And I said, 'That's why I'm a Republican. I always thought that we worried about the deficit, and Reagan doesn't seem to give a damn about it.'"

Weinberger, who declined to be interviewed or respond to written questions for this book, had come into the Pentagon with a reputation as "Cap the Knife," but he was soon signaling different branches of the service that the Reagan Administration would only be able to keep the funding spigot turned on for so long, so they'd better fill up as fast as they could. (Over on Capitol Hill, in the privacy of their office, Grassley's people derisively referred to Weinberger as "Cap the Ladle" for dishing out the gravy to the Pentagon.) Korb said, "In those first couple months, they came in and we said, 'No, ask for more.' . . . Of course, it was an overreaction of what happened under Carter. People just got carried away."

There was the feeling among Reagan's Pentagon appointees, Korb recalled, that they would avoid the mistakes of the past through better planning and analysis that would force costs down during production and make maintenance easier and cheaper. They also failed to take into account that too much money itself was a disincentive to good management. "I've been a student of this all my life, and I've seen some smart people—[Robert S.] McNamara and [Charles E.] Wilson and Clark Clifford—and I said to myself, 'If they couldn't figure it out, why are we going to be able to do it?'"

Reagan's people did not figure it out. With less than two months to amend Jimmy Carter's budget and present it to Congress, the new administration basically closed its eyes and threw a lot of money at the military. The action was the foundation of a costly trend.

Korb contended that he soon began to encourage colleagues to think long term, with the thrust of the Spinney analysis as a starting point. "I said, 'Guys, even [with] all of the optimistic assumptions you're making about efficiencies as we go along, we're still going to be $700 billion short over the next five years of doing what it is you say you want. . . . It's just not going to happen, so let's start making some hard decisions now before this thing gets away from us.' The brief was leaked to the press. Rather than confront the issue, we all ended up taking lie detector tests to see who leaked the brief."

That leak and others led to a press conference in which Spinney's superior denied the analysis existed. Reporters, who had their hands on a Pentagon report that cited Spinney's analysis and knew him as an authority on the "hollow defense," smelled a cover-up. So did Kolesnik.

He had heard Spinney's name in those news reports just as he was reaching the conclusion that the inevitable result of a Reagan funding frenzy would be that the Pentagon would spend more money for proportionally less effectiveness. "It was not just a matter of money; it was national security," Kolesnik said.

It was a Thursday in early January 1983 when Grassley called Weinberger, and the Secretary quickly agreed to send Spinney to the Senator's office the following Monday. "On Friday we started getting calls from generals, first one star, then two stars, then three stars. 'Spinney can't come over to give you his briefing,'" Kolesnik said.

He spent Saturday trying to clear the bureaucratic log jam. Grassley, calling from Iowa, told his aide to "tell whoever you're talking to that if Chuck Spinney isn't in my office by two o'clock Monday, I'm going over to Weinberger's office to find out why not."

The jockeying continued on Monday, with the Pentagon brass offering to send over Spinney's supervisor, Dr. David Chu, in his place. "Two o'clock came and Grassley said, 'Go get the Chevette.' He had this little orange Chevette. On the way out the door, he told the [administrative assistant] to tell them we were on the way," Kolesnik said. "We went over to the Pentagon. They had a spot for us to park at the River Entrance, and this colonel was waiting for us, nervous as heck."

Weinberger was at the White House, so Grassley told his subordinates to produce Spinney. They reassured him that Chu was on his way up to the office to present his cost-analysis briefing. "Grassley told Chu, 'I'll take yours and his.' Chu denied it. That's when Grassley said he was going to Spinney's office. Chu said Spinney wasn't there. I knew he was—I'd talked to him on the phone—but we didn't press it. We left and Grassley told Chu to tell Weinberger that he was very displeased, and Weinberger hadn't heard the end of it. As soon as they denied him access to Spinney, Grassley knew they were hiding something and that we were on the right track. The next day, Weinberger called up and said, 'Look, Chuck, you and I are good Republicans, let's stick together.' Grassley said, 'I wanted a briefing. You told me I could have it, and I'm not going to stand for this.' Grassley said he was going to pursue it on his own, and the reaction from Weinberger was 'you've gotta do what you've gotta do.'"

What Grassley did was line up the support of Budget Committee colleagues Nancy Kassebaum of Kansas and Slade Gorton of Washington to have Spinney come to the Hill to testify. He knew there would be no trouble getting Democrats to side with them and create a majority that would force action. Kolesnik recalled that Chairman Pete Domenici of New Mexico "basically had to do what we wanted."

However, Sen. John Tower, the Texan chairing the Armed Services Committee, was under no such obligation. In effect, he commandeered the proceedings by claiming jurisdiction. In a joint session with the Budget Committee, Tower demanded the hearing be held on a Friday, when almost everyone would be out of town. He would have Spinney testify behind closed doors for good measure.

"It became a real chess game," Kolesnik said. "We knew the press wouldn't stand for a closed-door hearing, and so we . . . told them there would be a hearing but they would be disallowed. So, all the members of the press corps called Armed Services and complained."

When only print reporters were allowed in, Grassley's people called TV correspondents to get them stirred up. The committee relented, but only agreed to one "pool" camera, which fed all the networks and local affiliates. Kolesnik said, "We called the same TV people and told them that, and the committee relented once more. Now, all cameras were allowed."

The committee regrouped and came up with a new strategy: hold the session in a tiny hearing room in the Dirksen Building. Grassley's staff countered by calling everyone they knew, urging them to reserve a seat in the hearing room. So many people called that the committee was forced to move to the cavernous Russell Caucus Room, site of the Watergate hearings and Lt. Col. Oliver North's testimony during the Iran-Contra inquiry. By the time the Spinney hearing began, midafternoon on a snowy Friday, the room was packed with reporters and eight television cameras. Tower's ploy had been short-circuited by Grassley's behind-the-scenes maneuvering.

Despite the heightened attention, Pentagon insiders, thinking the issue had blown over, were declaring a public relations victory. Then Caspar Weinberger arrived at his Monday morning staff meeting and was given the latest edition of *Time*. Spinney's face was on the cover. "It took two years to freeze the defense budget, but that hearing was the beginning of the battle," Kolesnik glowed.

It was the first time Weinberger had underestimated Grassley's tenacity, intelligence, and resourcefulness. Weinberger could hardly be blamed for the misjudgment early on, but he and his aides continued to view Grassley as "almost a joke," according to Korb. "You always have a couple flakes [on Capitol Hill] and I think they put him in this category. 'Who is this guy? Where the hell did he come from? He was in the House. He's some dumb farmer. We don't have to take him seriously, and if we ignore him, he'll go away.'"

Korb was stunned by the arrogance and stupidity of the strategy. "I'm saying to myself, 'Good God, he's a Republican. This is the old Midwest tradition. You've got to remember that Midwest Republicans are traditionally isolationist, very skeptical of government, and why do we want to make this guy an enemy?' If Weinberger had called Grassley over and said, 'Senator, you know, you're right. We're going to look into this. Why don't you go down and talk to Spinney, and if you've got any ideas, come back and we'll talk more.' I think that would have ended the issue right there."

Grassley went at the Pentagon policies from two directions—employing "macro-arguments" about spending from the Budget Committee vantage and "micro-arguments" via his Judiciary subcommittee—and by feeding stories to the media to build public concern. Some Senate Republicans thought Grassley was allowing himself to be used by Democrats or that he was motivated by his own reelection, still three years away.

Kolesnik said, "He wasn't making a lot of friends in his own party or the White House, but he was using nothing but conservative arguments. The same sort of arguments we would use for other programs, we would apply to defense. He was the first to talk about defense competition. He talked about improving efficiency in programs, integrity, bureaucracy. Every possible thing you can imagine that conservatives would use against social programs, we brought it up. We called the defense industry 'welfare queens.' They hated it. They thought that was below the belt, and we had people in the office that didn't want us to do the defense crusade. Defense people would contact them to try to get word to Grassley, saying, 'This is awful. It's going to hurt this or that.' I didn't know about it then but, to his credit, Grassley just said, 'Keep going on.'"

Grassley did maintain a few GOP allies—Kassebaum, Gorton, Bob Kasten of Wisconsin, Rudy Boschwitz of Minnesota, and Don Nickles of Oklahoma. Though they did not hang together on all issues, they did, along with Democrats, provide Grassley with enough leverage to force his agenda forward. Still, Grassley may have been tilting against Pentagon windmills for a long time, had the military contractors not begun to show a propensity for doing stupid things to illustrate Grassley's points. Much to the embarrassment of the Reagan Administration, revelations about contractors' excesses began to spring up like dandelions after a spring rain:

$435 for an ordinary claw hammer, mystically described in billing as an "impact device."
$659 per ash tray in Air Force planes under production.
$750 toilet seats in those same aircraft.
$1,118 for plastic stool caps.
$6,000 for aircraft arm rests.

Korb explained, "Grassley got into this thing before a lot of the spare parts horror stories and when they started coming out, it sort of proved what he was saying."

As the story grew bigger with each revelation, Grassley was nudged to the side, partly by his own doing because he wanted a bipartisan, bicameral attack on waste. According to Kolesnik, Grassley's staff let Representative Barbara Boxer, a California Democrat, break the news that the Air Force was paying $7,622 for coffee pots in its C-5 planes.

But more influential members also pushed their way into the picture. Rep. John Dingel, a Michigan Democrat who chaired the House Energy and Commerce Subcommittee on Oversight and Investigations, began to probe the Army's Bradley armored personnel carrier and the Air Force's MX missile and Stealth bomber programs. "By then," Korb said, "the whole Congress was up in arms, and the whole country was up in arms and you just didn't have to deal with Grassley, you had to deal with everybody else, the whole Congress."

Attacks on Weinberger's Pentagon, and lobbying of Reagan by senators including Grassley, persuaded the President to form the Packard Commission, an independent panel to try to clean up some spending abuses. The maneuver was a necessary step in the attempt to inoculate the administration from criticism that had gained legitimacy through Grassley's complaints.

"Remember what Reagan did to the Democrats. He got in there by talking about all the waste, the welfare queens, and people buying vodka with food stamps," Korb said. "Weinberger would put out these press releases saying we're getting the F-16 for only $45 million. People can't relate to that. The logic goes, if you screw up a hammer or a toilet seat then of course they don't trust you on the big ones because that's what they can relate to. And the interesting thing about Grassley was he was ahead of that."

The coffee pots, hammers, ash trays, arm rests, and plastic seat caps literally worth their weight in gold became potent symbols of Grassley's complaints. But Korb saw an overcorrection that was also problematic. "Then we went too far the other way and worried about the small things, not the big things. I would not fault him but I would say that somebody in addition to this needs to be asking, 'Why did you need 600 ships? Never mind if you can get them efficiently. What are you going to do with them?' Or, 'Why do we need a new bomber?' Because even if you buy it correctly and don't need it that's not a good thing. [Grassley] was not on Armed Services so you couldn't be saying,

'Well, you ought to be looking at those big things,' because that's the vehicle for looking at the big things."

Grassley and Pryor also worked with Rep. Denny Smith, a conservative Oregon Republican, and others to create an independent weapons testing office. Before then, test results were sent to the Pentagon officers whose advancement depended heavily on the apparent success of the weapons they were in charge of developing. Korb said, "The services would really slant those tests, and Smith challenged them."

Smith, a former Air Force pilot who flew in the Vietnam War, forced Weinberger into killing the Army's costly, unreliable "Sergeant York" antiaircraft gun after learning through the Pentagon grapevine that test results had been altered. Grassley teamed with Smith in efforts geared toward freezing the defense budget, as well as the overall budget. He played off Smith's focus on capability issues to hammer away at cost issues.

The Iowan scored three Senate victories during a single month in 1985 to reform the Defense Department budget, adding momentum to a cost-cutting crusade that he hoped would sweep throughout the federal system. Korb recalled, "'We had asked for a six percent increase for FY85/86. He got on the Senate floor and said, 'They don't deserve any increase. They deserve a decrease.' That, to me, was really pivotal. The bill was just going for routine floor debate; it had already cleared the committees. And remember, the Republicans still controlled the Senate until '86. It was a very critical thing, because the Democrats were terrified of the military and terrified at being seen as soft on defense. They didn't want to take on the Pentagon, but Grassley furnished them a perfect vehicle."

In leading the charge for a freeze, Grassley went up against a legend whom he deeply admired. During debate, Grassley told of proudly keeping a "Barry Goldwater for President" poster at his station at the Waterloo Register Company in 1964 and bearing the brunt of criticism from union colleagues. "I told [Goldwater] about that and that I respected him. Then I went on to say why he was wrong."

On May 2, Grassley won a defense budget freeze as the Senate rejected the President's defense budget by opting for his "freeze-plus-inflation" target on a 50–49 vote. "That was the end of the Reagan build-up from that point on, and that was a major accomplishment in my life," Grassley said.

Kolesnik elaborated, "The major impact was to plateau the defense budget. By 1991, events [such as the fall of the Berlin Wall and the collapse of the Soviet Union] would have caught up [to the defense budget], but there was still a lot of money saved. Billions of dollars. Even though we were making a big dent on the deficit, the deficit continued to grow. We didn't take drastic enough action because we underestimated other forces at work. But the result of the defense work was that we didn't spend ourselves into oblivion; we've only spent ourselves into near oblivion."

On May 23, the Senate accepted Grassley's provision on the 1986 defense authorization bill to reestablish a federal program to reward and protect defense whistleblowers who uncover excessive costs, abuse, or fraud. The bill would make whistleblowers eligible for cash awards and greater legal protection. "These loyal public servants who expose waste have too often been rewarded by demotions, undesirable transfers, firings or other penalties," Grassley said in a press release. Seeking to reform "a twisted system which rewards wasters and penalizes savers," Grassley's provision would allow whistleblowers to appeal their cases through federal courts when seeking just treatment.

On May 24, the Senate adopted the third Grassley reform, which would require the Pentagon to inform Congress of "real costs" charged by defense contractors as well as "reasonable or 'should' costs" based on industry norms. Grassley said the "should costs" information would help Congress quickly identify and block excessive charges passed on to taxpayers. He explained that "when listed next to its real cost of $450, as well as a reasonable cost of seven or eight dollars, the Pentagon-named 'impact device' could be cited by Congress as excessively priced, even without knowledge that we're talking claw hammers."

He also advanced other good management and cost control initiatives. Among those proposals was his "creeping capitalism" bill to mandate greater competition among contractors for billions of dollars in Pentagon business. Grassley went directly to the White House for a meeting with Reagan and Weinberger to seek protection for whistleblower George Spanton, who was pressured to retire after revealing in 1982 that Pratt & Whitney Aircraft Group had charged taxpayers $10,000 for Palm Beach parties, billed the Air Force $1.4 million for $531,000 in spare parts, and created pay scales far above industry averages. After a publicized campaign, Spanton's boss, Charles O. Starrett, Jr., was removed as director of the Defense Contractor Audit Agency and fined by the Merit Systems Protection Board for wrongful retaliation against Spanton.

In the Judiciary Committee, Grassley resurrected the dormant Abraham Lincoln Law—the Federal False Claims Act—to combat fraud against the government. There, too, he pressed forward with related whistleblower protection laws.

In its preview of the Senate that was returning to Democratic control, the *Almanac of American Politics 1988* provided a keen insight into Grassley's impact, more by looking back than ahead. "Legislatively, Grassley is not likely to be a power in a Democratic Senate. Yet he has shown the capacity to change the terms of debate, and future historians may date the end of the Reagan Administration's huge increases in defense spending to Grassley's initiatives."

Years later, Pryor said, "The thing about Chuck Grassley is, very few people realize the amount of courage it took during that period of time, in the early '80s, with the Reagan defense build-up and 'defense, defense, defense.' I remember one time I asked one of the Republican senators if they would join me if I offered an amendment to cut 25 cents—25 cents!—out of the defense budget and they said, 'Absolutely not.' That's where it was, and here was Grassley at that time going against his own party, challenging his own president to accountability. I tell you, this took a lot of courage for this man to do that. He never backed off. He always called them as he saw them."

Pete Conroy also saw something instructive in Grassley's clash with the Pentagon. "Chuck has [a method of operation] when he sees an issue and mostly what it is, is 'take on somebody big.' First of all, you make sure your cause is just and you've got enough issues. But if you're going to go, go big. Chuck is not a bully. For instance, he's not going to pick on a waitress. The Senate and House are full of bullies, first class bullies, throwing their weight around. A lot of staff is like that, too. But Chuck doesn't do that. When they slammed the door [on him at the Pentagon], it was the dumbest thing."

Conroy also noted that Grassley, "despite people thinking he was tearing the hell out of the Pentagon," maintained the respect and friendship of a number of current and retired military people, including executives at Chamberlain Manufacturing, a Waterloo munitions maker. "That's the interesting paradox in Chuck. Again, it's the politician in him. He's known in these circles. He's got all these arms guys with him. He's got an arms plant in his district."

Grassley continued to keep pressure on the Department of Defense throughout the late 1980s and into the early 1990s, drawing a brief, polite chiding from Reagan's successor. "After I became President, I did not agree with some of Senator Grassley's attacks on the Pentagon, but I always respected him for his integrity," former President George Bush wrote in May 1994.

Korb's analysis almost 10 years later was that Grassley left a lasting imprint on the Pentagon and the federal budget financed by taxpayers. "The procurement process is much better today, and there's a lot less waste and things like that. The Packard Commission pointed it in the right direction. They followed up the Packard Commission, and then they had the Ill Wind investigation [into defense contractor fraud]. So, now, I think people are much less willing to do stupid things in the process because you can get yourself in a lot of trouble. And the inspectors general in the Pentagon have become much harder to keep under your thumb. Nobody would dare touch the Inspector General."

Spinney, still inside the Pentagon in 1994, saw a harsher side than Korb. He indicted the government's accounting system and the congressional response to a fiscal crisis. "In the early '80s, there were a lot of people in Congress worked up about what was going on over here, partly because the Democrats had the Congress and a Republican president was throwing a lot of money at [the military]. Now that it's a Democrat president, those people have hightailed. [Senator] Barbara Boxer [of California] claimed to be for defense reform, but in my mind, she's just a shill for defense contractors now.

"The thing that stands out about Grassley was here's a conservative Republican with an extremely powerful conservative Republican presidency, and he said, 'I think we've got some problems over there, and I don't like what's going on.' He's doing it again, and some people might say he's playing [politics] because it's a Democratic president, but you've got to go back and look at the record. It's a theme."

In the post-Cold War era, Spinney saw continued exorbitant spending on weapons that did not work. He noted that Grassley, who had the "best staffer on defense matters in the entire

Congress," Charlie Murphy, was perhaps positioning himself for another assault on military waste in the late 1990s. "Grassley's the only guy in Congress doing anything about it. Everyone else has their head in the sand because they think if we turn it off we'll have a depression because there's obviously not a military threat. . . . The one thing about Grassley over the long term that has been a constant theme is government waste and accountability. If we can't account to ourselves, how can we account to the American people? We've evolved government accounting practices that have disconnected people from the budget. Politicians love that stuff because they can rape, pillage, and loot. Grassley is one guy that views that as a threat to our democracy."

Ultimately, according to at least one colleague, defense reform will be Grassley's Senate legacy. "It's a little bit like if all of a sudden Ted Kennedy was against a civil rights bill. It would have a significant impact if he was against it," Biden explained in May 1994. "Well, for a conservative on the far right of the political spectrum, as Grassley is viewed to be, to take on defense contractors, is like, 'Woah, wait a minute. This *must* be a problem.' So, I think, initially at least, it had that impact."

Still, it cannot be denied that the Iowan's vigorous campaign for military procurement reform also paid political dividends. "He's upset conservatives over the years by taking on the defense establishment. Now, that's good Iowa politics because defense has never been a real strong issue in Iowa for conservatives or liberals," Biden said.

The analysis would prove especially true in 1986 as Grassley prepared to seek a second term. Liberal groups kept reminding Iowans how much more they were paying for the big military build-up and how little the state's depressed economy was receiving in return. Deliberately or not, Grassley had insulated himself from partisan attacks and enhanced his stature with Iowa voters even before the opposition's criticism began.

# "All but Impossible to Beat"

In 1986, Grassley found himself in the same, unenviable position as John Culver six years earlier: an incumbent running in a particularly trying year. Grassley the studious plodder, however, was better positioned for a positive outcome.

As he had done after the election in 1974, he moved decisively to reinforce and expand his political base. Through his work on defense spending and other issues, he had also shucked the image as a Roger Jepsen clone. His six-year term had afforded the luxury of time to let Iowa voters get to know and like him.

But it dumped his reelection effort in the midst of a devastating farm-sector recession caused, according to Democrats, by Reagan Administration economic policies wholeheartedly supported by Grassley. The Senator had several advantages his predecessor had not enjoyed. He was in closer touch with his constituents. Not counting the 1980 campaign itself, Grassley was in the sixth cycle of his annual tour of all 99 counties. And he literally became the Republican Senatorial Campaign Committee's textbook example for success in 1986 by taking action on several fronts to protect himself politically.

First, he very publicly distanced himself from Reagan, widening the chasm opened by differences over farm policy and defense procurement waste and fraud. When White House political adviser Ed Rollins grumbled that he wished "that son-of-a-bitchin' Grassley would die" for not going along with the Administration's agenda in March 1985, the Senator's operatives leaked the story, and he played the defiantly principled, wounded party to the hilt. Correspondingly, signals were sent that Reagan wouldn't campaign for any candidate who didn't vote for the MX missile. Grassley said that was fine with him.

Reagan's popularity was, after all, lower in Iowa than anyplace else in the country. *The American Almanac of Politics 1988* observed: "But Grassley was not maneuvering. He is strong precisely because his popular stands reflect his genuine, long-held beliefs, and that he advances them as shrewdly as he has his own career. From that point on other incumbent Republicans rushed forward to record their dissents from this or that item on the Administration's agenda and tailored their reelection campaigns closely to the views and priorities of their home states. . . . Not all his colleagues were as successful as Grassley; but then he has been winning with this kind of formula for three decades."[1]

A second factor in Grassley's favor was the tremendous campaign fund he had amassed, due, in large measure, to his position on the Senate Finance Committee at a time when Congress was overhauling the federal tax system. Special interest groups lavished money on every member of the committee. Between January 1, 1985, and June 30, 1986, Finance Committee members were among the Senate's leading PAC-money recipients, including Robert Dole ($839,319), Steve Symms of Idaho ($870,560), and Grassley ($668,526).[2] From the PAC's perspective, a senator from Iowa who supported their views was just as good as one from California or New York, and he required less money to win reelection.

The media's fascination with Grassley also heightened as the election approached, affording him favorable national and statewide coverage. "It is now an established fact—in the way facts somehow get established in politics—that Republican Senator Charles Grassley of Iowa will be all but impossible to beat this year. And deservedly so," proclaimed the *Des Moines Register* on February 16, 1986.

Grassley had a better than 3-to-1 lead over Roehrick in the newspaper's Iowa Poll, holding the support of 68 percent of all voters. His 89 percent backing from Republicans vaulted him into rarefied air; Robert Ray in 1978 and Ronald Reagan in 1984 stood at 84 percent among GOP partisans.[3] He noted that his independent streak had helped him with voters, but he did not consider himself invincible. "My opponent is the Iowa economy not my Democratic opponent, and I don't think the economy will soon improve."[4]

Grassley campaign finance director Tom Synhorst was not as concerned about the economy's impact. "I felt like it could have lessened what we won by, but I felt like he had distanced himself enough from the Administration's problems with the economy."

Instead, the campaign was hyping the Senator's invincibility. A risky strategy with the potential to backfire, when it works it pays handsome dividends in the form of token opposition. Grassley's organization was worried early on that six-term Rep. Berkley Bedell, a well-liked, wealthy Sioux City Democrat, would enter the race. "But Berk told Grassley face to face he wouldn't run," Synhorst said. "Grassley had flat-out asked him."

A political comeback by former Sen. Harold Hughes was also rumored. "But part of our strategy was if we had $1 million in the bank a year out, people would have to think twice. The organization and [Grassley's early work], all combined, made a pretty daunting package. That was our objective."

And the objective was achieved. Emerging from a morass of Democratic fear toward a challenge of Grassley was a shaky, underfinanced challenge by Des Moines attorney John Roehrick, who reversed a 1985 vow that he would not run if Grassley's popularity remained high. "Let me put it this way," said Roehrick, "I'm not a kamikaze pilot."[5]

Roehrick began his campaign on January 23, 1986, with a broadside at military spending and a call to restore the nation's smokestack industries. He charged that Grassley "talks about $600 hammers and votes for $53 million to reactivate battleships. While he talks of the waste, he supports Ronald Reagan's gold-plated trillion dollar military expenditures, which directly affects the deficit and the economy of this state."

Iowa Democratic Party chairman A. Arthur Davis described Grassley as an "anti-union, anti-farm, anti-small town, pro-Pentagon senator."[6] But Roehrick wasn't well known, even in the capital city, and he lacked a fundraising track record. Davis quietly launched a search for a more viable candidate.

"I like John but knew he wasn't the guy," Davis said in a May 1994 interview at the Des Moines Club. With the deadpan skills of a great storyteller, Davis recalled, "There was one Democrat prominent in Iowa, who shall remain nameless, and I was having lunch with him here. And after the preliminaries, I said to him, 'Let me tell you what I really want you to do. I want you to run against Chuck Grassley.' He looked at me, and he said, 'I thought we were friends, Arthur.'"

Davis had a certain profile in mind, though he was uncertain that image stood the test of time. "It seemed to me you couldn't 'out-rube' him. Throw that rube out and elect our rube? No. So, it had to be somebody smooth. It had to be a [Pioneer Hi-Bred president] Tom Urban or [Meredith Corp. editor-in-chief] Jim Autry. . . . I thought the only way to beat him was to say we needed a different sort of United States senator."

Tom Harkin appeared to be directing a less discreet search, trying to counter Grassley with a pro-choice woman. State Representatives Minnette Doderer of Iowa City, Kay Chapman of

Cedar Rapids, and Guttenberg Mayor Karen Merrick were the publicized potential candidates, but state Rep. Jean Lloyd-Jones of Iowa City was suggested, too. Roehrick reacted angrily. "This is a Democratic firing squad. Everyone lines up in a circle and starts shooting."[7]

Roehrick wasn't the only angry Democrat. One account had it that when Harkin unveiled his list to state party leaders, he neglected the protocol of including Vice Chair Barb Leach. Sitting in on the meeting, Leach was incensed by the oversight.

Harkin eventually retreated, mission unaccomplished, with party activists grumbling that he had done more harm than good to the party's cause. Roehrick said later, "I'm not really blaming him, that's in the past . . . but it really ground everything to a halt. You know, your own Senator. You can't go to Washington and talk to PAC people about raising money so there you are."

Harkin insisted later that he had never intended to recruit someone to oppose Roehrick in the primary. Instead, he said, "Some people in the party came to me and said, 'You're our top-ranking Democrat.' I didn't even call the meeting. They wanted to draft someone to run against Grassley."

Ironically, Harkin had played a large role in Roehrick's decision to enter the race. Roehrick, who had long aspired to office, was impressed by Harkin's 1984 victory over Roger Jepsen, sensing that it foreshadowed the end of the New Right's brief dominance. By early 1985 at the latest, Roehrick was thinking that Grassley had just squeaked by Culver, the economy was down in the dumps, public sentiment was turning against Reagan, and "if everything came together, there was a crack at it."

He was, admittedly, betting on long odds by jumping into the "all but impossible" race. But there was always the slim chance that lightning would strike, literally or figuratively.

It nearly did.

Grassley, utterly disheartened by the pain and suffering caused by the agricultural recession, told his wife on a February 1985 flight home from Washington that he did not want to stand for another term. "[There was] terrible stress from the farm crisis in those first six or eight months in 1985. I said, 'If it's OK with you, I'm not going to run for reelection. I just can't take it.' The emotion of people losing their farms, you just felt a little like them."

Grassley would have felt more like them had he not had his Senate job as off-farm income. He was making the 20th payment on 120 acres, but he owed $65,000 on his remaining 80 acres. "Most years, I've had some off-farm income, not much sometimes, but always some. If I had just been farming [in 1985], I would have been in terrible shape. Maybe I wouldn't have lost the farm. But I don't know."

Grassley also worried about his son, Robin, who was having a tough time finding money to farm on rented land. The Senator opted, however, to remain in the race.

Meanwhile, Roehrick, who did not know then how close he had come to seeing that elusive lightning strike, found that raising funds was like pulling teeth. "The money was just unbelievably difficult. And that's something that I had no idea the amount of time that took and the amount of money needed. Until you do it, you cannot envision it. You cannot envision, a year out, laying out a budget and saying, 'My God! That's $5,000 a day,' and trying to raise it, and against an incumbent whose popularity and performance were up in the [60 percent range]. It was a real chicken-egg problem because unless you could drive [his popularity] down you couldn't get money, and in order to drive that down you had to have money. So, it got to a situation that was the most frustrating part."

Roehrick had no clear strategy to drive down Grassley's popularity. "That was something that we did realize, that you needed $1 million in the bank before you could do it, and that's why you have [millionaires] in the Senate. Unless you can bankroll it, you just can't do it."

Roehrick, a Minnesota native with a streak of Hubert Humphrey in him, had ties to some of the party's more liberal activists. He had been active in Gary Hart's 1984 presidential campaign and had connections with George McGovern's organization as well. "I had that network of Hart people around the state and McGovern people, so basically we just tied into that and were trying to expand that base out there."

The Hart-McGovern base wasn't much to work from, in retrospect. Hart had finished second in the 1984 caucuses, but he had only 16.4 percent of the small core of party activists who participate in the caucuses. McGovern, the party's 1972 nominee, was the third-place finisher with 10.2 percent.

Roehrick had to face another reality. No small part of Grassley's electoral success has been the ability to win healthy Democratic and independent support. The reason: constituent service second to none. "We used to, at the party [headquarters], send requests [to elected officials' offices] to see what the turnaround time was," Roehrick said. "His was generally under seven days. And you know . . . he personalizes his damn letters. I'm not saying personalized in the heading, 'Dear John,' I'm saying down at the bottom, 'P.S. I hope this helps you; Chuck.' You can't beat that."

Roehrick found himself seeking a nomination that no other mainstream Democrat coveted, then ran into a brick wall among party activists. "The reaction was 'Why? He can't be beat.' That was the biggest hurdle to overcome in our own party, was the fact that Grassley was 'unbeatable.' And you had within the party, people saying, 'You know, he's not a bad guy.' Because you cannot not like Chuck Grassley. It's a personal thing, and I don't understand it."

To get to Grassley, he had to first defeat Juan Cortez, a retired postal worker from Cedar Rapids who adhered to the philosophies of extremist Lyndon LaRouche. Roehrick got help from Arthur Davis, who denounced Cortez as an infiltrator and declared him persona non grata at the state convention and other events. Some liberals howled about freedom of speech; Davis did not listen. Roehrick rolled up 83 percent of the primary vote in brushing aside Cortez, but he found that getting his name "out there," as he put it, didn't get much easier. The state's largest newspaper, the paper in the very city where he lived, continually derided him as a little-known lawyer from Des Moines.

Roehrick attacked Grassley's record on the economy, social issues, even military spending and agriculture. "I was trying to pierce that armor that he'd put up of being the watchdog of the Pentagon when, in fact, he was voting for virtually every defense bill that came down the pike. . . . My belief was you go right at the strength. Because if you can't attack the strengths and pierce that or dent it or shatter it, then he's got that sitting there and it's available."

On Grassley's role in the farm crisis, Roehrick said, "He hadn't done anything to contribute to it and he wasn't doing anything to try to solve it, either."

During the course of the campaign, he criticized Grassley's vote for $100 million in aid to Nicaragua's *contra* rebels, claiming it would lead to U.S. military involvement in the region. Speaking of a military plane he had seen at the Des Moines International Airport, Roehrick said, "Someday I believe that C-135 will be unloading body bags of our young men and women who have been killed in Central America. When that happens, I say Chuck Grassley had better look at his hands because on them will be Iowa blood of young men and women."[8]

Roehrick accused Grassley of failing to respond to a NASA whistleblower's warning of thruster problems with the ill-fated Challenger space shuttle, which exploded January 28 and killed seven astronauts. Grassley's staff said the engineer had only alleged that a NASA contractor had overbilled for computers.[9]

He also charged that two interns on Grassley's staff in 1985, under the sponsorship of a Unification Church-linked group, raised questions about the Senator's wisdom. Grassley spokesman Allen Finch said the Senator severed ties with the Conservative Youth Foundation when the interns were "compelled to attend seminars on causes consistent with Rev. Sun Myung Moon and the Unification Church and coerced to attend a demonstration against the National Education Association."

Roehrick retorted, "You've got [Rev. Moon] who was a foreign agent convicted of tax evasion in this country who is trying to rehabilitate himself and he's doing it by putting out millions of dollars. Every other senator realized that except Chuck Grassley. It's not a question of who kicked them out but who let them in the door in the first place."[10]

Roehrick couldn't generate any movement in the polls during the summer, and couldn't goad Grassley into an attention-grabbing tit-for-tat. Where he needed $1 million to buy credibility and force Grassley to respond, his campaign was borrowing $20,000 just to keep from collapsing. He was not without allies, particularly in organized labor. He had represented striking United Auto Workers in the early 1970s against the Delevan Company in West Des Moines. "The problem," he lamented, "was one of targeting. You sit down and you look at all the Senate races and say, 'Which can we win and which can't we win? You show us some numbers and we'll take a look.' Unless you've got the money, you can show the numbers to get more money."

The Democratic candidates "showing the numbers" were in Minnesota, Illinois, South Dakota, and other states. PACs and labor unions responded accordingly. Roehrick conceded, "I knew by the end of August there was no hope because the big break we got we were never able to capitalize on. That was the multimillion dollar tax break for Ruan [Company of Des Moines]."

Grassley had inserted the $20 million transitional tax credit for Ruan in the massive Tax Reform Act of 1986. Such credits were provided to companies that could show potential severe losses because of the new tax code. The firms had to show contracts that could not be broken without financial penalties signed before 1986 for the future delivery of goods. Only two other Iowa firms, Teleconnect and a Cedar Rapids catering firm, had sought and were eligible for the credits. Yet Roehrick charged that Grassley had shown favoritism to a big-money contributor, trucking magnate John Ruan. "Iowans should know what it costs to get a special tax break on the floor of the U.S. Senate," Roehrick said.

Grassley spokeswoman Bev Hubble countered, "It doesn't cost anything. It's free." Roehrick, she charged, was grasping at straws after having "a hard time making news. Business people who are paying attention should be scared to death if a person who makes a very naive statement like that wins election and proceeds with that attitude."

Roehrick thought the credit was the most persuasive issue at his disposal. "Our polls showed when we brought up the Ruan matter . . . people didn't know it and when they did, they were furious. And Grassley's approval went right off a cliff. His electability was dropping, and we couldn't capitalize on it because we couldn't raise the money."

For all his attempts to get media attention, this was the one time Roehrick got it too soon. He had scheduled a seven-city fly-around to drop the bombshell himself, but while he was waiting for confirmation of details, the *Register* wrote about the tax credit. With the news element gone, Roehrick's accusations were relegated to the inside pages.

Synhorst believed the Ruan issue had potential. "It could've cut, and we knew that was going to be one of the seven or eight they were going to take at us. . . . Number one, we knew they didn't have the resources to put behind it, and number two, we were prepared. Roehrick had a considerable amount of baggage. And, on the positive side, we could point to all the corporations big and small that Grassley had fought for to help keep jobs. I don't think they would've gotten very far with it."

Unable to buy his way onto television, Roehrick wanted as many debates as he could get in hopes of capitalizing on a Grassley miscue. The incumbent, naturally, wanted a minimum number of debates and, aside from the traditional Des Moines Chamber of

Commerce event, he wanted them to be early, acknowledged Synhorst. "[Roehrick] argued that Iowans needed to know where we stand on the issues. We counted up several hundred meetings where Iowans could question Grassley and where he had fully aired his views on different subjects so that we didn't feel we needed to subject ourselves to his ridiculous request. But we definitely wanted to have a public forum. . . . We set the agenda, and he had to take it."

Appearing before the Iowa Newspaper Association convention at the Conway Civic Center in Waterloo on September 6, Roehrick portrayed Grassley as an ineffectual legislator who played "press release politics." Referring to "Grassley-Reagan policies," the Democrat said, "They have had six years to reduce interest rates, but the farmer who has to go borrow funds to plant his crops is still paying 13 percent or 14 percent. . . . I hear talk, talk, talk. We don't hear solutions."

Grassley countered that trade and monetary policies were even more important than simply passing a farm bill for the swift resolution of the agricultural crisis. He lauded his Pentagon spending freeze as a vote that "allowed money to be taken from arms and given to farms." The incumbent also cited his recent move to bring ambassadors to Iowa as evidence of his commitment to economic development. "It was my leadership that brought 31 foreign nations to Iowa. We're going to have to have more."

Roehrick snapped, "That was a political gimmick. Where have you been for six years in getting those ambassadors?" He also lashed out at the tax credit to Grassley's "millionaire friend," Ruan. "Senator Grassley has been the senator who can't say no." If approached under similar circumstances, Roehrick added, "I'm not going to say 'no,' I'm going to say 'hell, no!'"[11]

Roehrick walked off the stage that afternoon feeling buoyant about his performance, which had been broadcast statewide by Iowa Public Television. He thought it might be the breakthrough he had long awaited.

Grassley's camp disagreed. "I never felt he caught on, even after the Waterloo debate. He was going to have to deliver serious blows, and he didn't," Synhorst said. "Maybe in his mind he was thinking, 'All I have to do is look statesmanlike.' In reality, he had to do that and much more. It would've been difficult to do, and he didn't do it. Grassley looked good that day. He had his glasses on that day, his hair was starting to gray . . . he was just starting to become an attractive person, and he looked like a statesman."

The next day, the reviews in the Sunday morning papers were good for Roehrick, but time had run out. "We had to get the money, and it just wasn't coming. One of the most frustrating nights I spent was up in Mason City," Roehrick said. "We were heading across that northern tier. I was in a motel room watching the ten o'clock news, and he had the lead-in ad. He had the ad between the news and weather. He had the ad between the weather and sports, and he had an ad at the end. You know, you just can't overcome that bombardment."

One of those ads featured Grassley's well-hyped little orange Chevette pulling up to the Pentagon in a re-creation of his search for Chuck Spinney. The ad also included an imposter. A look-alike Chevette was used to tape the Iowa scenes. Schreuers, who had searched long and hard for the fill-in, laughed, "I was driving down a road in Cedar Falls and I saw an orange Chevette. I flipped the car around immediately, went up and pulled alongside this guy. He thought, 'I don't know what I've done, but whatever it was I don't want any part of it.' And I said, 'You've got an orange Chevette. We need to shoot a spot this weekend, and would you mind us using your car?' After he checked out whether we were for real and checked with his parents, he agreed to do it. But the orange Chevette we used back here had racing stripes on it, and the one we used in Washington didn't. You can see it in the [TV ad] spots. . . . That campaign had some good spots—the land of limousines, the orange Chevette, hogs at the trough, the typewriter spot [with a liberal columnist's laurels for Grassley], and one on attendance."

Roehrick, who was not a serious threat, was not even mentioned in any of those commercials.

Roehrick called the orange Chevette ad "pure corn." But, he conceded, "It worked. The East Coast and West Coast ads never sell, and Grassley understands that. He has great media people."

The Democrats were celebrating at the Jefferson-Jackson Dinner at Hilton Coliseum in Ames on October 18 when they got the kind of media they didn't need. Word rippled through the audience that the Iowa Poll in the next morning's *Des Moines Sunday Register* would show that Branstad had opened an 18-point lead over Lowell Junkins. Davis made the decision that no other candidate, including Roehrick, would receive party money for the duration. He explained to State Treasurer Mike Fitzgerald, "If I gave you $5,000 more or $10,000 more and Lowell loses by fifteen points, I think you'll lose. But if I can get Lowell close, I think you can win."

Roehrick's floundering candidacy desperately clawed for a financial lifeline from Washington money sources and wasn't getting much help from Harkin. Campaign manager Mark Farnen complained bitterly, "Tom Harkin explained it as 'senatorial courtesy.' I thought senatorial courtesy should have gone out the window in an election. Harkin was the titular head of the party. In an election, he should have had a large blunderbuss aimed at Republicans, and if he hit his friend Chuck Grassley, so be it. John Culver didn't pull that 'senatorial courtesy' crap. If it was a Republican, he went after them. I never did understand that with Harkin."

Harkin defended the practice, saying it was necessary for senators to work together for the state's good after partisan elections were over. "When someone is running against Grassley, I'll go out and support them, do fundraisers, say great things about them, do whatever to help him or her. What senatorial courtesy says is I do not personally attack Senator Grassley or his record or try to interpret his record, and he is to accord the same courtesy to me."

Roehrick eventually found one important ally who had an eye on his party's 1988 presidential nomination. Joe Biden made an impassioned pitch to the Democratic Senatorial Campaign Committee for $75,000; Roehrick got part of the money. One source indicated Roehrick did get help from Davis, who coaxed $25,000 from wealthy New Yorkers through his contacts with Gov. Mario Cuomo, who was considering his own presidential bid. Even though Roehrick's race was viewed as a lost cause, Davis made it clear that Cuomo would "have to start with someone in Iowa" if he wanted to run, and he could do a lot worse than receive the support of the defeated Senate candidate. The contributions came in 20 personal checks for $1,000 and 10 more $500 checks.

However, the Democrats' pervasive disinterest was a relief within the Grassley camp. Jim Gritzner, for one, felt the Democratic Party unfairly abandoned Roehrick. "I think they underestimated his ability. That was wonderful for us, but I really felt at the time that he was a better candidate than his own party gave him credit for. Anytime you have someone who is a high-profile party activist, they carry a lot of baggage within the party. That may explain some of that, but I think they decided at a very early time 'this is not a race to win,' and they failed to invest in probably what was a very decent candidate."

On November 4, Grassley, who had spent $2.21 million to Roehrick's $238,134, won 98 of 99 counties as he received 574,997 votes, compared to 300,461 for his challenger.[12] Grassley's was the biggest vote total in the state's history as he became the first U.S. senator in two decades to be reelected from Iowa.

The ebullient Grassley felt tremendous vindication as he addressed supporters in Des Moines about his detractors' conventional wisdom. "They said Chuck Grassley would be eaten alive by those smooth-talking senators in Washington. Well, we showed them. And then, after they looked at the history books, they said surely Iowa wouldn't break its tradition on incumbent senators. Well, we proved them wrong tonight."[13]

Mark Farnen revealed that the Roehrick campaign had been so hobbled by a lack of the three M's—money, media, and manpower—that the candidate's backup plan was to "walk out on the stage on debate day [in Waterloo], shake Grassley's hand and say, 'Brother, you've got it.'" [Roehrick denied he ever considered dropping out.]

Synhorst said later that the real secret to success was that Grassley had begun to position himself for reelection the day after the 1980 election with the 99 counties tour and crackerjack constituent service. "That's why he was untouchable, not because he'd sucked up all this money and had a great campaign organization. Those things helped, but they didn't just happen at the eleventh hour. They happened in the first two years of his term. It was very methodical, and it came from him. A lot of us helped—Bev Tauke, Charlie Jarvis, me, John Maxwell—but it was that work that put him in the position to be unbeatable."

Ken Cunningham, Grassley's agriculture staffer, observed, "When things are going bad in the economy, politicians are usually held accountable, even if they're working hard to stop the hemorrhaging. But Senator Grassley was working so hard [in the early '80s] that he was not hurt politically in 1986. Whereas others up for reelection in 1986 from farm states—James Abdnor from South Dakota and Mark Andrews from North Dakota—went down in flames because their economy was bad. Senator Grassley was out there working the grassroots, and farm people knew he was working for them. He didn't need any slick ads to prove it. He was out there working day in and day out."

Though he may not have been looking so far ahead on that happy night to recognize it on his own horizon, one suspects that the careful, calculating Grassley did sense an even sweeter victory that night. "What 1986 really did for Grassley," Davis said, "was close the door on the Democrats for 1992."

# Desert Storm and the No Vote:
## "One thing he can't do is accept death"

In the early morning hours of August 2, 1990, Iraq's army poured across the border of neighboring Kuwait. The assault followed the collapse of talks over oil production and border disputes, and a disagreement over whether Kuwait and other Arab countries would write off $30 billion in credits given to Iraq during its war with Iran. Iraq claimed its troops had been "invited" in to restore order after revolutionaries had overthrown the ruling Sabah dynasty. The tiny Kuwaiti defense force fought fiercely, but could not hold off the overwhelming Iraqi might.

Halfway around the world in Washington, D.C., it was still August 1 when the invasion began. President Bush needed only one day to ban almost all trade with Iraq and freeze its U.S. assets. International reaction was equally swift. Britain and France banned trade and froze assets, while the Soviet Union suspended arms shipments to its ally. The United Nations Security Council unanimously condemned the invasion.[1]

Grassley, preparing to return to Iowa for the August recess, thought to himself that it would end up as just another one of those disputes that gets worked out without ever amounting to much. He misjudged on both counts.

By August 6, the UN Security Council had imposed its own trade embargo. Ominously, Bush ordered U.S. troops and planes to Saudi Arabia to protect its oilfields from an Iraqi incursion. He indicated the commitment was open-ended and might increase to 50,000 American personnel, making it the largest U.S. military overseas build-up since the Vietnam War. Operation "Desert Shield" was under way.[2]

Iraqi President Saddam Hussein responded by annexing Kuwait. Tensions escalated through August, September, and October, as a well-orchestrated media campaign, managed by U.S. public relations firms on retainer to the government of Kuwait, detailed war atrocities against Kuwaitis.

On October 22, 1990, Saudi defense minister Prince Sultan ibn Abdul Aziz Al Saud raised the possibility of a deal with Iraq that included giving up the disputed Rumaila oilfield and the islands of Bubiyan and Warbah so Iraq could have a position on the Persian Gulf. President Bush said the next day that he would reject anything short of an unconditional withdrawal from Kuwait.[3]

Grassley, campaigning for fellow Republicans, began to hear from Iowans concerned about the National Guard being called up for active duty in the Persian Gulf. Several weeks later, Bush stepped up the pressure with huge new deployments of U.S. land, air, and naval forces on November 8, moving to double American personnel in the region to as many as 400,000 by early 1991.[4]

By the third week of November, Grassley urged Iowans to participate in his Adopt-a-Soldier program, designed to keep holiday spirits from withering in the hot sands of the Persian Gulf. Ironically, Grassley was opposed by Pentagon officials. His request for names of Iowans on active duty in the region was denied, based on the Privacy Act and national security concerns. Grassley contacted radio stations and newspapers to encourage Iowans to call his office if they wanted to "adopt" a soldier or had the name of a friend or relative who wanted to be adopted. "The idea was to say thank you and show our appreciation for the men and women serving over in Saudi Arabia at the holidays," Grassley explained. "But we want this to be a longer-term thing than just saying thank you at the holidays. Even if you don't send something to them until December 15 and they don't receive it until January 15, what difference does it make?"[5]

On November 29, the UN Security Council approved a resolution authorizing the use of force against Iraq if its troops were not out of Kuwait by January 15, 1991. Two days later, 134 reservists assigned to the Marine Corps' Battery D, Second Battalion in Waterloo, were to ship out for Saudi Arabia. Bunny Wiegmann said her brother wanted her to go to the send-off at the Waterloo Municipal Airport on that Saturday morning. Grassley stayed at his sister's Cedar Falls home the night before, a common practice when his wife remained in Washington. When he returned, he asked Bunny if she would go with him the next morning to see the unit off. Wiegmann said no. "I saw too much of that [during World War II]. I said good-byes too many years because Ed was gone 42 months.'"

Grassley went alone to an experience he remembered later as "very traumatic." He had tried to blend into the crowd, but of course he was recognized, and the family members of the departing soldiers poured out their feelings to him. "Maybe only one actually used the words, but it seemed to me everybody was saying we expect you to keep them safe or make sure they return," he said. "And all the tears. I felt a part of their anxiety." Grassley was also struck by a conversation with a departing Guardsman in his early fifties who was saying good-bye to his son and grandchild. "He had fought in Vietnam, and he was going to fight another one. His son had never been in the service."

After the band played, after the farewell speeches, after the Boeing 727 took off, Grassley lingered. "I have a feeling we'll have to make some tough decisions soon," he told *Waterloo Courier* reporter Larry Ballard. "I want to make the right one."[6]

Ballard told colleagues later that the way he spotted Grassley was a story in itself. "About 5,000 people surrounded the tarmac for the send-off. Every elected official and wannabe for miles was there. We heard several flowery speeches about how these guys were sacrificing for our freedom, and so on. I'd accumulated enough quotes for a good story and decided to head for the warmth of the terminal.

"I was about to head back outdoors when I noticed a tall, thin man in a brown trench coat, standing alone. His face was pressed close to the glass. He was watching intently as the Waterloo artillery unit marched single file up the ramp. 'Senator Grassley?' I said. He didn't turn around immediately, and for a moment I thought I'd made a mistake.

"Finally, in that unmistakable drawl of his, he said, 'How are you?' I asked him what he was doing. He said, 'If we're going to vote to send these young men over there, I think it's important that we see what it's like for their families.' He didn't go out there and make any speeches, even though his presence would have no doubt scored some big political points. From that day on, no matter how he voted on the issue at hand, I've thought of him as something more than just a 'normal' politician."

The Senator was glum when he returned to his sister's home. "He said, 'Oh, I can't take that.' He said, 'They all said to me, Don't send my son or don't send my husband.' . . . And he said, 'Now I understand why you didn't want to go,'" Wiegmann recounted.

Later in the day, she remembered he articulated the view that would become his position on the Gulf War Resolution. "He said, 'I promised those people I am not going to send those boys over there, and I have an obligation to them. Then somebody from the *Des Moines Register* had called me to interview me about it because they had heard I had been with him, and they [asked], 'Has he got a son in the service? Does he have any relatives in the service?' I said, 'As far back as a fifth cousin, I can't think of anybody that he has in the service.' So I said, 'It's nothing service connected, but he had almost made a vow to those people out there.' He saw how they felt and, of course, when I didn't want to go with him out there, he knew. One thing he can't do is accept death."

In the intervening days before the Iowa contingent departed for the Gulf, Grassley flew on a National Guard Kingair with Maj. Gen. Warren G. Lawson to the airfield near Camp McCoy in Wisconsin. "I just wanted to visit with them and encourage them, I guess, is what I was trying to do. They said the same things [about the war], only it wasn't the family. But everybody seemed committed to what they were doing. Nobody was complaining."

He had intended to visit other Iowans at Fort Leonard Wood near Rolla, Missouri, but that never materialized.

In the week before the January 12, 1991 vote, with 1,700 Iowa reservists and National Guard soldiers in the Persian Gulf region, Grassley told people how he was thinking but not exactly how he would vote. "I was still trying to get their view," he said. But by January 8 or 9, Grassley had resolved that he was not ready to vote for military action. He had publicly gone against the will of three presidents in the past; now it was George Bush's turn. But this time was different.

This time Chuck Grassley was voting against a resolution of war. And his independence wasn't much appreciated back home. Grassley's office phones were ringing with calls from disappointed and angry Iowans. "Maybe I misread public opinion, because I went back with a real certainty in my mind that Iowans really weren't for going to war, that they wanted the sanctions to work. Obviously I misread it, because less than a week after I voted, it was something like 60–30 to go to war from Iowa. The Iowa Poll showed that," he said.

It is plausible that Grassley did misinterpret the public mood, but it is just as likely that public sentiment shifted rapidly in a rekindled, rally 'round the flag patriotism when it became evident that the United States was going to war. When the *New York Times* had conducted a nationwide poll between January 5 to 7, 46 percent said the United States should go to war if Iraq did not withdraw by January 15, but 47 percent said the sanctions should be given more time to work. On January 9, a *Washington Post*/ABC poll indicated 86 percent of Americans believed war with Iraq was inevitable. On the question of whether the United States should attack after January 15, 68 percent said yes.[7]

Once Grassley had made up his mind, however, he dug in his heels with trademark tenacity. Bush did not personally lobby Grassley, but Vice President Dan Quayle and White House chief of staff John Sununu took on the task. When the Senator was quoted in the *Des Moines Register* as saying he would not be part of sending young Americans to die in defense of "money, macho, and monarchy," Quayle and Gov. Terry Branstad were infuriated. "I had announced my vote before I went back to Des Moines. I remember the Vice President called me at the Kiwanis Club in Boone . . . and just had to talk to me right now. Well, I was in the middle of my speech, but I never did return his call," Grassley said.

When Quayle couldn't get through to Grassley, he telephoned Branstad to track down the Senator and apply some pressure to his long-time political ally. "The Governor called me up and told me just how wrong and stupid it was," Grassley said. Sununu had also tried to contact Grassley that night, but "I got home at 11:30 and I didn't return his call."

The next day, Grassley went to the Senate Republican Caucus, took a seat in the back of the room, and just listened. All the time he had been in Iowa, he heard his constituents expressing reservations about going to war. He expected to find at least 10 or 12 colleagues on his side. He found none. "The people I expected [to oppose military action were] all cranked up to say why they decided to go to war," he said. "I didn't say one thing in the caucus, and before it was over I got up and left."

Sen. Sam Nunn, a hawkish Georgia Democrat and chairman of the Armed Services Committee, led the opposition to the resolution in favor of continued sanctions. Nunn and Senate Majority Leader George Mitchell, a Maine Democrat, offered a resolution that did not rule out the use of force at some point, but would have required Bush to return to Capitol Hill for approval. Specter, the Pennsylvania Republican, countered that the time had come to show Iraq's petulant leader that "we mean business and are prepared to fight."[8]

The next day, Friday, January 11, 1991, Grassley cloistered himself in his Capitol hideaway. He recalled later that his old friend Bob Dole may have called to ask if there was anyone at the White House with whom Grassley wanted to speak. Grassley didn't want to talk to anyone, not even his own staff. Caran McKee, who had served as Grassley's press secretary, said, "I know he spent the day praying, reading his Bible and thinking. It was such a personal decision."

Fifty-two students from Wartburg College in Waverly traveled to Washington that weekend of January 12–13, struggling through ice, sleet, snow, and rain to urge members of Congress to continue the sanctions rather than give Bush the authority to use military force. Reps. Dave Nagle and Jim Nussle met with the delegation. Grassley did not. The students were told he wasn't meeting with anyone before the vote because he wanted nothing to change his position.[9]

Nor would he return the calls of his old friend Evan "Curly" Hultman, who was a major general in the Army Reserves. Hultman got nowhere when he called Grassley's administrative aide, Bob Ludwizcak, in hopes of lobbying the Senator to support a call-up of reserve units. "I felt guilty for not talking to him, but I just made up my mind I wasn't going to be bothered by anybody," Grassley said.

Hultman was amused later by this revelation. "If there's one thing about Chuck, he's a guy who never fails to return your call or respond." He added with a laugh, "He lost his 100 percent record on that one. He's a 99.9 percent guy now."

Hultman, who was executive director of the Reserve Officers Association headquartered across Constitution Avenue from Grassley's office, had guessed exactly what was running through the Senator's mind. "I think he was afraid I was going to convince him of something, and rather than take a chance in the process, better to not respond at all.... I had to work diligently on the thing because, first, we had some difficulty getting the President convinced. Then we had to get the support in the Senate, and that was a tough go."

Yet, Grassley's opposition did not anger Hultman. "I respect him very much for his decision because it's genuine. On tough issues, there's going to be some solid arguments on both sides of the issue. That's why we elect people to make those judgment calls. When people don't sell out or make a deal, I have no problem with that."

Grassley had mapped out his own precise strategy for the day of the resolution vote, Saturday, January 12. The office where his wife Barbara worked, RBC Associates, was about six blocks from the Capitol, west of the Senate Office Buildings. That was where he went, waiting for the scheduled 11 a.m. vote. "I waited until the bells rang [signaling the vote and he was paged] and I had about a ten-minute walk. I went in the north door and up the Democrats' steps, on their side, and came in the back door and sat down," Grassley said. "They had called my name the first time, and I just stood up and said no. I didn't talk to anybody. What had happened in that last week or so was the [small number of] Republicans . . . who said they had their doubts, leaned on the side of going to war in analyzing their doubts.

"After we voted, [Quayle] came down from the podium and said, 'How come you didn't return my call? I'm disappointed you didn't return my call.' Well, I wasn't going to be beat over the head. I'd made my mind up."

The final vote was close, 52–47; the absent member, Sen. Alan Cranston of California, would have voted no had he not been hospitalized. But only Grassley and Mark Hatfield of Oregon broke ranks in the 44-member Republican caucus and opposed the resolution.[10]

Asked later if it was his toughest vote, Grassley didn't hesitate. "Yeah, yeah." Then he paused, reflecting for a minute. "I hate to say it was the toughest vote, but [it was the one with] the most emotional strain connected with it. And for three or four days before that, I never felt such weight, but then just as soon as I cast my vote, it was just like a whole load had gone off my back."

Grassley's conservative colleagues and supporters, not to mention many Iowans, felt shocked and betrayed. One, in particular, resided at 1600 Pennsylvania Avenue. "Needless to say, I was disappointed," Bush wrote in a May 1994 letter, "when Chuck Grassley did not support the critical resolution leading up to Desert Storm; but, again, he reached his decision honestly and I have respect for that."

But respect and acceptance are two different things. "You may recall that I had to work very hard to get the Congress to give me their *imprimatur* to fulfill the UN resolutions," Bush continued. "The war went so well that many people have forgotten that chapter."[11]

Grassley rose on the Senate floor to deliver a brief speech on January 12, 1991, to "express my hope on the Persian Gulf resolution since I refrained during the debate. There is in my state a principle of Iowa politics that a representative of the people should vote in Congress the way that we speak to our constituents in Iowa. So my vote or votes today should surprise no constituent of mine. I voted as I related my principles and thought processes to my constituents." He expressed his support for U.S. forces, and argued that the policy of containment against Iraq had been successful. "If we are ready to give up on sanctions now, then we will be giving up on sanctions forever. If we cannot bring a tin-horn, Third World dictator to his knees through sanctions that are being nearly universally enforced, then sanctions will never be successful against anyone.

"Are we ready to accept that defeat? I, for one, am not ready to cast the present or future use of sanctions onto the dust heap of history, because the only next step is likely to be war. Much has been said about the so-called new world order and what it means. Well, Mr. President, I certainly could never be accused of being a Cold War pacifist. But I am not ready to be a new world warrior either."[12]

Bombers and fighter jets from the UN coalition—principally the United States, Britain, France, and Italy—unleashed a devastating attack on Iraq in the early morning hours of January 17, 1991 [local time]. It was still the evening of January 16 in Iowa when Grassley was notified of the offensive by his Washington staff when he arrived at his Des Moines office. He canceled a scheduled trip to Greenfield and returned to Capitol Hill. "Those of us who voted against the resolution," he said, "are all in the mode of being behind our troops. Hopefully, it will be very short. . . . This is a time for all of us to be very prayerful."[13]

During the following four weeks, allied forces flew 52,000 bombing sorties over Iraq and Kuwait, laying waste to Iraq's infrastructure and resistance, and negating Grassley's privately held vision of massive American losses in the deserts of Iraq. By February 14, confirmed U.S. combat losses had reached 14, with 12 wounded, 28 missing in action, and eight prisoners of war.[14] Thirteen days later, allied forces had liberated Kuwait, and Iraq agreed to end hostilities. U.S. deaths were reported at 79 in the six-week conflict; Iraqi military casualties were estimated at between 25,000 and 50,000.[15]

With the 1992 election approaching, some state Republican Central Committee members thought that Grassley should be publicly rebuked for his vote. "I remember John Maxwell telling me several days or maybe weeks [after the vote] about how stupid it was from the standpoint of getting ready to run for reelection," Grassley said.

Maxwell added, "I've never told him I thought he should vote one way or another for political purposes. I'll tell him how I think we should handle what he's done, for political purposes, but never the former. We didn't talk about it in advance nor did I attempt to influence him on it; but, yeah, I really felt it was the wrong decision."

Maxwell's positions were not just based on political considerations. He argued energetically later that the use of force would empower future sanctions, which, in the case of Fidel Castro's Cuba, for instance, had not proven effective over more than three decades.

Grassley was not worried about the effect the vote would have on his 1992 prospects. Nonetheless, his vaunted personal touch with constituent service helped take some of the edge off the anger directed at him. "All these nasty letters we had to answer, I made a point of trying to put a note on the bottom of every one of them so they'll know I personally answered them," he said. "Because, probably, a lot of it was from people who were personal friends of mine besides being political supporters."

The Associated Press reported that Grassley received a "tongue-lashing" at the midwinter conference of Iowa Veterans of Foreign Wars in Des Moines on January 26, 1991. "You broke my heart on your vote," said Maurice Pentacost, a Korean War veteran from Independence. "I submit that three-fourths of the people who influenced you on your vote are now on the streets demonstrating." State VFW commander Carl Johnson of Waukon told Grassley that he was among the members of Congress who "took the easy way out" by voting against the resolution then supporting troops in the Gulf.

Grassley defended the vote, telling the veterans that he thought the economic and diplomatic sanctions he had voted for should have been given more time to work. "I think a lot of the principles that I go by are the same ones that you go by. . . . I'd like to sometimes have a 'maybe' vote, but you don't. You either vote 'yes' or 'no.'"[16]

Grassley continued to publicize the Adopt-a-Soldier program. He also introduced tax measures to help farmers and small business people serving in the Reserves, and brought Secretary of Veterans Affairs Ed Derwinski to the state to hear Iowans' concerns directly. With American patriotism surging, even anger over Grassley's "no" vote did not stop Iowans from contacting his office to buy flags flown over the U.S. Capitol. Requests, which usually numbered a thousand per year, topped several thousand a month in early 1991. It was well into the fall before all the orders were filled. "They just weren't able to manufacture enough flags in this country, but we're not going to have a bunch of American flags made by foreign entities flying over the Capitol," the Senator said.

Three years later, and undoubtedly for the rest of his life, Grassley remained unswayed. "I thought I was doing the right thing, and I guess I still think I was doing the right thing. I don't think I would have ever said this in the press or used this as a reason, but I kind of thought our nation was still divided from the Vietnam War . . . and you can't go to war as a divided nation. Now, obviously, after the polls came out, I have to admit I was wrong on that, but I sincerely believed we couldn't fight a war divided. I honestly felt people had doubt about going to war."

# The Judiciary Committee's
# Non-lawyer

Sen. Arlen Specter, a Pennsylvania Republican, was walking out of a political breakfast in Washington, D.C., when Attorney General William French Smith passed. "He said, 'Nice to have you here, Chuck,'" Specter recalled with a smile. "When I told Grassley about that, he was seriously offended. I think that may have been the reason he was so tough on the Attorney General."

"Tough" meant citing the attorney general of his own party's president with contempt of Congress just two weeks before the 1984 election in a dispute over prosecution. Months later, Specter ran across Smith again, just before Ronald Reagan's lawyer friend returned to California. After Edwin Meese had been sworn in as Attorney General, Specter approached the departing Smith to say hello. "He said, and I didn't understand it at the time, 'Why are you trying to hold me in contempt?' or 'Why do you think I'm contemptible?' Something like that. He was confusing me with Grassley again."

Grassley insisted later he was more amused than angered by the mistaken identity, and that he had already clashed with Smith before those incidents occurred. But they illustrated that his position on the Senate Judiciary Committee was noticed by friends and foes. Grassley got on the committee as much for what he wasn't as for who he was. "Strom Thurmond started recruiting people because he knew liberals who wanted to be on the committee," Grassley said. "One was Arlen Specter, who eventually got on. But he asked me because one issue I had a long interest in was the congressional veto."

Grassley set two conditions: chairmanship of the subcommittee that dealt with the veto issue, and the authority to have his own staff with a $120,000 budget over and above his personal office account. Things worked out.

John Maxwell set a condition of his own for returning to Capitol Hill. He wanted to be able to put his law degree to use, and the only way he wanted to do that was as chief counsel of a Finance or Judiciary subcommittee. Through his deal with Thurmond, Grassley was able to fulfill his trusted adviser's request, and both men went about the business of the Courts and Administrative Practice Subcommittee.

Grassley immersed himself and the subcommittee in the congressional, or legislative, veto issue. The National Federation of Independent Businesses and the U.S. Chamber of Commerce were hot on the idea, which would have given Congress a certain number of days to reject regulations written by a federal agency. "The concept being that regulations were an extension of legislative authority and, like OSHA, a one- or two-page bill ends up being 200,000 pages of regulations," Maxwell said. "When Congress passes a law and the agency puts on a regulation in conflict, Congress has to go through the whole process of passing another law."

The veto had been supported by candidate Ronald Reagan and included in the Republican platform, but when Grassley tried to advance it in his subcommittee, he got no support from the White House. "All roads led back to George Bush, who Reagan had named as chairman of the President's Task Force on Regulatory Relief," Maxwell recounted. "It took a while for it to all play out, but the bottom line was that Bush and [counsel] Boyden Gray had determined that the legislative veto would be wrong, and that actually developed into an official administration position of opposition."

Grassley and Sen. Harrison Schmitt, a New Mexico Republican and veto-backer, ended up meeting with Bush in the Vice President's office. "Bush came in and started off with something to the effect, 'Look, I know what was in the platform, and I know what was said on the campaign trail, but that was the campaign and this is the government, and I'm not going to talk about the campaign baloney. We're going to talk about this thing on the merits,'" Maxwell said. "I sat there thinking, 'You SOB. What you're telling me is you'll say or do whatever it takes to get elected, then all bets are off. You'll do what you please because you're an elitist, and you know better than the rest of us.' I was never so mad. Then one of his aides says why it's unconstitutional. He says they've got three cabinets full of opinions back to the FDR administration that say so."

Grassley, by Maxwell's account, was none too happy, either. "It's one of the few times I've seen him lose his temper. He starts pounding his fist in his palm in front of Bush and says, 'Listen! The Reagan landslide was a mandate for change,' and he's punctuating each word with his fist in his palm. 'The people are tired of business as usual, and I don't care how many file cabinets of old opinions you've got.' Bush just sort of sat there. It was not a pleasant meeting, and Grassley and Schmitt decided that Bush could go back on his campaign promises but they couldn't. That was probably the first confrontation between Grassley and the Administration, and Grassley and Bush."

The two senators moved the veto through the Judiciary after Thurmond allowed a vote, over vigorous administration opposition. Grassley came in for more pressure as a White House official told him that he ought to remember that he'd only won his Senate seat because of the Reagan landslide. Grassley bluntly pointed out that he had run ahead of Reagan, and if anyone should be grateful for the coattails, it was not him.

The Senate approved the legislative veto with more than 70 votes, but that was the end of the road. As it awaited House action, the Supreme Court ruled 8–0 again, that the legislative veto was unconstitutional. Grassley moved on to other work, a complicated difference of opinions involving the extension of the Voting Rights Act of 1965. The battle was over drawing the lines of political districts, revolving around the intent of line-drawers versus the effect on election outcomes. Such questions would have little meaning in Iowa, but in states throughout the South, they were important to the balance of power and the integrity of the individual vote.

Proponents of the effects test were accused of wanting to manipulate political lines to further their own liberal agenda. Backers of the intent test, concerned that the effects test amounted to a quota system and imposition of federal will over local control, were labeled racists.

Grassley approached Biden, then ranking member on the Judiciary, and offered to help work out an acceptable compromise. Dole also wanted to break the deadlock. Grassley and Dole, in Maxwell's words, "had very strong civil rights records and didn't want to be—or be seen as—opposed to the Voting Rights Act, but they also saw significant areas that needed clarification and improvement."

Under pressure from the Administration and fellow conservatives on one side and civil rights groups on the other, Grassley and Dole sought and found an acceptable middle ground. Compromise came when Harvard University law professor Alan Dershowitz, acting on behalf of Sen. Edward Kennedy, met with Grassley's counsel. Maxwell contended that the Kennedy-led forces were sending mixed signals, offering legislation that was far broader than the legal case they cited as their foundation. He indicated that Grassley and others could accept the case as the basis of new law, but no more.

In the end, Kennedy, whose close friend had been defeated by Grassley just 19 months before, included Grassley among the colleagues worthy of praise for playing an important role in the legislation. Biden, meanwhile, concluded that his first impression of Grassley was off the mark. In a 1994 interview, he said Grassley stood out among Republicans as "more open-minded about the plight of blacks and minorities in the country."

Biden, who became Judiciary Committee chairman in 1985 when the Democrats regained power only to relinquish the post after the 1994 elections, observed, "Chuck is not a lawyer. He does not pretend to be, although he's mastered some fairly complicated constitutional concepts. I don't think he is a force in and of himself in trying to move the committee on any major, legal, constitutional question."

Specter, another Judiciary member, praised Grassley for bringing a fresh perspective to the committee's work. "I have said that we could use on the Supreme Court some non-lawyers. The Supreme Court is the one judicial body that you don't have to be a lawyer. The Constitution does not require it. I thought, for example, that Senator [Mark] Hatfield would be good on the Supreme Court because of his background as a professor of history, governor, long-term senator, and I think Senator Grassley brings that kind of background."

Where Grassley excelled, Biden, Specter, and others agreed, was in using his subcommittee to dust off the neglected Lincoln Law, enacted in the Civil War years to prosecute military contractors who were gouging and defrauding the Union Army and federal taxpayers. The "new and improved" bill would allow whistleblowers to keep as much as 30 percent of the money recovered from those convicted of defrauding the government. It would also allow the government to force convicted companies to repay three times the damages, pay an additional criminal penalty of up to $1 million, and a civil fine of up to $10,000.

A year-long clash with the Reagan Administration ensued. Obtaining information from the Department of Justice about audits of companies such as General Dynamics Electric Boat Division, proved difficult. "We just wanted to review the records they reviewed. I think it was because we thought Justice had taken a dive on this case," Kris Kolesnik said. "The hearings we had were basically with the head of the criminal division, Stephen Trott, this real smart-aleck lawyer from California who refused to sit at the hearing. We subpoenaed him; he showed up without the documents. We canceled the hearing and we ended up with a contempt citation against William French Smith. It was really a big, emotional tug of war right before the election.

"The argument Grassley [accepted] was if we don't do this, it's going to look like we're playing politics and we're not pursuing the issue on the merits. There was a lot of substance to that argument because around here the norm is to play politics. Our whole purpose and our reputation was becoming 'Grassley doesn't play politics and he's going to get to the bottom regardless.' That notion appealed to him, so [the contempt citation] was almost inevitable."

Ronald Reagan's attorneys general only reinforced Grassley's belief that stronger laws were needed to help individuals sue on behalf of the government, and at government expense, in instances where fraud was suspected. Kolesnik said, "William French Smith was bad enough, not being aggressive against fraud among defense contractors. Meese was even worse. . . . We thought if the Justice Department is not going to do it—and even if they did, they didn't have enough resources—this is a terrific series of incentives to help out the government and, more important, to help out the taxpayers."

Defense contractors mobilized against the Lincoln Law update, formally known as the Federal False Claims Act, by recruiting other business groups to lobby against it. Grassley met individually with representatives of eight groups that had signed a letter of opposition to the law, and peeled them off, one by one. Opposition within the Senate was dealt with in similar fashion, in one case by helping a journalist with a story that reported two opponents had received campaign contributions from a Florida defense contractor just before they went public against the Lincoln Law. After winning House approval on October 7, 1986, the bill was sent to President Reagan, whose rhetoric about stopping government fraud and waste really left him no room to veto it.

"Chuck's been very, very tough on the defense industry because part of his ethic, which is admirable, is 'a penny saved is a penny earned; don't waste any money,'" Biden explained.

"Now, that's good Iowa politics because defense has never been a real strong issue in Iowa for conservatives or liberals, but in fairness, I think he believes it, too. It's consistent with how he is on other matters relating to tax policy, relating to spending federal tax dollars."

There was, of course, much more to Grassley's work on the Judiciary than chasing crooked contractors.

Shortly after Grassley was appointed to the committee, Ronald Reagan nominated his first appointee to fill the vacancy of retiring Justice Potter Stewart. Sandra Day O'Connor, a former Arizona legislator and appellate judge, was the first woman selected for the high court. Confirmed 99–0 on September 21, 1981, O'Connor's was the first of seven Supreme Court nominations in which Grassley had direct participation through 1994.[1]

Grassley and Senators John East of North Carolina and Jeremiah Denton of Alabama took the lead in questioning O'Connor on her views on legalized abortions.[2] "I think what was going through my mind was the first high-profile televised nomination, and I guess I felt a need to do the very best I could," Grassley explained. "The big issue was whether or not she was going to say she was for abortion. This is just the inverse of what Democrats did [in later nominations]. They were lecturing the Republicans that you shouldn't have a litmus test for O'Connor. There were a few of us that felt we should get something out of her on abortion. Looking back, we were wrong. You can ask about the issue, but that she should have to give us the right answer on any current political issue is wrong."

That philosophical shift was just the opposite of Biden's read on his colleague from Iowa. "Chuck started off with a view that I think has moved—my impression—on the issue of what is appropriate to inquire of a nominee. I think Chuck was like I was in the beginning, without having thought it through, which was if you're a nominee for the court I should just check if your moral compass is functioning, whether or not you committed a crime of moral turpitude, whether or not you are academically qualified, and whether or not you have a judicial temperament and that's it.

"I think that as time has gone on, at least as it relates to the Supreme Court, Chuck has acquired the view that it's also kind of important what you think and how you're going to interpret the Constitution because you're part of a coequal branch of the government, and you could affect the lives of people as much as any elected official can.

"So it's appropriate to know what your judicial philosophy is. I may be mistaken, but I sensed a kind of movement . . . in that direction from the Bork hearings through other hearings. But I also think that on social issues, on the social agenda, he still tends to be very rigid."

Grassley later countered, "I suppose I am kind of rigid on social issues, but not as they apply to the questioning of potential Supreme Court nominees. When he is talking about the application of broader principles, I think he's right. I'm not sure he's right about where he's starting from with his principles. The Democrats, who have been very rigid on questioning Republican nominees on abortion, were the same ones saying it was wrong for me back then, some of the leading Democrats, not necessarily Biden. As you move into the present day [1994], as Biden was trying to describe it, he would put more emphasis on philosophy than I would . . . sometimes that emphasis on philosophy tends to get you into more current political views than long-term judicial philosophy."

After O'Connor came the tense 1986 nomination hearings for William H. Rehnquist to succeed Warren Burger as Chief Justice, and the confirmation of Associate Justice Antonin Scalia in 1986. Grassley remembered Scalia for expressing a contrarian view from the rest of the nominees who were quizzed on congressional intent. Typically, nominees said if intent was unclear in legislation, they would review the committee report, then, if necessary, records of the debate. Scalia said only the statute mattered.

"By golly, to this very day, he's been a justice that's adhered to that principle," Grassley said. "I always want a justice to lean over backward and do everything to determine congressional intent. Every bill has a committee report and record of debate, why not use it? Where I disagree with the court is in making law contrary to what we meant in the statute."

Biden, however, contended that Grassley's votes did not reflect a philosophy of judicial restraint on legislative matters. "He says what he wants is a strict constructionist, but what he means by 'strict constructionist' is he wants someone who constructs the way he strictly thinks it," Biden said with a laugh. "There's a big difference. It amazes me, you know, all these conservatives say, 'We want a strict constructionist' and I say, 'OK, great. Well, there's a liberty clause in the Fourteenth Amendment that says there's a right to choice.' They say, 'Woah! Woah! Woah! Wait a minute, now! That's not what I want.'

"Think about it. Who are the most interventionist people? Who are the least strict constructionists? The conservatives. The conservatives say, 'Look, we don't like the Warren Court. We want you to go back and change what the Warren Court did.' You say, 'Wait a minute, now. You just want them to call the laws the way they are, right?' They say, 'Well, no, change them and then call them the way they see them.' But I don't think Chuck views it that way. Chuck thinks, 'I'm just being a strict constructionist.'"

That philosophy was at the heart of the September 1987 hearings on Robert H. Bork, nominated by Reagan to succeed moderate Justice Lewis F. Powell, Jr., just as several Democrats on the Judiciary Committee, most notably then-Chairman Biden, were looking to define themselves in the 1988 presidential sweepstakes.

Grassley considered Bork, a U.S. Court of Appeals judge from the District of Columbia Circuit and premier constitutional authority, to be "the smartest person appointed to the Supreme Court since Felix Frankfurter in 1939." He "hit it off" with the judge, who had copious scholarly papers to his credit. Grassley attributed his enthusiasm in part to the tremendous admiration that his brother, Gene, harbored for Bork. "[He] had read what Bork had done as Solicitor General in the Nixon Administration and as a professor at Harvard. I had Bork in my office when he was appointed to the Circuit Court of Appeals and remember telling him in 1982, 'My brother thought you should be on the Supreme Court.'"

Grassley liked that Bork was a strict constructionist, though he worried later that he might be too much of one to win Senate confirmation.

"Secondly, Reagan won the election on the proposition he was going to turn the court around, and he had a mandate to do it." But Bork's Supreme Court prospects dimmed, in Grassley's estimation, when President Reagan "took off the month of August, riding horses on his ranch. He let the civil rights groups mount a political campaign, particularly in the South, against conservative Democrats and scaring the black people of America. Reagan or nobody else was defending Bork and he was defeated before the hearing was held."

The hearings, a formality or not, still had to be held. Things only got uglier for Bork when Biden gaveled the committee to order the week of September 15, 1987. Bork was introduced by former President Gerald R. Ford who called him "perhaps the most qualified nominee to the Supreme Court in more than a half century."[3] Five Republicans, including Grassley, supported Bork, and five Democrats, including Biden, opposed him. The balance of power was with Democrats Dennis DeConcini of Arizona, Howell Heflin of Alabama and Robert Byrd of West Virginia, and Republican Specter.

Bork insisted he was "neither a liberal nor a conservative" but an adherent of the "original intent" philosophy, which had it that the only way for a judge to interpret a law or constitutional question was by "attempting to discern what those who made the law intended."

Senator Patrick Leahy, a Vermont Democrat, accused Bork of being a hard-line conservative who had made a "confirmation conversion" to moderate, mainstream views. Kennedy charged that Bork was an ultra-right-wing zealot who was "hostile to the rule of law" and "instinctively biased against the claims of the average citizen in favor of concentrations of power, whether that is governmental or private."[4] Odd repudiations, indeed, considering that the committee had unanimously recommended Bork to the Court of Appeals in 1982, and he was unanimously confirmed by the Senate twice, the first time as Solicitor General in 1973. Senator Alan Simpson pointed out that retiring Justice Powell had agreed nine out of 10 times where he had voted on Bork's decisions.[5]

In his opening statement, Grassley said, "Make no mistake about it, the critics of this nominee know the law they prefer is judge-made, and therefore susceptible to change by other judges. Their loud protests underscore that the law they prefer is not found in the Constitution or the statutes." If such were the case, he continued, Bork's foes "would have no fear of any new judge pledged to live by the credo of judicial restraint. Instead, these critics prefer judges who will act as some kind of 'super legislature' who will give them victories in court when they lose in the legislature."

Privacy rights became a flashpoint in the hearings, and Bork told the panel that his position on original intent meant the Supreme Court had no reason to follow previous rulings if it felt those rulings had created rights not intended by the framers of the Constitution. Clearly, abortion was involved. Bork said he would not discuss the 1972 landmark case *Roe v. Wade* because it was possible he would be ruling on it in the future. He did, however, engage Biden in a lengthy discussion about *Griswold v. Connecticut*, a 1965 case in which the court overturned a state statute that prohibited married couples from using artificial birth control. Bork did not support the law, but opposed the court's reasoning.

Liberal interest groups, particularly women's groups, took to the television airwaves in an unprecedented campaign against a Supreme Court nominee. They hammered away at Bork's position in *Griswold* and another case in which Bork concluded that a battery factory had a right to bar women of child-bearing age from hazardous areas where chemicals could injure a fetus or, otherwise, the company could require that women working in those areas be sterilized.

"The groups came and put out ads saying Bork was for forced sterilization. Well, that's simply not true," Biden said. "He wasn't for it. The irony is of all the people on there, Bork personally supported abortion choice. The question was whether legally [the company] could do that, and there's a legal argument that . . . it is within the law for the employer to say, 'You can't work in this section if you're pregnant or unless you're sterilized. I'm not proposing you be, but just so you know, we have to worry about the impact on the child for liability reasons, for a lot of other reasons.' [Interest groups did not frame it] in terms of his legal philosophy but in terms of his motivation, which was an unfair characterization." Biden accurately sensed that the special interest attacks on Bork "offended Chuck's sense of what he felt was fair."

Bork was also questioned at length about free speech, and his previous statements that the First Amendment only applied to political speech that did not advocate the violation of laws. Bork broadened his definition before the committee but declined to say where protected speech and unprotected speech began and ended. He said unprotected speech included pornography and obscenity, but because he did not read current bestsellers or watch more graphic movies, he said he could not comment on whether he thought they would be protected speech. Foes scoured Bork's neighborhood video stores looking for evidence that he had rented dirty movies. "The civil liberties groups who wanted to protect everybody's civil liberties were prying into his past," Grassley said, indignantly. "We got a bill passed later that those were private records."

At the end of an unprecedented five days of hearings, Bork maintained his criticism of the court for upholding an individual's right to privacy, the right established by the courts in preventing laws against abortion. But abortion was never mentioned by him. Sen. Howard Metzenbaum of Ohio noted Bork's thorough, even-tempered, and engaging testimony by observing, "You're not a frightening man, but you are a man with frightening views."[6]

On October 6, Specter joined eight Democrats as the committee voted 9–5 to reject the Bork nomination. Three days later, Bork announced he would not withdraw even though a majority of senators had announced their opposition to him. "A crucial principle is at stake," Bork said, noting that if he quit, "public campaigns of distortion . . . would be seen as a success."[7] He also warned that such campaigns would be mounted against future nominees.

Grassley and other Republicans met with Bork in a strategy session in Dole's office. The meeting was a microcosm of the disagreement between pragmatic moderates concerned about getting the next nominee through the Senate, and Bork's allies who thought the opposition had to be confronted. Sam Gerdano, Grassley's chief counsel at the time, recalled that the Senator urged Bork to "hang in there and press it for a vote to get people on the record, have a floor debate and not let it die informally. It's not simply a matter of counting noses at that point; it's a higher matter of principle. [Bork] would have been left with this unfair caricature painted of him, which no one of that stature ought to have left of him."

Bork's nomination was defeated on October 23 when he received only 42 votes. "He was a scholarly writer, but he wrote too much, and they used it against him. And he always tried to give scholarly answers to the liberals, and he should have given political answers," Grassley said. "He was the only one who understood what he was talking about. He was probably right, too, but he should have been giving a political answer."

Already disappointed, the Senator found that his brother was disgusted with him. "He said, 'You didn't do enough to save Bork.'" The former judge certainly didn't express such sentiments in his 1990 book, *The Tempting of America: The Political Seduction of the Law*, in which he wrote of his gratitude to Grassley and several other committee Republicans who "labored at length to expose the misrepresentations."[8]

He was more effusive about Grassley in a July 1994 interview from his office at the American Enterprise Institute for Public

Policy Research in Washington, D.C. "I was very pleasantly surprised by his knowledge of the legal issues involved. I didn't know he was into that kind of thing. He was well prepared and asked very good questions. I hadn't thought that he would be one of the leading exponents of the point of view I was trying to get across but he was."

The former federal judge was particularly impressed because Grassley was not a lawyer. "That's why he surprised me. I thought he had a much better grasp of the issues than the lawyers did. Specter, who thinks he is a constitutional scholar, didn't understand any of it. I had to be polite to him, but Grassley had a much better grasp of the Constitution."

With Bork's defeat, Reagan offered Harvard professor Douglas H. Ginsburg's name on October 29, but his nomination was the Court's first to be shot down by marijuana use. "Early on, I made statements to the press that with people his age, if you're going to discount someone who smoked marijuana, you're probably not going to find anyone to fill these offices. There's very few people who would pass that test. It was a case originally where he didn't admit to this, then he said something like he'd used it one or two times. If he'd been upfront and open, he probably could have survived it," said Grassley, a self-professed teetotaler who said he hadn't had a "John Collins in the last 40 years."

That apparently is no exaggeration; the drink is a Tom Collins. But Ginsburg was also caught in another act of deception on November 1 with the disclosure that he had led a Justice Department effort to extend First Amendment protection to cable television companies when he had $140,000 invested in a cable company.[9] Ginsburg withdrew his name on November 7.

On November 11, Reagan announced his third choice, Anthony M. Kennedy, an appellate court judge who served in San Francisco. He breezed through committee hearings in mid-December, professing "no overriding theory" on constitutional interpretation and saying that trying to decide what the Founding Fathers would have done about modern problems "doesn't seem to me very helpful."[10] He was confirmed 97–0 on February 3, 1988.

George Bush proved he had learned a valuable lesson from the rebuke of Bork when he nominated David Souter in 1990. The U.S. Court of Appeals judge from New Hampshire had few written opinions or papers to provide the philosophical smoking gun the Democrats desperately wanted. During his confirmation, Souter told the panel that he felt the Supreme Court had to act when Congress left a vacuum.

Specter recalled, "I leaned over to Chuck and said, 'You're a big guy on judicial restraint. Why don't you give him the business on the grounds that when Congress leaves a vacuum, the inference is that Congress intended to leave a vacuum, that it is not inadvertent.' I didn't think Chuck was necessarily going to pursue that. Then Grassley did such a job on Souter, there was nothing left for me to do but gasp."

Grassley asked Souter to explain whether he really believed Congress was supposed to make public policy. "It seems to me he didn't give a very satisfactory answer, and we did catch him in a very confusing, contradictory opinion," the Senator said later.

Specter added, "Souter said afterward that he made two mistakes in the hearings; one of them was the comment on judicial vacuum."

But Souter couldn't lose; Bush made certain of that. "The nominees answer just as many questions as they have to, and Souter didn't have to answer questions," Specter said.

Bush ran into troubles with his second "no paper trail" nominee, conservative African-American Clarence Thomas, chosen to succeed Thurgood Marshall. Iowa's two senators split on Thomas' nomination when it was announced July 1, 1991. Sen. Tom Harkin was blunt: "Clarence Thomas is a zero." Grassley, meanwhile, described Thomas as "an outstanding jurist and public servant," but his sense of honesty was taxed by Bush's rationale for the choice.[11]

"I was glad to see a black appointed. I may argue with Bush in saying he picked the best qualified person. I think he would have been best to say, 'I want a black American. I think he's qualified and he's a black American' rather than saying, 'He's the most qualified.' Beyond that, I guess I was happy to see a conservative black appointed to the court because I think about 40 percent of blacks are fairly conservative," Grassley said. "They want a job; they want to walk the streets safely; they want their kids to have a good education. They don't want government meddling in their lives. I thought he'd be a good role model on the Supreme Court."

Grassley also knew that in his prior appointment to the Equal Employment Opportunity Commission [EEOC], Thomas had been confirmed by the Senate. Still, with memories of the Bork nomination still fresh, conservatives launched a preemptive strike of their own, questioning whether Thomas should be judged by Edward Kennedy of Chappaquiddick notoriety, savings and loan scandal-rocked Alan Cranston, and alleged plagiarist Biden.

Grassley was puzzled by the attacks and publicly asked, "What are they up to? This nomination is not in trouble. I haven't heard any negative ads against Thomas. If I had heard any, I'd say this is fair game." He finished with one of the bedrock principles of his political truce with Democrats. "When things are going well, it makes no sense to rock the boat and I think they're rocking the boat needlessly."[12]

Thomas' nomination was opposed by the Congressional Black Caucus, women's groups, and four black law professors during two weeks of confirmation hearings in mid-September 1991.[13] But Grassley, who had predicted a 60–40 Senate vote, upped the margin to 75–25, glowing, "I think it's directly related to how he presented himself."[14] On September 27, the committee tied 7–7 on the question of a confirmation recommendation. Shortly after, members voted 13–1 to send Thomas to a full Senate vote with no recommendation.[15]

The nomination was seriously jeopardized on October 6 when a former Thomas aide, University of Oklahoma law professor Anita Hill, accused Thomas of persistent sexual harassment between 1981 and 1983 when she worked for him, first at the U.S. Department of Education, and then at the EEOC. The next day, she charged that the Judiciary Committee had not fully investigated her complaint and claimed she had come forward because she felt Thomas' alleged conduct showed he felt no compunction to comply with federal guidelines against sexual harassment. The Senate postponed for one week an October 8 vote.[16] Three days later, Hill began testifying in a riveting, unprecedented televised hearing. Hill said she was forced to refuse Thomas' requests for dates and endure his graphic discussions of pornographic films.

From the Democratic side, Thomas was grilled by a former prosecutor, Patrick Leahy of Vermont, and former trial lawyer and Alabama Supreme Court chief justice, Sen. Howell Heflin. Specter, Hatch, and Simpson were directed to lead the Republican effort to discredit Hill. Each was given 30 minutes to question Hill and Thomas, often in graphic detail, while others, including

Grassley, were limited to five minutes. Ironically, some Iowa Democrats later criticized Grassley, not for attacking Hill, but for sitting silent most of the time.

Grassley saw his role as giving Thomas "an opportunity to state a position that was within the mainstream of America when [opponents] to a considerable extent were painting him as an extremist." The Senator released a statement on the morning of October 15, declaring that "the only conclusion I can draw is that the hearing was nonconclusive. Professor Hill accused Judge Thomas and she bears the burden of proof. . . . On the merits, Professor Hill's story just doesn't add up."

At the same time, he said Hill had "done a great deal of good for American society by highlighting" sexual harassment, which he described as "a serious problem." He also expressed distress that one of the committee members' staffers had leaked the confidential FBI report about Hill's allegations. That report had not been disclosed during the hearings because agents said the evidence was inconclusive.[17]

Grassley later observed that when the Hill accusations against Thomas became public, "most Americans were against him. As that hearing went on, you could see people weren't convinced by Anita Hill or maybe they were trying to be fair to Thomas, but it got to the point that not only was a majority of the American people supporting him in rolling polls, but he was also getting his biggest majority with women, and even a majority of black Americans, which told us he was doing a good job of defending himself. In fact, he probably saved his own skin."

Calls to Grassley's office from Iowa constituents ran about 3–2 in favor of Thomas after Hill testified. Harkin, unable to reach a conclusion about the charges, felt compelled to vote against Thomas. "The benefit of the doubt does not rest with either the accused or the accuser in this case; it rests with the Constitution. . . . For the protection of the Constitution," Harkin said on the Senate floor, "we should not vote to consent to this nomination."

On October 15, Thomas was confirmed by a 52–48 vote and became the 106th U.S. Supreme Court justice.[18]

Grassley found the silver lining in the dark clouds over the Thomas confirmation, noting that the trial by fire that almost destroyed his judicial career had left the newest justice more sensitive and compassionate to the views of others. Invited to Thomas' home for a victory celebration, Grassley saw a man who was "jovial, thankful, caring, and forgiving as opposed to the Clarence Thomas who sat across from the committee for two days just stone cold staring in disgust at both friends and foes. The Clarence Thomas I saw last night is the Clarence Thomas that's going to be on the Supreme Court, and all that adds up to his being a very good, impartial arbiter. I don't have any doubt he's going to show a great deal of sensitivity on the court, and he's going to be very forgiving of the groups and philosophies that opposed him." He also suggested that Thomas might evolve into a judicial moderate, a role then filled consistently by only two of the court's nine members.[19]

But who did Grassley believe told the truth? "To this very day," he said in 1994, "I don't know who's lying. You just don't know. But I adopted the philosophy you give the benefit of the doubt to the accused. I agonized not over making the decision; I agonized over the process that we were on television with such a back-alley subject as sexual harassment and all the descriptive terminology that went with it and the descriptive picture-writing on television. It was really the gutter-type subject matter and language, the form, that I really detested. I suppose it was really difficult, too, because I didn't know who was lying, but when it came to Clarence Thomas, I didn't have any hesitancy about voting and giving him the benefit of the doubt. I was probably happiest for him, even with Bork's defeat, because he really was a guy who had come up the hard way."

Was he not troubled that he helped put a relatively young man who may have told a horrendous lie on the United States Supreme Court for life? Clearly, he was not. "I still think if somebody says you lied or did something wrong, well, he should have been charged and it should have been proved. I've seen this guy pilloried when he was before the Labor Committee, when he was being appointed to the EEOC, and what it amounted to was there were civil rights advocates in America that just couldn't stand having a black man in a position of leadership who was saying, 'You can pull yourselves up with your bootstraps and you didn't have to have government help.' Because it was contrary to their view you had to have big government help. These campaigns against him were approaching hate mongering—I wouldn't say they were hate mongers—but they approached it. It was worse than [the Bork hearings]."

Grassley, who had been quiet for all but five minutes of that searingly dramatic televised hearing, was not spared from some indignation back home. "Senator Grassley told me that people came up to him in Iowa and said, 'Why were you so strong on Anita Hill?'" Specter said. "They were confusing him with me."

Grassley echoed, "I ran into a couple women at the Clear Lake band shell and they just jumped all over me. She didn't say it, but by implication it was Specter she meant because she said, 'I can't believe how rude you were to Anita Hill. I'm so ashamed. What am I going to tell my daughter?' The only question I asked Anita Hill was about did anybody coach her or did any lobbyists work with her. I told this woman she got me mixed up with Specter, and she said, 'He shouldn't be reelected either.' Right around the Hill, including the cleaning ladies, they'd say, 'You did such a beautiful job of questioning Anita Hill. You should run for president.' I said, 'I'm Grassley; that was Specter.' And they'd say, 'Oh, I'm sorry.'"

Iowa Democratic Party Chairman Eric Tabor later mocked Grassley's performance as woefully inadequate. Grassley's only question to Thomas had been an inquiry about how the nominee's grandfather would have thought of the nomination. Tabor said, "It was ludicrous and off-the-wall. If that was an attempt to get his colleagues to underestimate him, I think he probably achieved that. If it was an attempt to embarrass Iowa, I think he probably did that."

Across the nation, a wave of anger swept over feminist groups and Democratic women, infusing them with a white-hot intensity and steely sense of purpose. The complaint rose that committee members "just didn't get it" on the issue of sexual harassment and their anger over the treatment of Anita Hill. They mobilized, strategized, and coalesced in the final days of 1991 and into 1992.

In Illinois, little-known Cook County recorder of deeds Carole Moseley-Braun, an African-American, would stun two-term Sen. Alan Dixon in the three-way March 17 Democratic primary. In Pennsylvania, Lynn Hardy Yeakel would emerge from a primary to give Specter a real run for his money. In California, Rep. Barbara Boxer and former San Francisco Mayor Dianne Feinstein would become the Democratic nominees for the state's U.S. Senate seats, one up for grabs in a special election to fill the vacancy left by retiring Sen. Alan Cranston.

In Washington, Patty Murphy would capture the Democratic nomination. In Maryland, the Democrats already had Barbara

Mikulski in the Senate, and she was running for a second term. In Kansas, Grassley's good friend Bob Dole would be challenged by Gloria O'Dell, a state treasury official.

In Missouri, Sen. Christopher "Kit" Bond would find himself running against St. Louis County Council member Geri Rothman-Serot in the general election. In Arizona, civic activist Claire Sargent would challenge Sen. John McCain, a former Navy pilot and Vietnam War POW. Charlene Haar, a school teacher, was the lone female GOP candidate, challenging Sen. Tom Daschle in South Dakota.

In the House, the 1990 record of 69 women candidates would be shattered as 106 women were nominated by Republicans or Democrats.[20] And in Iowa, Jean Lloyd-Jones, a sophisticated millionaire and state senator from Iowa City, would cite the Thomas-Hill controversy as a major impetus for her candidacy for the Democratic nomination for the U.S. Senate.

Suddenly, 1992 was the Year of the Woman in politics, a direct result of the handling and content of the Clarence Thomas-Anita Hill episode by the all-white, all-male Senate Judiciary Committee.

It was against that backdrop that Charles Grassley—one of the committee members who, according to liberals and feminists, "just didn't get it"—entered the campaign for his third Senate term.

# "Seeing How High He Could Make the Rubble Bounce"

Considering the national trend—the Year of the Woman in politics was a direct product of the Clarence Thomas-Anita Hill episode—things should have gone Jean Lloyd-Jones' way in 1992. But this was Iowa, where political and economic conditions often run counter-cyclical to other parts of the country. And Lloyd-Jones wasn't running against just anyone. She was up against Charles Grassley, the aw-shucks New Hartford farmer who had engineered 13 straight victorious campaigns since 1958.

For some time, John Roehrick had harbored serious hopes of a 1992 rematch with Grassley. His second campaign would have been in a presidential year, which he felt would have been beneficial. He would have had the knowledge earned from the stinging 1986 defeat and the benefit of contacts made as the 1988 presidential campaign wound through Iowa, and from his place on the Democratic National Committee. All three components were vital to Roehrick's rematch strategy.

His intent was to keep in touch with Iowa voters while simultaneously spending the year before the election coaxing several million dollars from the pockets of wealthy East and West Coast Democrats. "If I had to do it over again, I would have spent 80 percent of my time in New York, Texas, California, and Florida. That's the reality. Forget about going to, with no disrespect to Grundy Center, forget about going there. If you're doing the same handshaking in L.A., that's where you're raising the money," Roehrick said.

In the real world of modern politics, 25 or 30 handshakes in a place like Grundy Center might translate into a handful of votes on a good day, but 25 or 30 handshakes in Hollywood would likely get a Democratic candidate enough money to pay for TV commercials that would reach 200,000 Iowans. On the home front, Roehrick secured the state party's vice chairmanship, which gave him a reason to travel the state and build his network and name recognition. But he threw in the towel in 1989 when, he said, "I looked at my bank balance. I had given a year and was in debt and had to practice [law]."

He estimated his out-of-pocket expenses were close to $35,000 in the 1986 campaign, while lost income was probably around $200,000. As the 1990 campaign approached, Roehrick, boosted to the role of party chairman, had more immediate concerns than Grassley. There was Harkin's reelection and the open Second Congressional District seat. He didn't even have a list of candidates he'd like to see running against Grassley two years down the road. Some Democratic-leaning organizations still listed Roehrick as the likely candidate even into late 1991.

Grassley's political apparatchiks had been expecting former Attorney General Tom Miller, loser of the 1990 Democratic gubernatorial campaign, to jump into the race. But they also viewed Representative Dave Nagle as a potential rival. Nagle was considered the strongest candidate "on paper," partly because he operated from Grassley's old power base. The Cedar Falls Democrat, who had broken the GOP's 52-year hold on the Third Congressional District in 1986, opted for a difficult and ultimately unsuccessful reapportionment showdown with Second District Representative Jim Nussle.

Throughout much of 1991, there had been a long-running, though not necessarily public debate about whether Lloyd-Jones or former state Rep. Paul Johnson of Decorah would wage the Democrats' campaign. Johnson, a sheep and tree farmer with sterling credentials as an environmentalist, told the Associated Press in May 1991 that he was pondering a challenge to Grassley. "I'm thinking about it, that's all. I'm not sure the Democratic Party is interested."[1] Johnson, who later went to Washington as director of the U.S. Soil Conservation Service in the Clinton Administration, concluded by year's end that he wasn't interested, either.

With Johnson and Roehrick out, the field of seemingly credible contenders was gone. It was down to Lloyd-Jones and former teacher and Peace Corps volunteer Rosanne Freeburg, a political novice from Cedar Rapids with no discernible base. But the protracted process of winnowing the field, combined with the appearance that neither Johnson nor Lloyd-Jones was particularly eager to run, chewed up valuable campaign, fundraising, planning, and research time.

Lloyd-Jones had a bigger problem on her hands as Senate Ethics Committee chairwoman. The assignment was normally a prestigious title with no heavy lifting involved, but just weeks before the start of the 1992 legislative session, news broke that the manager of a California investment firm known as Institutional

Treasury Management had lost or stolen $75.4 million in money deposited by 87 Iowa schools, cities, and counties. Thus began the Iowa Trust Fund scandal and, though no one knew it yet, the effective end of Lloyd-Jones' candidacy. A disclosure came on December 11, 1991, that Senate President Joe Welsh, a Dubuque Democrat, was a well-paid sales representative for Institutional Treasury Management. Accusations were leveled that Welsh had peddled his influence as Senate Appropriations Committee chairman to persuade local officials to invest in the Iowa Trust Fund.

Lloyd-Jones, as stunned as anyone by the turn of events, presided over the Democrat-controlled Ethics Committee that voted in mid-January 1992 to terminate its investigation on the advice of independent counsel Patrick Roby of Cedar Rapids, despite evidence that indicated Welsh had lied under oath about his efforts on behalf of the fund. Citizen member Lucas DeKoster had pressed for a formal reprimand of Welsh, but Democrats squelched the move by arguing that Welsh had been punished enough by resigning from the Senate presidency and suffering the resulting loss of public esteem.

The public saw it otherwise. In the ensuing protest, Lloyd-Jones announced a week later that she was reopening the investigation. Voters now added "vacillating" to their short, largely unfavorable list of impressions about Lloyd-Jones. The assessments may have been unduly harsh—the committee was operating in uncharted waters without the benefit of all the facts—but first impressions were what counted, and Lloyd-Jones made a terrible first impression.

In the end, no charges were filed against Welsh, but the two-year, part-time job that paid $53,850 had destroyed his public career. He announced in December 1993 that he would not seek reelection.[2] For her part, Lloyd-Jones was a mortally wounded candidate when she made her March 17, 1992 formal announcement, which included a variation of the old David vs. Goliath theme. "Mr. Grassley may be a political Goliath, but he's about to learn David has a sister." The line sounded contrived—and Lloyd-Jones unconvincing—after her unsteady performance in the Welsh hearings, which also seemed to undermine her criticism of his performance on the Judiciary Committee during the Thomas-Hill hearings. Lloyd-Jones accused Grassley of supporting Bush Administration policies that had "literally assaulted the economy of Iowa. Our workers take home smaller and smaller paychecks, when they can get them, and our family farmers struggle just to survive." But the picture she painted of Iowa was much bleaker than most saw it, particularly when contrasted with memories of the mid-1980s farm recession.

She also charged that the incumbent had "a long and consistent pattern" of ignoring children's needs, citing the bipartisan nonprofit Children's Defense Fund rankings that indicated Grassley voted "wrong" on such children's issues as education and nutrition on two-thirds of 105 crucial votes.

"I'm told that Mr. Grassley is a good family man, and I have no doubt that is true," she said. "I'm sure that where his own family is concerned he puts his children's needs first, but the fact is that his pattern of votes is so insensitive to children's issues that it can only be characterized as serious neglect."[3]

Iowans who had listened to the debate up to this point undoubtedly found that hard to believe about the man many called "Chuck," especially coming from the chairwoman of the committee that had investigated Joe Welsh. But at least her candidacy was finally off and running. It did not take long, however, before she wounded her cause again with the announcement that she would not accept PAC money.

She assailed Grassley as bought and paid for by special interests. In fact, several sources, who asked not to be identified, insisted it was Harkin who persuaded Lloyd-Jones not to accept special interest money, perhaps to benefit his presidential campaign.

"I had a lot of arguments with Jean on that issue because Jean really cares, but nobody else [did]," said one prominent Democrat. "You've got to go out and raise your money, and if you cut your PAC money out, you're cutting off our base of support here in the state, and that's labor. You cannot afford to do that. But with Lloyd-Jones out of the running, who gets all the PAC money?"

Tim Raftis, who managed Harkin's 1990 presidential campaign, scoffed at the assertion. "There were any number of persons who gave her advice one way or the other. On the one hand, one might legitimately think that it might be an Achilles' heel for Grassley and a point of attack that might catch on with the press. At the same time, she had to figure, 'I'm up against a member on a big committee; I'm not going to be able to raise as much money anyway, so maybe the cost benefit is one that I could wage a campaign on.' But it never caught on, and she never had enough money to take it on the tube for it to catch on. As far as we were concerned, we were operating from a much bigger pool than Iowa. Hers and ours were two separate races, and PACs make those decisions separately. And besides, Tom was out March 7, and she didn't announce until March 17."

Whoever was responsible, the no-PAC pledge turned out to be the worst of both worlds for Lloyd-Jones. She had no money to wage a meaningful media campaign against Grassley, and his ads pummeled her as a hypocrite who had taken a lot of PAC money in the past and was only engaging in political hucksterism by not doing so in 1992. That stinging criticism was only reinforced by Lloyd-Jones' gimmickry. Always perfectly dressed, she carried a knapsack so she could declare, "This is my only PAC."

Curt Sytsma, a Des Moines attorney who managed the Lloyd-Jones campaign, later said he did not regret the no-PAC money decision because "some of our most telling arguments against Senator Grassley and the ones with the most logical clout, however far they went in the polls, ultimately had some ties to the financing of campaigns." But, he added, "I don't know for the life of me how you can run a campaign without substantial money and without PAC money."

In the primary, Lloyd-Jones and party leaders ignored Rosanne Freeburg, who was running as someone outside the political system. "People really do not like the way that Jean Lloyd-Jones has conducted herself with the Ethics Committee and her leadership as a whole," she said.[4]

Freeburg ran the type of amateurish, low-budget, no-respect-from-the-media campaign common among first-time candidates. Yet with public wrath over the Iowa Trust Fund on Freeburg's side, Lloyd-Jones stumbled into the general election with an embarrassing 60,615–38,774 victory. Heartened by receiving 40 percent of the vote, Freeburg quickly launched an independent campaign. What she failed to comprehend, even though she emphasized she was an alternative to Lloyd-Jones, was that many votes were not cast *for* her but *against* Lloyd-Jones. Tracking polls would later prove that when those same voters had a chance to vote against Lloyd-Jones with Chuck Grassley on the ballot, they would turn out for him in droves.

The opposition's missteps were of little consolation to Grassley or his operatives. Caran McKee, Grassley's Senate and campaign spokeswoman, said his early, seemingly insurmountable lead didn't count for much, either. "It was a funny year, and we didn't know what attacks of hers would stick. She attacked continually, so each was taken very seriously and was responded to."

Lloyd-Jones did enjoy a moment in the spotlight at the Democratic National Convention at Madison Square Garden in New York. In a two-minute speech, which was carried live by CNN, Lloyd-Jones described herself as "part of a people's movement for change in this country." She said Grassley's treatment of Anita Hill has "embarrassed and insulted Iowa."

"I want a government that's not for sale to the highest bidder, a government that guarantees equal opportunity to all Americans and a Supreme Court that will uphold a woman's right to choose," she said. She then shared the stage with other women seeking high elective office across the country, joining hands in a triumphant wave to the cheering crowd.

Roehrick predicted the appearance would cause big-dollar contributors to see the candidate in a new light. "This whole event is a matter of perception, particularly the race between Grassley and Lloyd-Jones. What [two minutes of national exposure] does is send a message to fundraisers and activist groups that this race has moved from 'they can't win' to 'at least take a look at it' and 'maybe it will become hot.'"[5]

For his part, Grassley had former Iowa Republican Senate Caucus staffer Bob Haus raising money for more than a year. The campaign was headquartered in the Haus' basement for the first six months, sharing space with the washer, dryer, and furnace in a deliberate effort to keep overhead costs down. Grassley's campaign brain trust—Maxwell, Wythe Willey of Cedar Rapids, Don Byers of Newton, State Auditor Dick Johnson of Sheldahl, Kayne Robinson, Jim Gritzner, Harlan D. "Bud" Hockenberg (who is Arthur Davis' law partner), Katie Roth of Des Moines, Dundeana Langer of Cedar Rapids, and Grinnell businessman and broadcasting executive Frosty Mitchell—met monthly to sign off on policy or spending decisions.

Grassley began his campaign staff build-up in March 1992, but the pressure on one potential foe began earlier. "We had fun with Nagle, rattling his cage by telling Second District voters that he really didn't want to be a congressman, that he wanted to be a senator," Haus said. "He'd vehemently deny it, then [Jim] Nussle would yank his chain from the other side."

Grassley appeared with Lloyd-Jones only twice.

Roth, who had met her future husband, Luke, in the 1980 campaign when he was working for Grassley and she was backing Tom Stoner, played Lloyd-Jones for Grassley as he prepared in the

West Des Moines offices of Schreuers & Associates for the first debate at the Clay County Fair in mid-September. She reprised the role for a second debate, the traditional day-before-the-election appearance at the Des Moines Chamber of Commerce's luncheon that occurs too late to change an election's outcome.

The first debate's site virtually guaranteed light press coverage. Grassley further deflected attention from Lloyd-Jones by opting to include independent candidates Freeburg and Mel Boring of Rockford. Talk centered on trade, health care, and agriculture. Grassley and Lloyd-Jones attacked the Bush administration for blocking the use of corn-based ethanol as a gasoline additive to reduce air pollution in major cities. Grassley called for the resignation of Environmental Protection Agency director William Reilly.[6]

In boxing jargon, Lloyd-Jones needed a knockout, but never laid a glove on Grassley. Nothing she tried over the summer and into the fall seemed to work. When she questioned his commitment to equality for women, he would point out that three of his five top-paid employees were women. When she tried to take advantage of the anti-incumbent fervor sweeping the nation, he would point out that he had remained in touch by visiting all 99 counties at least once each year since 1981. Her admission on the program "Iowa Press" early in the race that she had no agricultural policy negated her weak criticism that Grassley was not the only working farmer in the Senate. And she couldn't break through his defenses on trade, health care, defense, or fiscal policy.

Sytsma said Grassley had formed an impenetrable barrier as a very adept politician who tended to constituent service. "He knows when to say what, better than most and . . . he runs a 'strongly politic' constituency service. He does a better job of getting letters to people and letters that reflect their concerns."

In fact, Sytsma frequently heard from dedicated Democrats who had a favorable, or at minimum neutral opinion of Grassley, because of a letter he'd written in response to a family concern, such as a Social Security glitch. "From a public service standpoint, you can't fault that. It's what every public official should do. From a political standpoint, that kind of service . . . protects him from attacks on the issues. We didn't know a really good way to get around that, obviously, fighting with limited resources."

Grassley's weak point, in Sytsma's mind, was an apparent attempt to have it both ways. "Where I thought there was a vulnerability was the letters for opposite things. We found out that was true, but couldn't get the documents. One letter on the Brady [gun control bill] made it sound like he was in favor of the controls. That went to everyone who signed a letter in support of it, including Jean Lloyd-Jones' daughter. He had another letter to a National Rifle Association mailing list that made it clear he was against it. While people read it to us off the record and we promised anonymity . . . they had the feeling he had written it just to them and that he'd know it was them who gave us the letter.

"In terms of getting correspondence that looks friendly and using technology to do that on a large scale and promptly, he's got it down. It's a technically sophisticated operation. I'm advised that's not just because of delegation; that's a hands-on thing making it work," Sytsma said.

When the Lloyd-Jones campaign managed to scrape up enough money to air TV commercials critical of Grassley, he unloaded with a withering response that his opponent "didn't bother to show up for work" because she had missed more than 600 votes since 1981. That averaged out to about 55 a year, not all that many, considering the crushing volume of inconsequential votes, but it provided another opportunity for Grassley to highlight his 100 percent voting record. Lloyd-Jones went public with her plea that he stop running the ad. "The amazing thing was that [the Lloyd-Jones camp] went negative in the first place," Schreuers said. "He never would have done that negative [spot] had she not done it. But once they did, Grassley did, and it was like, 'Gee, there's even more room to grow.'"

For the most part, though, Grassley said he felt compelled to treat his opponent with kid gloves. Gender was a motivating factor. "It was just that I guess I knew in my own mind I had to be more cautious, and probably more sensitive in how I responded to questions from the press," Grassley recalled.

He gave credit to Beverly Hubble Tauke, his press secretary during the end of his House tenure and his first years in the Senate, for preparing him for just such a campaign. "She knew and I knew I couldn't have a record where I was going to be out in front on all the liberal issues, but we were careful enough to do what we could do, and when we did what we could do, of documenting it well and having it and remembering, maybe even doing press on it at the time. Probably [less] the general press, but press that would go to specific publications.

"By 1992, we'd probably had eight or ten years, even though I had different press secretaries, of a sensitivity toward the issues so we didn't feel like we had to take a back seat even if I wasn't for the litmus test of *Roe v. Wade.* And if I wasn't OK on that, that somehow we did enough other things to protect ourselves. It wouldn't have been recognized by Emily's List as being a very good record, but we did enough things so that we could establish a record so that we couldn't be painted as an extremist."

He also praised other women on his staff, including McKee and Jill Hegstrom, for continuing to foster sensitivity toward the "women's issues" such as pay equity, sexual harassment, family leave, and health research and care.

As if Grassley did not already enjoy enough advantages, Sen. Phil Gramm of Texas, the Republican Senatorial Campaign Committee chairman with designs on the 1996 presidential nomination, poured thousands of dollars into Grassley's race, which had never been in jeopardy. "He was trying to buddy up to Grassley," one Democratic official groused in a campaign postmortem.

The pragmatic Grassley wasn't above accepting Gramm's largesse because, at that stage, it came with no strings attached. By the time Election Day rolled around, he had raised more than $3 million; Lloyd-Jones had less than $400,000.

When the speeches were over and all the votes were counted, Grassley had bettered his 1986 showing against Roehrick. He won all 99 counties as he received an astounding 72 percent of the vote. Grassley's 899,761 votes shattered Harkin's record for the most votes in a U.S. Senate race in Iowa, which had been 716,883 in 1984.

Lloyd-Jones received 351,561 votes. In Dubuque County, the Democratic stronghold that was home to Joe Welsh, Lloyd-Jones lost badly, 28,334 to 12,713. But the story played out the same everywhere, including her home county, Johnson. Despite the strength of Iowa City's liberal base, Grassley buried her, 29,663 to 19,494.[7]

The Thomas-Hill episode never jelled as an issue. McKee contended one reason was because Grassley had used the debacle as a springboard to renew his fight to extend sexual harassment penalties and other workplace laws to Congress. "The other point about Grassley and running against a woman is that he's not the naive, sheltered '50s politician she tried to make him out to be.

When he sat down with editorial boards, his human experiences came through. His wife was raised on a farm and went back to college after the kids were raised. He's got daughters and daughters-in-law that work full-time and grandkids in day care," McKee said. "He has a liberal maternity leave policy, and he's willing to work with families. . . . It came out that you shouldn't paint him as a Norman Rockwell senator because he's someone who's had normal living experiences. That's why he ran so well against a woman, and why he's as popular as he is. And that's why every newspaper in the state that endorsed, including the *Iowa City Press Citizen*, endorsed Grassley."

Nor did Grassley's vote on the Persian Gulf Resolution become a vulnerability. "The minus side was you had Republicans really mad," John Maxwell said. "In retrospect, it ended up that, in fact, it was a very big positive. At the time, the thrust of what was being written was Democrats were enthused about going after Grassley where they hadn't been previously, for two reasons. One, because he was so actively engaged on Tom Tauke's behalf against Harkin, they didn't view him as being some kind of benevolent figure they didn't have to worry about. He really represented a threat. Secondly, they saw what happened to Rudy Boschwitz, who was supposedly unbeatable, and if Boschwitz could be defeated in Minnesota, then Grassley could be defeated in Iowa. So they were out looking for a strong candidate, but after the war vote, they just pulled the plug on all that. It took the heart out of it for them."

Boschwitz's defeat became a motivator for Grassley and his team. McKee said, "He and Rudy Boschwitz were good friends so it wasn't a trite thing around here to say 'Remember Rudy Boschwitz.'"

In the minds of some Democrats, Grassley's margin of victory was nothing but bitter evidence of a classic case of overkill. "He was just seeing how high he could make the rubble bounce," said former Iowa Democratic Party spokesman Joe Shannahan. Word from GOP insiders of the goals Grassley set for the campaign would seem to reinforce the contention. "He wanted the record percentage for a U.S. Senate seat in Iowa and he wanted to end the campaign with $500,000 in the bank," one source said. "The percentage was for a sense of history, I think. I don't know why it had to be $500,000, but he did both."

Bob Haus contended that Grassley's motivation was more altruistic than the typical politician's ego at work. "There were two reasons. One was personal, the other was party-oriented. The personal was he knew if he went back with a 60 or 65 percent margin and money in the bank his colleagues would think, 'This guy is a very strong voice in his state,' and it would increase his effectiveness in Washington.

"Second, we felt all along that he was leading the ticket in Iowa, not George Bush. Grassley was going to be the fire wall—that was the term we used, fire wall—in the November election between the presidential race and the rest of the ticket, and if there were going to be coattails, it would be him. Some voted for Bill Clinton, some for Ross Perot, a few for Bush. He got people back on the Republican side."

There seemed to be little doubt that Grassley had helped rescue Rep. Jim Ross Lightfoot, whose reputation was tarnished in the House Bank bounced-check controversy. And Grassley had a hand in the GOP's return to power in the Iowa House. Grassley had campaigned hard in the new Third District that covered southern Iowa in the final days, giving Lightfoot his personal seal of approval for voters to see, and doing what he could to help legislative candidates in tight races.

The Senator's campaigning in parts of his old congressional district, which had become the new Second District through reapportionment, also helped boost Nussle in his narrow victory over Nagle. And Grassley's record victory, with a pile of money left in the bank, had raised him to the status of a political giant in Iowa. Whether it would raise his stature on Capitol Hill remained to be seen.

# Public Service, Personal Gains

In September 1979, as he prepared for his challenge to Sen. John Culver, Grassley told a reporter that his wife Barbara had OK'd his entrance into the race. "And I don't take that lightly. We've been partners in all of this over the years, and she has as much to lose as I do."

At stake were the family finances. "If I wanted economic security, I would run for reelection to my House seat. If I go back to the farm, it will mean an income of under $20,000 again," he told *Waterloo Courier* associate editor Jack Bender.[1]

At the time, representatives and senators were paid $57,500 a year. But even more was on the line than indicated by that rare, though cursory, acknowledgment that public office had been good to the Grassley family finances. There was also the matter of honoraria.

In 1981, the year after he had accused Culver of "getting rich" in office, Grassley reported that he earned $21,580 for giving speeches. That amount alone, of course, exceeded what Grassley, by his own accounting, would make back on the farm. And that was before the agricultural crisis hit Iowa, and sent incomes plummeting and debts soaring. Grassley gave 23 speeches with fees ranging from $200 to $2,000. He was also paid for one radio performance, a magazine article, and a chapter in a book. It was not exactly the type of off-farm income that most Iowans would receive.

Getting to that point had been a financial gamble in itself. Grassley's 1974 congressional rival, Stephen Rapp, recalled a conversation that occurred as they rode from Des Moines to a candidates' forum before the primary. "He really did worry about how difficult it would be after the election if he lost . . . because he really didn't have anything to fall back on. He was obviously very worried about it."

Grassley's worries began to ease, predictably, in the '70s and '80s, as his children began to gain their financial independence. His increasing public salary, coupled with generous honoraria, helped at least as much; but the Grassleys were far from Easy Street. Election to Congress improved Grassley's cash flow, while simultaneously presenting the new expenses of living and working in two places, especially when one was as expensive as Washington, D.C.

In the 1980 primary against Tom Stoner, Grassley released summaries of his own 1978 and 1979 tax forms. His total income in 1978 as a little-known member of Congress was $62,228, including his $57,500 congressional salary. In 1979, it was $65,655, counting his $58,027 congressional salary. "In 1979, Grassley earned $1,797 from outside speaking engagements. In 1978, he made $7,929 in charitable contributions and in 1979, contributions totaled $8,431," the Associated Press reported.[2]

After his Senate victory, other disclosure statements revealed that "Grassley and his wife reported earning up to $113,000 on dividends, interest and rent in 1981," the Associated Press reported in a May 19, 1982 story about financial disclosure statements. "The senator's 200-acre Butler County farm complex was listed as being worth at least $250,000, but about half of that was mortgaged."

Grassley received $41,950 in honoraria from speeches and gave $17,961 to charity in 1984. He listed assets of $505,000 and income of $17,000. He listed most of his outside income as coming from his Iowa farm, but said most of it was absorbed by operating expenses.[3]

Members were not required to list their official salary or the value of their residences during those years; nor do they today. Grassley had two homes—a modest, split-level house on his New Hartford farmstead, and a similar though larger home near Mount Vernon in Alexandria, Virginia. He sold the house in Virginia in late 1994, and purchased a townhouse near the Senate.

By early 1994, Grassley reported assets ranging from $611,000 to $1.8 million under the vague Senate disclosure requirements. Most of those assets were in farmland, equipment, and related property. He reported gross farm income of $74,000 from his Butler County farm that was, by then, more than 557 acres. However, gross receipts of more than $67,000 left him with a net farm income of just more than $6,000.[4]

That Senate salary of $133,600 proved quite handy, indeed. Grassley's acceptance of speaking fees from special interest groups throughout the '80s was absolutely legal. Still, Pete Conroy sensed that Grassley was uncomfortable with what critics such as Common Cause charged was easy money from corporations or organizations looking for access and influence. "One thing he'd always say if he'd do something was, 'I don't want to let the dollar signs get in my eyes,'" Conroy said. "One time he was coming back from a speaking tour and, God, he was going to be late. At that time he had an unbroken voting streak and he said, 'Maybe I let the dollar signs get in my eyes.' He always had that in mind as to where is the line that you go out and give speeches and get honoraria and stuff like that.

"I think that he grapples with it all the time but he's got these mechanisms and they're not artificial, they're real—legal, moral, religious, all of that—which assuages [Grassley's worries]. Those things help him, and I think he's got all those parameters in mind. Of course, when you see some of these other guys, I doubt if they've got one of those parameters."

Lawmakers banned honoraria in 1992 when they voted themselves a controversial pay raise. Grassley, as he had done on past occasions, opposed the raise. He did, however, accept the higher pay. And he did not confess to any epic moral struggle over accepting special interest money. "I had dealt with that sometimes in my life, but I suppose that I didn't let it sway me because this is what the rules of the Senate provided. I saw an opportunity to do speaking for money, and you could keep [fees equal to] 20 percent of your salary. That was the way it was until [1992] when you had to give it all to charity."

From a political standpoint, he said, he viewed the big honoraria offers as "a way of expression of some power within the Senate, as a way to stand out with key leaders. On one or two occasions, out of 100 members of the Senate, I would have been sixth or seventh when I made a concentrated effort to do it. It's a recognition that your view is important in Washington because other people want to hear it and pay you for it."

He added, "I never made much money throughout my life. Even as faithful as I am, I never tithed. I've given a lot, but probably until I got to Congress I never really tithed, so here I had an opportunity to make a lot of money and give it to charity, and I suppose, do some good."

In 1993, Grassley gave $6,500 in honoraria and more than $14,000 of his salary to his church and charities. "It's not a lot of money, but it's more than tithing." Of course, it could be argued that the issue was not Grassley's good intentions in accepting the money as much as what was in the hearts and minds of the contributors. He conceded, "They probably thought they were buying access. But that's stupid. I spend two hours a day talking to people. I don't have a list of PAC contributors. [Scheduler] Mary Jo [Archibold] doesn't have a list. So anyone who says they give PAC money or honoraria to get access to me is stupid."

Grassley answered with his usual candor when asked if he thought PAC money had ever influenced his votes. "No. But what would you expect me to say? But I honestly believe that." He noted in July 1994 that he had accepted PAC money and honoraria from military contractors during the '80s, which didn't stop him from going after defense fraud, waste, and abuse. "Last night I was at a dinner where I sat next to the vice president for governmental relations for McDonnell Douglas a week after trying to eliminate a $348 million bailout for his company. I hope I smiled and caused him to be civil."

Such is the reality in Washington. "People don't understand, and it doesn't do me any good to blame anyone. I don't think we teach appreciation of our political system, and that lack of understanding in people early in life breeds a lot of cynicism today," the Senator lamented.

Some people who did understand the intricacies of election financing in the post-Watergate era, however, expressed cynicism about the millions of dollars Grassley collected from special interest groups to finance his House and Senate campaigns. Conroy acknowledged, "The whole money deal is tough for him—how do you equate all the big money that's involved in politics with your own personal view of what part money should play and where it stands in your priorities? I know that has been a constant struggle for him, too—first of all, to raise it, then when it starts coming in and the way it comes in and the amount it comes in. The only thing I can think of is he has complete confidence in the people handling it, not that he turns it over to them *carte blanche*."

In the days when honoraria flowed freely, the staff also played a role in winnowing out the offers for paid speeches that just didn't feel right. Conroy said, "You get a guy like Bob Ludwiczak; he can't be any better at keeping track. See, these [public officials] get in trouble when their staff lets them do things they shouldn't. . . . Of course, your friends are going to be the ones to get you in trouble. Your enemies you're careful with. This is subjective, but I believe the staff will be as good as the member."

No matter how good a staff is, history has shown all too clearly that underlings can't always make amends for their employer's conduct. During 36 years of public service, Charles Grassley never put himself, his family, friends, staff, supporters, or constituents in the position of having to explain away his personal conduct, and there is no indication that he will deviate from that pattern in the future.

# Grassley and the Media: Assertive, Accessible, and a Different Standard

Like almost every political success story, Grassley's well-polished image as an unpolished, unconventional public official could be directly attributed to his skillful massaging of the mass media to shape and reshape public opinion. He achieved, or at least enhanced that image in standard fashion—surrounding himself with smart, talented, loyal people who understood and agreed with his philosophy and objectives and adopted his agenda as their own. And, like most politicians, Grassley insisted he rarely won any special favor from the Fourth Estate, though he certainly had the respect, friendship, and admiration of such professionals as Jim Gritzner, Bob Bradsell, and *Waterloo Courier* reporter Mike Kelly, all of whom joined his congressional or campaign staffs.

Grassley also had his share of press-related scrapes, usually with the state's dominant newspaper, the *Des Moines Register*, and particularly during the latter part of his Iowa House career and into his first Senate term. No experience with the Iowa media, however, prepared him for the embarrassment he experienced in the second half of 1982 when *Washingtonian* magazine labeled him the least intelligent member of the United States Senate. (Roger Jepsen was named the chamber's least effective member.)

"I was hurt," Grassley said years later. It was not quite the reaction Buster Lynes would have coached. "He would have gotten mad and told them off." But that wasn't Grassley's style. "I figure people are entitled to their opinion. I just don't think that particular opinion was right, based on their approach to it. I never pretended to be a Rhodes Scholar, *summa cum laude*, Harvard. I try to represent my people."

Reporters rarely confess to such lapses in judgment, but the denunciation may have been at least partly attributable to a media bias against the New Right and evangelical Christians and the reasonable perception that Grassley was "one of them." Conroy had been concerned about the fallout from the 1980 election and the stories that immediately followed. Profiles surfaced in the *Washington Post* and *Washington Star* describing Grassley as a member of the

Moral Majority, a Christian organization founded by the Rev. Jerry Falwell. Conroy recalled, "First of all, Chuck was never a member of the Moral Majority, and I called the papers. Nobody seemed to be able to track down the original stories so we could correct them. I wanted to get that profile out of their morgues and out of the files of members of Congress because they keep files on other members. So leadership had all this stuff on Chuck, and it wasn't true. Chuck would say, 'Oh, Pete, don't worry about it.' But that's the job of the staff, to try and clean up some of that stuff."

Grassley's press secretary, Beverly Hubble, shared Conroy's clear-the-air philosophy when it came to the knock delivered by the *Washingtonian*, which, ironically, had listed its own editors as having made the year's "worst goof" for picking as the "Best D.C. Divorce Lawyer" an attorney subsequently censured for negligent practice.[1] Hubble said, "Normally I think it would be masochistic to pursue this kind of story because it would invite follow-up. But they do this story every year. And the question was, if you didn't respond, would they do it next year and the next and the next? And then do you have this whole series of stories like that?"

Nevertheless, Hubble persisted with John Samsing, editor of the *Washingtonian*. She presented a picture of a freshman senator who had more victories on amendments and legislation in committee and on the Senate floor than 60 percent of his colleagues. "I said, 'If this is someone with low wattage, how do you explain that? Someone hasn't done their research.'"

Samsing regrouped, indicating the description of Grassley must have been based on stylistic considerations.

Hubble replied, "If we're talking style, why don't we report it as style?" She made it clear that a few stories alleging a lack of brain power could put a big dent in Grassley's effectiveness, not to mention drastically shorten his political career.

She reported back to Grassley that Samsing had listened with a fair and open mind. Grassley's reply was, Why don't we invite him to dinner? Hubble was taken aback, and even more surprised that the editor accepted. They had dinner at The Monocle, a Washington landmark a block from the Senate Office Buildings. No one brought up the article during a pleasant evening of superficial chit-chat, but the next month the *Washingtonian* "clarified" its position on Grassley.

Still, the flap caused ripples in Iowa. John Hyde of the *Des Moines Register* had met with Hubble before she had talked to

Samsing. Faced with a deadline, he reported the story in his weekend column based on the information at hand. He noted that a previous recipient of the dubious distinction had ended up at the *Washingtonian*, pounding on a table and shouting, 'I am not stupid,' which led many to conclude that he certainly was. It was not the image Grassley and his staff wanted to take root back home. All was not lost.

Ken Sullivan, then the *Cedar Rapids Gazette's* political reporter who had covered Grassley extensively, bristled publicly when he learned of the *Washingtonian* story. "I observed in a column that he may not be clever and sophisticated, but he's not a dumb guy. As close as he is to a Ph.D., he's nobody's fool," Sullivan recounted. "I instantly got this response from Grassley, a letter that expressed his appreciation that anybody in the media would take that attitude and rise to his defense."

The *Washingtonian* episode was a testament to the damage control that can be performed by a good press secretary. In fact, Hubble had keen instincts and was in tune with Grassley's characteristic manner on other matters—confront the issue head-on, state your case clearly, and hope to win points for honesty and reason. But she also could plan and execute an effective end run, devising a "trickle-down" strategy to short-circuit any potential trend of troubling stories back in Iowa in the wake of the "Dumbest Man in the Senate" story.

"I came to the conclusion we could more effectively get the message out dealing with the national media, and if we did, papers in-state that had some kind of intrinsic opposition to him would have difficulty continuing to sell that. If a senator is getting rave reviews in the *Wall Street Journal, Los Angeles Times,* and *New York Times,* which one might expect to be negative, it becomes a little more difficult to be credible selling to the public a slant that presents him in a different way. I'm sure in Iowa nobody said, 'We'll let the *Wall Street Journal* or *New York Times* dictate coverage.' But, of course, I made sure they all saw them, and it's a little difficult not to affect your perception, and I think appropriately so. These are big operations that have armies of reporters down here scrutinizing this guy."

At the same time, she also knew the *Des Moines Register* was not the big, bad boogey man that bewitched and bewildered so many Republicans, including Grassley. Stung by the newspaper's liberal, Democratic editorial leanings and refusal to endorse him,

Grassley was positive that *Register* news coverage of him was unfair. Hubble recalled, "Somebody was coming to do a story from the *Register* . . . and he kind of rolled his eyes and said, 'Why do we do this? Because you know how the stories are inevitably negative.' I went back to my office and pulled out all the *Register* stories, this was about 18 months into the term, and separated the negative from the positive. The negative stack was about a quarter-inch. A much bigger stack, I'd say about two inches, reflected [Grassley] positively or just factually."

As she had done with Samsing, Hubble laid out the evidence before Grassley, and convinced him.

David Yepsen, the *Register's* chief political reporter, recognized early on that Hubble was teaching her boss about the art and science of feeding the hungry press just as she was teaching reporters to appreciate some of Grassley's overlooked fine points. "When Chuck Grassley ran in the early stages, he was a basic, right-wing Republican who thought most media people were liberals and out to get him. And he was viewed as a hick in Washington by the national media. I think Bev did a good job of sort of sitting down, saying to him, 'These folks have a job to do; they're not evil. Some of them agree with you, and let's work with them.' If you look at Chuck Grassley's growth as a public figure in 1981 and 1982, Bev did that."

Allen Finch, who left WQAD-TV in the Quad Cities to become Grassley's assistant press secretary in 1983, elaborated, "Bev provided at a very important time in Grassley's career a level of polish, it's safe to say, he didn't have in coming to the U.S. Senate. The instincts were there, all the elements were there, but not the level of polish. And she provided it in a way Grassley was able to absorb and use. She was very personable and had a strong relationship with God and Jesus Christ, mirroring the Senator's religion and beliefs. As a consequence, I think there was a spiritual as well as professional and personal connection that allowed them to get through some really tough times those first few years."

Hubble also expanded Grassley's vistas, working with liberal groups and other unlikely venues. One such meeting was a breakfast with NAACP president Benjamin Hooks. Hubble also wrote a speech for Grassley on race relations, landing him in the African-American magazine, *Jet*. Her base-broadening drive coincided with Grassley's move to assist in the 1982 reauthorization of the Voting Rights Act of 1965. "I don't think she was having me do anything that deep down in my heart I wouldn't believe, but I wouldn't have sought out the dialogue just in the course of doing what you believe. When you do it, they question whether you're doing it for political reasons. The staff felt I ought to do it to enhance my communications, respect, and eventually my power in this town."

No other run-in with the press before or after bothered Grassley as much as the *Washingtonian*, but, with Hubble's coaching and coaxing, it did not change his willingness to cooperate with reporters. It did not stop him, however, from bristling in a post-victory interview in 1986 at the suggestion that he had been viewed as a slow-witted country bumpkin. "That was mostly the Eastern press. They just didn't know Chuck Grassley, and they didn't bother to ask."[2]

Those who did ask and listen invariably ended up coming away with respect, Conroy insisted. "What creates that is his knowledge. No reporter goes in to talk to him that they don't learn something if they're paying attention, because he gives them background—that, plus showing no animosity, not only no animosity but no strong feeling against anybody. He doesn't say mean things."

When Grassley's media reputation turned from the negative, it turned with a vengeance. With Hubble's behind-the-scenes prodding, Grassley became something of a national media darling because he broke the conventional mold. He himself recognized that some of the fawning could be traced to the fact he was a conservative who would take on the Pentagon and stand up to a president of his own party. It had dawned on the big-time reporters that his agenda mirrored theirs; he was a maverick, and the media loves mavericks.

Throughout the mid- and late '80s and into the '90s, he was not criticized much and was typically accorded elder statesman status from the generally civil Iowa reporting corps. Grassley acknowledged that bad press "doesn't happen too much. I suppose part of it is I've been around politics long enough to get people to understand the true Chuck Grassley. Or else, I outlived them."

Accessibility was another characteristic for the Grassley press operation. Big, medium, or small. Print, radio, or television. It made no difference to Grassley's crew. Finch said the operation's formula for success was that "the media are treated no differently than our constituents."

"If a particular reporter or editor had a request, it's answered promptly, factually, and with concern to ensuring that the information provided is what that individual needs," Finch said. "In Grassley's history, he's been shown to do as well with Democrats as Republicans. Why? Because he doesn't ask their ideological bent when they have a particular problem to deal with, he just deals with the problem. Neither does he question the individual reporter or editor's ideological bent as much as he meets the request.

"It harkens back to the old saw: you can catch more flies with honey than vinegar. So, over time, you develop relationships. If you have a relationship with a senator, you have a harder time voting against or arguing with him. It's not to say you won't have a different opinion, but you will act upon it differently. It's an extraordinary lesson in communication skills. As a politician, Grassley is a master, and few on Capitol Hill practice it as well."

Finch, who left Grassley in 1989 to serve as press secretary for Tom Tauke's failed challenge of Sen. Tom Harkin, saw a second, active agent. "The magic of Chuck Grassley is that nothing changes over time. He is what he says, and he does what he says he does." Those simple, but difficult-to-meet standards are the difference between a Charles Grassley and, say, Sen. Bob Packwood, whose voting record in support of women's rights in general was found to be in sharp contrast to his personal conduct toward individual women.

"Grassley's operation is not unique as a strategy, everybody tries to do it. What's unique is the man," Finch said. "Communication skills are simply that—skills. It's what you're communicating that counts. No amount of communications work could have pulled some people out of the depths they plumbed. Grassley, in contrast, is a gold mine in terms of raw materials and skills."

By the time the 1986 campaign cycle rolled around, Grassley was not only the beneficiary of largely favorable press, but he caught another break. The challenge from Des Moines attorney John Roehrick attracted relatively little media attention because reporters and editors had already declared a Grassley victory and turned their focus to the gubernatorial and Third Congressional District contests.

Grassley was also proving surprisingly adept at conquering that modern-day phenomenon known as the sound bite, that fleeting amount of time television and radio newscasts give a person to state their strongest points. "When you're down to, what do they say now, 10 to 15 seconds," Roehrick said later, "you can't do much."

Grassley, with a tendency to ponder, pause, and shift direction of thought, would seem to be at a distinct disadvantage. He personified the argument that Abe Lincoln would not have been handsome enough or smooth enough to be elected in a modern campaign. But, in fact, Grassley had mastered a sort of common sense, bite-size philosophy that could be backed up with numbers and logic. In a very true sense, his "don't spend what you don't have" mantra is a perfect example.

Roehrick observed, "He's a great sound bite guy. 'We've got to bring our POWs/MIAs home, and we shouldn't negotiate with Vietnam until we do.' That's a 10-second sound bite, OK? 'Child pornography is wrong. The Clinton Administration is doing nothing about it. I'm going to fight it.' There's another sound bite there."

Democratic complaints of a roll-over-and-play-dead media arose almost three decades into Grassley's career. Eric Tabor, a Baldwin farmer-lawyer who ran for the Second Congressional District seat in 1986, 1988, and 1990 before becoming the Iowa Democratic Party chairman in 1993, contended that Grassley was held to a different, kinder standard for several reasons. When a young Tabor campaign worker falsely registered his family as voters living at his residence, Republicans pounced on the opportunity just days before the 1990 election. They also rolled out their biggest gun—Grassley. He called for an investigation into statewide voter fraud, which pushed the story to the top of newscasts and the front pages of newspapers on the crucial final Sunday. After Tabor narrowly lost the race he had been expected to win, talk of a full-scale voter-fraud probe cooled.

Tabor submitted that episode as Exhibit A in making his case that Grassley was not above manipulating the media to get what he wanted. "He runs, from every sign I have seen, an extremely aggressive kind of press operation where he makes himself available to reporters very easily. And when you make yourself accessible, reporters like that, and I think they tend to treat you better. The other thing is that he has had extreme electoral success, and I think the press, both reporters and editorial boards say, 'Well, this guy has strong support in the state of Iowa, and he ought to be treated with a little more respect than someone who is kind of on the edge.'"

Tabor conceded that "part of that has been the failure of our Democratic candidates and the party to mount aggressive challenges to him. In '86 it was weak and in 1992 it was even weaker—weak candidates, not enough money, not enough organization to really get to the true Chuck Grassley. And that's the thing that upsets me most about Grassley and the press is how the press, I think, fails to adequately characterize the Senator as a very, very conservative senator.

"In no sense of the word can he be called a moderate, and I think he is much more conservative than most editorial boards, most reporters, and most Iowans. And when he does things that indicate that extreme conservatism, I don't think those are reported or they are not put in context. I think that you compare Chuck Grassley today to the fellow he beat, John Culver. Culver was bright. He was a towering figure but took a lot more abuse in the press for what was viewed as liberal leanings . . . far more than Chuck Grassley's conservatism.

"There is not an even hand. Part of it is Grassley is kind of likeable, kind of just down home. He's an easy guy to get along with, intellectually not threatening, certainly unlike a John Culver, who could wrap most reporters around his little finger in an intellectual argument. Chuck Grassley won't do that, and reporters don't have to fear that about him. It leads to some actions on Grassley's part that are extremely cynical, and the one I faced in my own political life, really, was the ultimate in the willingness of the press to bite on what Chuck Grassley had to say, without analysis."

Ironically, Grassley agreed with Tabor that he had not been the subject of enough in-depth reporting. Of course, Grassley believed he would stand the test well. "People don't get the full measure. Like the person who said to me, 'How come you don't ever fight this wasteful spending?' The only thing I can write back is 'just because you don't read it in the newspaper doesn't mean I'm not doing it. I don't control the press. I can issue press releases and give speeches, but it's not my fault if it's not there. If you don't like what the press is doing, write them, not me.'"

Yepsen dismissed the arguments of special media treatment for Grassley, calling the charge "a typically partisan shot."

"The Democrats have not been able to lay a glove on Chuck Grassley, and they're looking around for a scapegoat. Whenever you don't like a politician, it's always easy to blame the media for the fact you can't beat them. Republicans say the same thing about Tom Harkin, and I just don't think it's true.

"The fact of the matter is Democrats can't run lawyers from Des Moines, they can't run liberals from Iowa City and beat this guy. That's number one. And number two, Chuck Grassley is a very good campaigner. He goes to every county every year. He just does a good job of electioneering, and I think that comes from the way he grew up, running every two years [for 22 years]," Yepsen said. "I'm sorry, the Democrats just can't run candidates flawed from the get-go. Jean Lloyd-Jones went on 'Iowa Press' and said she didn't have a farm program. I don't think you can run for the United States Senate in Iowa and say you haven't developed a farm program yet. They're looking for scapegoats and they ought to look in the mirror."

Ken Sullivan suggested that if Grassley did get different, though not necessarily special treatment, he had earned it by operating on a higher plane. In April 1981, Sullivan had picked up the rumor that Grassley was going to hire Wythe Willey away from Governor Ray's staff. "It was not common knowledge, but [*Waterloo Courier* reporter] Bob Case and I nailed Chuck after a House Republican caucus and said, 'This is what we hear.' Chuck said, 'I can't lie to you. I didn't want to announce it now, but I can't lie.' That was kind of refreshing candor."

Sullivan admitted to finding "relatively little reason to criticize" the Senator. "Grassley has an almost instinctive ability to identify and become identified with the kind of subjects and issues that people around here can appreciate. You don't see him taking a lot of very hard positions on the real controversial and tough issues. The things he becomes very vocal on, who can argue with? Defense reform. This Vietnam POW/MIA thing. He's on the side of the angels on most of these issues. Nothing stands out in my mind on where he's really taken a hard stand on a controversial issue. He just manages to, and I assume it's by design, avoid it. If you don't get yourself cornered like that, you don't expose yourself to a lot of criticism by the media."

While Sullivan considered Grassley fairly easy to get to know, he did not always find the Senator easy to cover. "He's not always the most cogent in his delivery. He sometimes meanders, and I'm still not convinced when he butchers a metaphor that he's not doing it on purpose. But from all appearances, what you see is what you get. He says he's a farmer, and he knows all the right words. He says he's a small-town guy, and you go into a cafe or one of those places and it's 'Hi, Chuck.' If there are warts, he does a superlative job of hiding them."

He mused, "God, in how many other states would the media have the hometown phone number of their senior U.S. senator?"

John Maxwell saw yet another angle to explain the rarity of media potshots. "Perhaps he gives fewer opportunities for that. Because I'll tell you, his rise in popularity happened, and he went into the Senate without getting any breaks from the *Register*. They were antagonistic. For years they insisted on running his old picture of him in the Legislature with his polyester suit, and he had this kind of funny look on his face. Even the '86 endorsement was strained, but they've probably throttled back on him," Maxwell said in June 1994. "But basically he got to the Senate and got to be the most popular politician in the history of the state, fighting them. So if you're inferring he's as popular as he is because he's getting a free ride, that's demonstrably disprovable. I'm suggesting you don't have good reason to be going after him."

What of the charge that Grassley has the same voting record as arch-conservative Jesse Helms of North Carolina, and the media ignores it? Maxwell retorted, "He's got the same voting record as Bob Dole, too."

And the argument that Grassley never takes on the tough issues? Maxwell replied, "He's taken on the Justice Department and the Clinton Administration on kiddie porn. He's taken on the Pentagon on POW/MIAs, calling those generals liars. [Senator] Bob Kerrey [of Nebraska] said, 'I didn't see Grassley going after George Bush on ethanol.' Well, baloney! Yes he did go after Bush on it, very vociferously, as he did with Reagan. He's been gutsy."

Conroy felt the *Des Moines Register* and, in particular, editor Michael Gartner were out to get Grassley in the '70s and early '80s. Grassley avoided any bitterness, though Conroy could not.

"The most disappointing thing I saw in the newspaper business was when Chuck was running for his second term [in 1976] and the *Register* went through these motions. They invite you up for a lunch up in the hallowed editorial room, and they have liveried waitresses waiting on you. I'll never forget, they were serving tomato surprise," Conroy said. "It's a big skinned tomato and has tuna fish and all these kinds of things, and they're all sitting around, Gartner, and [publisher] David Kruidenier and all these guys, and of course Gartner's leading the charge. They didn't even have the decency of letting him finish his meal when he was done [being interviewed]. But this is typical Chuck; after all the grilling, the cheap-shot stuff and everything, we got out and the first thing he said was, 'What was that we had for lunch?' That's so typical. See, he wasn't mad."

Eight years later, the *Des Moines Register* endorsed Grassley for the first time. Yepsen, who knows all too well how so many Republicans view the newspaper for its liberal editorial philosophy, subjected the Senator to some good-natured ribbing at their next meeting. "I said, 'I hope it doesn't hurt you too much,'" Yepsen recounted. "He said, 'It feels pretty good,' and I said, 'How good?' He said, 'I guess I know now how it feels to get into the country club.'"

# The Global Grassley

A U.S. military helicopter swooped down from the salty, humid air over the Mediterranean Sea and landed in front of the U.S. Embassy in war-shattered Beirut on Thanksgiving Day, 1983. Charles Grassley, dressed in a flak-jacket and helmet, clambered out of the aircraft and into an armored personnel carrier.

Five weeks earlier, at 6:22 a.m. on October 23, a Mercedes truck filled with six tons of high explosives plowed past two unarmed sentry posts, and rammed into the four-story Lebanese Aviation and Safety Building that had become a temporary barracks for U.S. peace-keeping forces.[1] The explosion killed 239 men, a greater death toll than all but one day in the entire Vietnam War.[2]

Just five days before the attack, President Reagan had met with his foreign policy and national security advisers about finding an end to Lebanon's civil war and withdrawing U.S. troops. After the blast, Reagan said that the United States had "vital interests in Lebanon . . . in the interest of world peace." The presence of such forces, he said, was "central to our credibility on a global scale. We must not allow international terrorists and thugs such as these to undermine the peace in Lebanon."

Grassley, detouring from his second trip to Israel in just over two years, chose to size up the local situation for himself. As his body armor suggested, the region's deadly volatility had not diminished. The experience was an eye-opener for the Iowan with no military record, little foreign travel, and certainly no life-threatening ventures into a killing field like Beirut.

Checking on the safety of U.S. troops, he sensed that the redoubling of American resolve had done nothing to further peace in this dangerous place so far from the safety and serenity of home. "We drove around the city and, my gosh, they had all this thick steel inside the truck, and afterward I started thinking how stupid it was to be out there. I still remember all these darned shell-pocked buildings and there'd be somebody restuccoing the side of his building, and it didn't make sense. And people [were] going right about their own business, just like nothing was happening."

He departed after sharing Thanksgiving dinner with the troops in a sandbagged bunker. A week after the visit, eight

Marines were killed when their observation post near the airport took a direct hit from Syrian-backed militia.[3]

Grassley concluded that the Reagan Administration had made "a doggone big mistake by not letting the Israelis have a free hand in there. We stopped them, you know, several weeks before. We should have let them go."

For all the cultivated perceptions that Grassley's feet were always planted firmly on Iowa soil, he would develop an impressive record of world travel and knowledge of international events. The catalyst for much of that jet-set travel—the likes for which he had sharply criticized John Culver in the 1980 campaign—was a concern for Soviet Jews persecuted for their religious beliefs yet barred from emigrating to another country. It was first instilled in him by voices in Des Moines' Jewish community while Grassley was still in the House. He nurtured it through the Senate Judiciary Committee, where contacts with immigration law became the vehicle to carry him into the realm of international human rights.

Ally Milder, one of his subcommittee lawyers active in Soviet Jewry issues during her college years, also encouraged Grassley, but not much coaxing was necessary. "I think he has always had an interest in religious freedom and had gotten involved in some of these issues when he was a House member," she recalled.

During a 1983 visit to the Soviet Union, Grassley proved himself, Milder said, as the "quintessential caring conservative who was able to communicate the ideals of freedom to government officials and would not be put off by the pat answers of various Soviet officials. He gave them a sense of 'we care about trade in Iowa, and that's very important to us, but we also care about other issues in Iowa and they're also very important to us.' It was very important that a man from a grain state sent that message. He wasn't saying, 'We're going to cut off all trade if we don't get all the people out,' but I don't know how many people from grain states went to the Soviet Union and said, 'Human rights are important to us.'"

The trip was, recalled Tom Synhorst, a "wild experience."

Milder and Synhorst, a Kansas City businessman who was Grassley's scheduler at the time, were detained at the huge, virtually empty Sheremetevo 2 Airport for hours. Synhorst recalled, "We had really stuffed his suitcases with a lot of black market stuff because we didn't think they'd check his bags, which was pretty stupid. They didn't check him or Barbara. They did check Ally and me, and everybody else went on. We had to stay at this huge airport in the middle of the night. They strip-searched Ally. We'd wait for an hour or more on end. It was like being in the middle of LaGuardia with not any other person around. Then five or six guys would come surround us, take Ally away and then bring her back. It was really a frightening experience."

The forbidden items Grassley carried included Bibles, blue jeans and sunglasses, and cigarettes for bartering with cabbies. Synhorst and Milder spent their days lining up night-time meetings with dissidents. "We'd get on one bus, get off it, get on another, make a fake call on one phone, get in a cab and go to another phone to call these people. We were in one cab, and the guy was drunk," Synhorst said. "The streets were really snow-packed and this bus was coming right at us from our left. We yelled at the guy, but the bus hit us and ran us into a light pole. We were wedged in [on one side] so we got out on the other side and ran off. We didn't want to be in the car when the police got there because we figured they'd take our list of names, so we hid in the alley for an hour before we thought it was safe again."

At night, the Americans left their hotel rooms and took separate cars to a rendezvous point. Then they moved on to the apartment of one of the dissidents. "The one night," Synhorst said, "we had this meeting until like midnight or one in the morning, and [the host] said he'd get us somebody to give us a ride back to the hotel by flagging somebody down as they drove by. Certainly the KGB knew we were there. Somebody had knocked on the door twice during the meeting, but no one was there when we answered. So, we were concerned about not getting in a car with somebody from the KGB. The host said it was better just to flag down a car because it was less likely to be KGB, and because the driver could make more than a whole year's salary for the ride." Grassley's contingent did not fear for themselves, but knew there would be KGB reprisals for some of the dissidents if they were caught meeting with the Senator.

Once, Grassley and Synhorst were squeezed into the back seat of a car, with the Senator rambling on about the type of transmission he thought was in the vehicle, judging by its rudimentary shift and other traits. "The driver was as quiet as he could be, and then finally Grassley, just talking in general, says, 'I wonder if it's gas or diesel.' The driver says, 'It's gas,' and in perfect

English starts talking about whatever kind of stick shift and transmission it was and how he read *Popular Mechanics* and how this car was 'just a piece of junk compared to your cars in America.' He knew everything. It was hilarious."

Grassley told his story in a September 1983 article for the *Saturday Evening Post*, noting that his "official" visit was to meet with Soviet agricultural officials. "However, at night I would see the country from a different perspective. I had come to visit Russian Jews who wished to emigrate but have been denied permission, the so-called 'refuseniks.'"

Grassley literally sneaked around in the shadows to meet first with dissidents in Moscow, where he heard "stories of persecution and intrigue that could fill an American spy novel," then in Leningrad. Writing of the second visit, he noted, "As we exited the cab we waved a cheerful good-bye to the unmarked car that had been following us, undoubtedly our KGB shadow, and entered the home of Aba Taratuta, our host 'refusenik'. In the modest two-room apartment we were joined by 15 other Jews. The word of our visit must have been passed by personal messenger because the government had disconnected the phones of most of the 'refuseniks'. . . . I left Aba's apartment that night with a better understanding of the problems of the Soviet Jews as well as a greater appreciation for life in the United States."[4]

Grassley returned home sounding every bit the Cold Warrior he was perceived by many to be, concluding that "naive Western appeals for 'compassion' and 'human rights' do not remove the hardened occupants of the Kremlin. Saber-rattling may not change Soviet policy, but reasonable bargaining will. If we as Americans recoil from solidarity with millions of the oppressed around the world, we must confront the truth that we share the blame for their suffering and that our waning wills may ultimately assure our own undoing."[5]

The Senator demonstrated his willpower in dealing with the equally stubborn Soviets by needling them with a proposal to change the address of the Soviet embassy in Washington to One Sakharov Plaza. State Department officials had tried to block the new address for the Soviet embassy, arguing that it unnecessarily rocked the diplomatic boat, but Grassley prevailed with the unanimous support of colleagues. The new address would serve as a daily reminder to its occupants that some American officials were not willing to overlook the plight of dissidents such as scientist

Andrei Sakharov, exiled to Gorky in 1980 for criticizing the invasion of Afghanistan. Milder said, "Grassley viewed this country as being founded on the basis of freedom of religion and to see people denied that basic right affected him a great deal. He also saw the parallel between political freedom and economic freedom and how linked they are. Without one, you don't have the other."

Grassley also concluded it would not be enough for the United States alone to champion the cause of Soviet human rights. He decided to create a worldwide coalition of parliamentarians devoted to the cause. "So we got some foundation money to do that, and we had our first meeting over in Paris," he said. "About 700 officials from 14 countries participated." He also traveled to Switzerland, Austria, Germany, Nigeria, Sierra Leone, Somalia, and Kenya to encourage the coalition's growth.

His commitment showed in other ways. Enraged by a PLO attack on the cruise ship *Achille Lauro* in which American Leon Klinghoffer was killed, Grassley won passage of legislation to combat terrorism. He also cosponsored a resolution to indict PLO leader Yasser Arafat for the 1973 slaying of American Ambassador Cleo Noel and Chargé d'Affaires G. Curtis Moore in Khartoum, Sudan.

And, motivated by his frustration with Republican Presidents Ronald Reagan and George Bush, he spoke out on the Senate floor against international terrorism. "It was probably as much related to the fact our government wasn't always pushing it, that our government was sending [mixed] signals; they were doing certain things and then not doing them, and sometimes maybe even doing some things that seemed like they were aiding and abetting the whole deal," Grassley recalled.

Through his efforts, which earned him a National Recognition Award from the Union of Councils for Soviet Jewry, Grassley demonstrated a willingness to go far beyond simple constituent service. His involvement was driven by his powerful sense of right and wrong.

"It had to do with the proposition we had signed, the Helsinki Accords; Russia had signed them and it was to guarantee family reunification, freedom of religion, freedom of communication, and freedom to emigrate, to go in and out of the country," he explained. "Russia signed the doggone agreement . . . I saw it as a way of making sure, too, that the Russians lived up to their law. The moral authority was on our side. We weren't trying to get the Jewish people any more than just what the Helsinki Accords gave them."

But Grassley's involvement in the international arena and government's duty to live up to its word also took him back to the steps of the Pentagon on the other side of the Potomac River from his office. His efforts to reform the weapons procurement process had opened a tangled network of underground military sources disgruntled with the official handling of the issue of American POWs and MIAs in Vietnam.

"We heard one of our sources telling us to look at the conclusion the [Department of Defense] was making that they were doing everything possible to turn over every stone and there was no evidence of live people or people left behind," Kolesnik said. "That was our point of departure."

Grassley served on a Senate Select Committee on POWs/MIAs and traveled to Vietnam in April 1992. But he found America's former leaders and top military brass, not to mention the stonewalling Vietnamese regime, to be more formidable adversaries than the Soviets. He had his suspicions, based on some military sources, that the Nixon Administration left behind live Americans in Southeast Asia when Secretary of State Henry Kissinger signed a 1972 peace accord with North Vietnam, but he could not uncover any concrete evidence.

Throughout his Senate tenure, it can be said that Grassley's global vision broadened and evolved. His view that U.S. officials should have given Israel the nod in 1983 to impose its will through military might over terrorists operating from bases in Lebanon, a sovereign country, would, in some ways, contrast with the perception he was just another right-wing isolationist. But it also accurately reflected his recognition that international issues were not as black-and-white as his sense of values.

He acknowledged years later that "each country and each circumstance is a little bit different." But, he added, "basically, you've got to have a broad framework of foreign policy that applies throughout the world. There's got to be some flexibility in that framework, but everything you do ought to be in that framework. My framework is that the United States, even more so today than in the Cold War because we're the only superpower, has to be in the forefront, at least diplomatically and politically and economically, in the processes of international relations.

That's a very general statement, but you've got to be engaged. Maybe not in every country, but almost in every region to some extent. Maybe to a lesser extent in Africa, but very surely in Europe, Eastern Europe, Russia, China, and Southeast Asia, and even in the Western Hemisphere, we have to be engaged.

"You want to make sure you've got enough military to carry out any mission you have to have, but you hope just the projection of [armed forces] or the ability to do that gives what you're going to do politically, diplomatically, and economically some clout, some meaning."

But, as he showed with his Persian Gulf war vote, Grassley did not always advocate military force. He voted against keeping U.S. troops in Somalia in October 1992 as part of a UN peace-keeping mission. Grassley was one of 23 senators supporting a proposal to, in the words of press secretary Jill Hegstrom, "get out now or as soon as possible" in the wake of attacks that killed and wounded American soldiers. Meanwhile, Senator Harkin, considered Iowa's leading liberal, sided with 75 colleagues to authorize President Bill Clinton's plan to maintain a military presence in the war-torn African nation through March 31, 1994. Noting that two Iowans had already been lost in the fighting, Grassley said on the Senate floor, "The President's greatest mistake was turning over policy and command to the United Nations. The Congress' greatest mistake was letting President Clinton get away with it."[6]

Grassley showed some hurt in July 1994 when reminded of a 1980 campaign appearance where Culver excoriated him for bragging that he had never given a penny of foreign assistance in his six years in Congress. "Some 600 million people are starving tonight," Culver said. "Ninety million have starved to death in those six years of Grassley's. I believe this country has a moral obligation to help those people."[7]

Grassley conceded, in retrospect, that his explanation "might not be as intellectually honest as I want it to be or appear, but in the House, I felt I was in the shadow of H. R. Gross, and one thing people expected of him and his successor was to be cautious with every dollar. Maybe I was parochial, too. Or both. I have not been [parochial] in the Senate because I have supported foreign aid. I don't mean to imply that's a legitimate reason, but I have a bigger constituency. Iowa City, Des Moines, and Cedar Rapids are very trade-oriented. The universities are very sophisticated from a policy standpoint. You don't have just a sliver of northeast Iowa that's rural. I suppose I heard from constituents a different point of view."

He noted that "there isn't a poll that you'd see today that wouldn't show foreign aid is the most unpopular of all issues. I probably have not been a proponent of foreign aid, but I do support a minimum amount of foreign aid, and for sure I feel a need to help out where we can on a humanitarian basis."

That's part of the metamorphosis of Chuck Grassley—from the shadow of H. R. Gross to statewide officeholder, and a body, the United States Senate, that tends to be more involved in international relations than the House. "I hadn't even traveled overseas until I finished my service in the House. I think traveling overseas is a way of understanding, which can be difficult to do from Iowa, that the world is a very small place," Grassley said.

# 'It Ain't Over'

Charles Grassley, like virtually every other Republican in the nation, was euphoric about the GOP's rise to power on November 8, 1994, which abruptly ended 40 years of Democratic control in the House of Representatives and eight years in the Senate. But power has its pitfalls. With majority status came new legislative responsibilities, and new political burdens for the Republicans. No longer could they rail about the dire need to balance the budget; now, the power was in their hands. The question was whether they would use it or cave in to special interests and the fear that voters would turn on them if the cuts hit too close to home.

For Grassley, the election created a personal moment of truth. Did he really have the talent and stature to accomplish any of the initiatives he had advocated for so many years, or would he prove to be an earnest but largely ineffectual member of the new majority? Would he make the necessary tough choices—such as slowing Medicare spending, reducing and eliminating agricultural programs, and even means-testing Social Security—to put us on the road to annual balanced budgets, or opt for the politically expedient "not in my backyard" attitude when cutting appropriations?

An early answer to questions about his ability to move legislation came just days into the 104th Congress, when President Clinton signed into law Grassley's Congressional Accountability Act, which the Iowan cosponsored with Senator Joseph Lieberman, a Connecticut democrat. "It says Congress will be covered by the laws that Congress has exempted itself from. It was the first bill passed by the new Congress. It was the first bill passed by a Republican Congress in 40 years, and it delivers on a promise I made to the people, and a promise the Republicans made to the people," Grassley said.

The quick, joyous triumph was tempered by other events. Grassley had little reason to be particularly excited about how the watershed change brought by the election would alter his clout on committees. Years of waiting had lifted him well up the seniority ladder, but real, recognized power remained outside his grasp as long as the Senate still included mossbacks like 92-year-old Strom Thurmond of South Carolina.

Just six months earlier, friends and aides, either overly optimistic or insufficiently versed in the intricacies of the committee assignment process, gleefully boasted about the possibility of Grassley becoming the first non-lawyer in 70 years to serve as chairman of the Senate Judiciary Committee. The assignment went instead to Orrin Hatch, a lawyer with more seniority than Grassley.

Blocked from ascension at every turn on the Budget and Finance committees, Grassley and his staff put the best face on things, emphasizing that the absence of the demanding additional responsibilities of committee chairmanship gave him the luxury of continuing to act as a free agent who could pursue whatever issue most demanded attention at a given moment. And even as the Senate awaited an Ethics Committee recommendation in mid-1995 that eventually resulted in Finance Committee Chairman Bob Packwood's resignation on charges of sexual harassment and other breaches of conduct, Grassley conceded that Packwood's departure would "only move me one slot closer to chairman of Finance."

"Either [John] Chaffee [of Rhode Island] and [William] Roth [of Delaware] would take that, so it doesn't help me much, Grassley said. "I'm in a situation where if I'd chosen, 15 years ago, committees that are not so powerful or well-liked, like Labor or Government Affairs or maybe Natural Resources, I could be chairman today. When I got on Finance, I was at the bottom of seniority. I was on [the committee] for six years, and went off when we lost control [he returned to the committee in 1991]. The chances of me being chairman of that committee are pretty nil. Same with Judiciary. I sacrificed the chairmanship of other committees so I could be on Finance and Judiciary." In the same breath, he insisted he does not regret the decision. "Not when 70 percent of the budget comes out of there," Grassley said. "Is it better being there or being chair of some committee that two percent [of the spending] comes out of? I think I can serve my people better by being on that committee than by being somewhere else."

Nevertheless, John Maxwell suggests the greatest challenge facing Grassley in the second half of his third Senate term is in finding his most effective place in the shifting political tides. "His career has really been defined by kind of going against the grain for what he thought was right," Maxwell said. "Standing up to Reagan . . . is what solidified the opinion of him for most Iowans.

His independence, and showing people he was willing to stand up to a president of his own party on behalf of constituents. Now he's got a Democratic president, and if he stands up to Bill Clinton, he's doing what's expected. And there's nothing on Clinton's agenda that he's going to applaud, so that can't be, either."

However Grassley attempts to find his political course in the next few years, he will rely heavily on his true, moral compass, which has directed him time and again to the right place at the right moment in his political history. Most assuredly, he will not care one whit about those people inside the Beltway and outside the Senate circle who know little of him or his background, and have recently begun to re-form the caricature of him as a slow-witted, knee-jerk conservative. He will, after hours of contemplation, decide where he wants to go, and how he wants to get there. And he will reveal his intentions on *his* terms, and no one else's. That may not be as easy for Grassley as it has been in the past.

In the spring of 1995, just about six months after the Republicans had swept the Democrats out of power on Capitol Hill in the stunning 1994 general election, Senator Larry Pressler of South Dakota felt compelled to speak out about balancing annual federal budgets, and the unpleasant side effects. Pressler spoke in the Senate chambers, but his words were directed at his constituents more than 1300 miles away.

In the weeks and months ahead, he warned, he would be required to make some difficult choices—a euphemism for unpopular votes that would probably include cutting agricultural programs, slowing the rate of Medicare's growth, and affecting other programs that middle-class, voting South Dakotans liked so much but, like everyone else across the country, didn't necessarily want to pay for. Pressler knew, though he probably would not want to admit publicly, that his constituents, like other senators' constituents, believe other people's programs are "pork," and programs that benefit them are not only a necessity but a right.

Grassley, who had waited two decades for his party to win control of the legislative levers of government, has not yet shared Pressler's need to explain himself. First off, he was not up for election in 1996, as was Pressler. Secondly, the absence of any *mea culpa*, preemptive or otherwise, may stem from his conviction that Iowans will understand and accept painful cuts as necessary. They will bite the bullet, he surmises, so long as the spending reductions are shared and shared alike. Given Grassley's deep-rooted zeal for fiscal responsibility, he may also have decided, though it is less likely, that the need to balance the budget is so pressing that political consequences be damned.

Regarding farm programs, however, Grassley the budget cutter sounded decidedly unstatesmanlike and parochial at the outset. He opposed the call from Senate Agriculture Committee Chairman Richard Lugar, an Indiana Republican, to dismantle the farm subsidy program with the argument that agriculture already had been forced to suffer disproportionately in recent years. He was not, however, for completely cocooning the U.S. Department of Agriculture's appropriations. "As much as I'd like to have a situation where Agriculture does not contribute a dollar, it has to contribute, too," said Grassley. His intellectual integrity remained intact.

Whatever his mind-set as budget talks and the prospect of "difficult choices" unfolded, Grassley certainly recognized that after years of harping about the Democrats' lack of desire or ability to balance federal spending with revenues, it was put up or shut up time for the Republicans. As far as the overall budget was concerned, Grassley was positive that he and his colleagues were up to the task, if for no other reason than that they had promised to cut government and delivering on that promise could well cement a Republican majority for another 10 to 12 years. "Not only will I be able to do it, I'll have to do it," he declared.

The remark demonstrated that difficult choices were not so difficult at all for Grassley, whose strong convictions prompt him to see many issues in black-and-white. "In most cases," he explained, "we don't have to cut anything. We have to restrain our current 5.5 percent to 3 percent across the board. Not every area of the budget can or will be [restrained to that level]—some will be cut, some will be eliminated—but the overall budget can be." In Washington, and in the hearts of many special interest groups, the black-and-white, 3 percent increase that Grassley spoke of amounted to a 2.5 percent cut, and an all-out assault on their causes. And every vote that Grassley recorded to "restrain" spending during the spring and summer of 1995 was certainly being tallied by Democrats and liberal organizations for future use against him.

That chance will come in 1998, when a Grassley bid for a fourth Senate term remains a very viable possibility. His success depends in part on the Republicans' ability to maintain a comfortable margin of control after the 1996 election. "About the only thing I can tell you about 1998 is the Republican majority has energized me in terms of not thinking about retirement. Could I say that's absolutely out the window? No, it's not. But had I been in the minority, I might have been more lackadaisical. Being in the majority, the results of the 1994 election signal to me that the tough work of being a senator will be enjoyable and allow me to do it for a longer time, or at least allow me to stay in politics a longer time." He added with only the slightest hint of humor, "Don't forget Strom Thurmond is getting ready to run for reelection."

But even then, Grassley could grow weary of the Senate grind and the reality that he will probably never chair a major committee. His political career could very well turn full circle to the time he spent in Iowa City in 1957, rooming in the basement of 707 River Street as he prepared to write his dissertation, "Reorganization of the Administrative Branch of State Government in Iowa." In the past, Grassley has expressed some interest in working out an arrangement to teach government and political science at the University of Iowa. But it is much more likely that his full circle would instead take him to the Statehouse, where he can apply his theories on the subject of that proposed dissertation.

Though he insists that his enthusiastic support of Terry Branstad in the Governor's 1994 primary challenge against Congressman Fred Grandy was simply an act of assistance for an old friend and the repayment of a debt from his own 1980 Senate campaign, Grassley had a personal tactical reason for wanting Branstad to succeed. Just as he had helped rid himself of a formidable opponent by ensuring that Congressman Cooper Evans defeated Lynn Cutler in 1982, Grassley's high-profile support of Branstad helped remove any impediments to his own run for the governorship in 1998, if he desires. The reasons are clear: If Grandy had beaten Branstad, and defeated the Democratic nominee, Attorney General Bonnie Campbell, Grassley would have little justification—aside from raw political ambition—to challenge Grandy in 1998. On the other hand, a Campbell victory over Branstad would have given Grassley the perfect political cover—the argument that only he could defeat Campbell. And, although Branstad has maintained he will not seek a fifth term, should the Governor renege on that promise, Grassley could argue that his old friend has served too long, and that he, Grassley, is the only politician guaranteed to bring a fresh start to Iowa state government.

Grassley neither confirms nor denies that he's got his eye on the governorship. "I have never said no to any possibility about the future," he has said. "It's a long time before I make the decision to run for the Senate or another public office. I intend to be very politically active [through 1997] so I am well-positioned, so I am not digging myself out of any hole." Clearly, Grassley, like any three-term United States Senator, has a variety of options in 1998, the year his current term expires and he turns 65. Grassley could seek reelection, run for governor, return to his Butler County farm, or retire.

He has nothing left to prove, this farm boy from New Hartford who engineered a remarkable string of political victories. He set new levels of voter approval in his 1978 House race and 1986 Senate contest, then raised the standards again in 1992. He received the highest total percentage ever in a contested U.S. Senate race in Iowa and was victorious in all 99 counties. He also received more votes (899,761) than any candidate in Iowa history, eclipsing the previous record (808,906) set 40 years earlier by Dwight D. Eisenhower's presidential campaign. He earned a performance rating of 81 percent approving (with just 9 percent disapproving), according to the *Des Moines Register* January 1993 Iowa Poll. He also insulated the rest of the Republican ticket from the collapse at the national level in 1992, playing varied but crucial roles in the victories of Reps. Jim Nussle and Jim Ross Lightfoot, and in the party's restoration to power in the Iowa House of Representatives after a 10-year hiatus.

On Capitol Hill, colleagues praised him for setting other standards. David Pryor, the Arkansas Democrat, said that Grassley's record for decency and integrity had become the benchmark in the Senate, where members treasure those values even more than philosophy, party loyalty, and wisdom. John Maxwell said those same qualities were what endeared Grassley to voters back home, too, even those who did not share his conservative viewpoint. "In a time of diminishing faith in public institutions and public service, he's really given people reason to believe there are some good people in the system, that it's not all bad, it's not all corrupt. I suspect that if he could chose a legacy, it might be that—to show that public service is honorable and being a politician ought to be honorable." Grassley did perform with the highest courage and honor in singlehandedly setting in motion the beginning of the end of the Reagan era military build-up, and by later voting against the Persian Gulf Resolution George Bush had so strenuously sought.

He would not be without his detractors; no one is. John Roehrick still insisted years after his 1986 defeat that Iowans "deserve someone better than Chuck Grassley." It was not a criticism uttered in anger or bitterness. "You get what you vote for," Roehrick shrugged. "He's surely not a Strom Thurmond or Jesse Helms, he's not bad for the state, but I don't think he's been as effective as he could. He hasn't done anything to really hurt us; he hasn't done anything to really help us." Roehrick contends Grassley has placed personal popularity above results on difficult and divisive issues of statewide importance. The Senator could have made a difference, especially during his third term, had he shown more willingness to risk giving up just a little of his record popularity. "That's the difference between a proactive politician and a nonproactive politician."

Regardless of such criticism, Grassley is in control of his political future. "He blows hot and cold on the governor thing. He was definitely hot on it [in 1990]," said one friend, who easily visualizes Grassley teaching at the University of Iowa. "If they went to him and said, 'If you decide to retire, we've got a professorship for you, we want you to do graduate seminars in political science and you can complete your work on your doctorate,' that's something I think he'd really like to do." A number of ambitious Republicans with their eyes on the governorship would unabashedly love to see Grassley as a molder of young minds rather than a candidate for the office they covet. "He's the 800-pound gorilla in this race," one observer said. "He can do anything he wants to, and everyone else just has to wait and see what that is."

Barbara Grassley conceded that she opposed her husband running for governor in 1990 because she did not believe he should resign in mid-term to take another political job. She has not expressed objections to another campaign in 1998—either for governor or the Senate. She smiled, "He might decide to throw in the sponge totally and just retire and drive me nuts." Turning serious again, she added, "You hope to Lord he never takes a Cabinet post, but if a Republican president came in and offered, you'd have to look." Such an offer would be particularly difficult to resist if it were tendered by Grassley's old friend Bob Dole.

Pete Conroy, one of those who knows Grassley best, scratches retirement or lobbying from Grassley's list of future options. Recalling his former boss's fishing trip to Minnesota years ago,

Conroy said, "He had to call in [to the office], and I said, 'Chuck, have you been out for walleyes?' He said, 'I did that yesterday.' It was like, 'OK, I got that out of the way.' He was sitting and reading, but he's action-oriented. He isn't peripatetic, but he's got to be involved in getting something done. He just can't stand not being busy."

Conroy leans to the theory that his old friend will eventually return to Iowa politics, even if it means an unconventional return to the Iowa Legislature. "With Chuck, surface things and appearances don't mean much—like going to plays at the Kennedy Center. People get Potomac Fever; he hasn't got it. You know what the Kennedy Center means to Chuck? It means the roof starting leaking three years after they finished it, and he raised all kinds of Cain because they were spending a million dollars to put a new roof on something they just built. Oh, it just drove him up the wall!" Conroy said. "But he definitely would miss the give-and-take and the intrigue and all that kind of stuff involved in the legislative and governing process because that's his life."

Noting that Grassley had a framed print of Terrace Hill, the Iowa governor's residence, in his Washington office, Conroy provides perhaps the clearest hint of what Charles Grassley's future holds. "He always liked to look at that and say, 'I'd sure like to live there.' I wouldn't rule out ever that he wants to be governor some day. If I were writing the last line on the thing, I'd say, 'It ain't over yet,' and the only office he hasn't held is the governor of the state. He hasn't had enough, and he isn't going to have enough, because he's born to serve."

# Endnotes

**More than Meets the Eye**
1. Barry Goldwater, letter to author, June 9, 1994.

**W. W. Ballhagen, J. W. Lynes, and the Iowa Legislature**
1. Iowa Official Register, 1957-58.
2. Iowa Official Register, 1959-60.
3. *Cedar Rapids Gazette* editorial, week of May 6, 1962.
4. United Press International story, May 6, 1962.
5. Iowa Official Register, 1963-64.

**"The Inflation Fighter"**
1. "Rapp pulls 3rd District upset; Grassley scores easy victory," *Waterloo Courier*, June 5, 1974.
2. Mark Mittelstadt, "Rapp stays on top in 3rd District rerun," *Waterloo Courier*, July 3, 1974.
3. "3rd District race costs: $360,000," *Waterloo Courier*, Feb. 9, 1975.
4. Larry D. Spears, "GOP keeps hold on 3rd District," *Waterloo Courier*, Nov. 6, 1974.

**Mr. Grassley Goes to Washington**
1. "Rapp quits demo post," *Waterloo Courier*, July 3, 1975.
2. "Rapp to seek office again," *Waterloo Courier*, Feb. 2, 1976.
3. Bob Case, "Mondale plea: participate," *Waterloo Courier*, Sept. 8, 1976.
4. "Grassley gives his raise back to U.S.," *Waterloo Courier*, Sept. 6, 1976.
5. Bob Case, "Grassley: will take pay raise," *Waterloo Courier*, Sept. 12, 1976.
6. Bob Case, "Rapp: I don't plan to lose," *Waterloo Courier*, Oct. 17, 1976.
7. Bob Case, "Grassley accused of misuse of mails," *Waterloo Courier*, Sept. 9, 1976.
8. Bob Case, "Grassley 'changes' noted," *Waterloo Courier*, Oct. 17, 1976.
9. *Ibid.*
10. "Did all we could on pay: Grassley," *Waterloo Courier*, June 30, 1977.
11. "It's good feds bow on change to road metrics," *Waterloo Courier*, June 10, 1977.
12. Charles E. Grassley, "Grassley urges: dignify elderly," *Waterloo Courier*, June 27, 1977.
13. Bob Case, "Grassley's style relaxed, Knudson 'gives 'em hell,'" *Waterloo Courier*, Oct. 29, 1978.

**David Takes on Goliath**
1. Brad Church, "Stoner kicks off Senate campaign in the heart of 'Grassley country,'" *Waterloo Courier*, June 11, 1979.

2. "Stoner steps up attack in Senate primary race," *Waterloo Courier*, April 13, 1980.

3. "Grassley opens campaign office: responds to Stoner criticism," *Waterloo Courier*, April 27, 1983.

4. Bob Case, "Stoner trips on connection," *Waterloo Courier*, May 11, 1980.

5. "Remedies for ag woes given," *Waterloo Courier*, May 21, 1980.

6. Bob Case, "Grassley plans positive campaign in final days," *Waterloo Courier*, May 27, 1980.

7. Bob Case, "Stoner criticizes 'ultraconservatives' groups' involvement in primary race," *Waterloo Courier*, May 28, 1980.

8. Bob Case "Dismissed soldier doing battle with Culver," *Waterloo Courier*, May 29, 1980.

9. Bob Case, "Abortion issue enters primary," *Waterloo Courier*, June 2, 1980.

10. Bob Case, "Culver emphatically defends his record in official announcement," *Waterloo Courier*, Feb. 11, 1980.

11. Bob Case, "Corey disavows attempt to link Culver, Chappaquiddick actions," *Waterloo Courier*, Aug. 19, 1980.

12. Bob Case, "Christian rally hears plan to oust Culver—group sings, prays in Marshalltown," *Waterloo Courier*, Sept. 3, 1980.

13. Bob Case, "Hits election efforts by non-Iowa groups," *Waterloo Courier*, Oct. 1, 1980.

14. "Grassley blames Culver for defense woes," *Waterloo Courier*, Oct. 14, 1980.

15. Meta Gaertnier, "Culver attacked at meeting," *Waterloo Courier*, Oct. 29, 1980.

16. "Culver raps Grassley, 'new right,'" *Waterloo Courier*, June 8, 1980.

17. Bob Case, "Culver draws firm campaign line," *Waterloo Courier*, July 10, 1980.

18. Bob Case, "Culver claims pride in record, Grassley votes draw criticism," *Waterloo Courier*, July 31, 1980.

19. "Culver hits Grassley stand on elderly aid," *Waterloo Courier*, Aug. 17, 1980.

20. "Senate rivals meet, 'come out swinging,'" *Waterloo Courier*, Sept. 7, 1980.

21. Nancy Raffensperger, "'Purse strings' are top issue for Culver, Grassley," *Waterloo Courier*, Sept. 22, 1980.

22. Bob Case, "Culver, Grassley step up attacks on each other," *Waterloo Courier*, Oct. 7, 1980.

23. Bob Case, "Culver says he's addressing issues, claims Grassley isn't," *Waterloo Courier*, Oct. 2, 1980.

24. "Grassley sees 'double standard' in Sen. Culver's voting record," *Waterloo Courier*, Oct. 8, 1980.

25. "Literature against abortion and ERA being distributed," *Waterloo Courier*, Oct. 27, 1980.

26. "Senate contest opponents move into home stretch," *Waterloo Courier*, Nov. 2, 1980.
27. Meta Gaertnier, "Julian Bond touts Democratic hopefuls," *Waterloo Courier*, Nov. 3, 1980.

**Goodbye, Tweedledumber**
1. Bob Case and Andy Montgomery, "Iowa senators in AWACs limelight," *Waterloo Courier*, Oct. 28, 1981.
2. *Ibid.*
3. *Ibid.*
4. *Ibid.*
5. Bob Case, "Jepsen irate at story," *Waterloo Courier*, Oct. 29, 1981.
6. "Profiles in Politics," *The Hawk Eye*, Oct. 30, 1981.
7. "Hultman will testify about alleged perjury," *Waterloo Courier*, Oct. 1, 1981.
8. Andy Montgomery, "Hultman quickly preparing for hearing before panel," *Waterloo Courier*, Oct. 6, 1981.
9. "Abuse of power by Sen. Hatch merits a probe?" *Waterloo Courier*, Oct. 11, 1981.
10. Bob Case, "Hultman overcomes adversity again," *Waterloo Courier*, May 12, 1982.
11. Carl Cannon, "Iowa's Grassley: Folk-Hero Image Considered," *Wichita Eagle-Beacon*, Oct. 20, 1985.
12. "The 'class' of the Senate GOP class of 1980," *Washington Post*, April 13, 1986.
13. John McCormally, "Grassley consistency earns credibility," *Hawk Eye*, June 4, 1983.
14. Helen Dewar, "Proposed one-year spending freeze is rejected decisively by the Senate," *Washington Post*, May 2, 1984.
15. Letter to author, June 9, 1994.

**"All but Impossible to Beat"**
1. "Iowa," *The American Almanac of Politics 1988*, National Journal Inc., 1987: 424.
2. Jeffrey H. Birnbaum and Alan S. Murray, *Showdown at Gucci Gulch*, Random House, 1987.
3. Iowa Poll, *Des Moines Sunday Register*, Feb. 19, 1986.
4. *Israel Today*, April 18, 1986.
5. *Boston Sunday Globe*, April 14, 1985.
6. Eric Woolson, "Roehrick begins campaign," *Waterloo Courier*, Jan. 24, 1986.
7. The Associated Press, "Harkin recruits women to run against Grassley," *Waterloo Courier*, March 5, 1986.
8. Eric Woolson, "Roehrick attacks Grassley's vote on Contras," *Waterloo Courier*, Aug. 24, 1986.

9. Eric Woolson, "Roehrick: Grassley failed to respond to shuttle warning," *Waterloo Courier*, Oct. 23, 1986.
10. Eric Woolson, "Roehrick questions Grassley on interns with Moon group ties," *Waterloo Courier*, Oct. 16, 1986.
11. The Associated Press, "Grassley, challenger spar over arms, farms," *Waterloo Courier*, Sept. 7, 1986.
12. The Associated Press, "Grassley paid out $2.21 million in Senate race; Roehrick $238,134," *Waterloo Courier*, Dec. 11, 1986.
13. Eric Woolson, "Grassley cruises in race that might not have been," *Waterloo Courier*, Nov. 5, 1986.

**Desert Storm and the No Vote**

1. "Iraqi Forces Invade, Occupy Kuwait; World Condemns Move, Oil Fears Stirred," *Facts on File World News Digest*, Aug. 3, 1990: 565.
2. "U.S. Sends Forces to Saudi Arabia; Iraq Annexes Kuwait; U.N. Imposes Sanctions," *Facts on File World News Digest*, Aug. 10, 1990: 581.
3. "U.S. Rejects Signals of Possible Deal With Iraq," *Facts on File World News Digest*, Oct. 26, 1990: 789.
4. "Bush Orders Major Boost in U.S. Persian Gulf Forces," *Facts on File World News Digest*, Nov. 9, 1990: 829.
5. Eric Woolson, "Grassley pools Iowans to lift spirits of troops," *Waterloo Courier*, Nov. 23, 1990.
6. "Come home soon," *Waterloo Courier*, Dec. 2, 1990.
7. "U.S.-Iraq Geneva Talks Fail; U.S. Congress Debates Persian Gulf War," *Facts on File World News Digest*, Jan. 10, 1991: 11.
8. *Ibid.*, 10.
9. Elizabeth Bloom, "Peace trip's loss is still students' gain," *Waterloo Courier*, Jan. 14, 1991.
10. "U.S.-Led Coalition Attacks Iraq After U.N. Deadline for Withdrawal From Kuwait Passes," *Facts on File World News Digest*, Jan. 17, 1991.
11. Letter from former President George Bush to the author, May 4, 1994.
12. *Congressional Record*, Jan. 12, 1991.
13. Eric Woolson and Joy Powell, "Somber war mood may alter inauguration plans," *Waterloo Courier*, Jan. 17, 1991.
14. "U.S. Officials Leave for Saudi Arabia to Evaluate Possibilities for Ground Attack on Occupied Kuwait," *Facts on File World News Digest*, Feb. 14, 1991: 73.
15. "U.S., Allies Retake Kuwait After Four-Day Ground Assault; Iraqi Forces Are Routed, Cease-fire Set," *Facts on File World News Digest*, Feb. 28, 1991: 125.
16. The Associated Press, "Cooks activated for duty; vets critical of Grassley," *Waterloo Courier*, Jan. 28, 1991.

## The Judiciary Committee's Non-Lawyer

1. "Senate Confirms O'Connor in Unanimous Vote," *Facts on File World News Digest*, Sept. 25, 1981: 687.
2. "Senate Judiciary Committee Approves O'Connor Nomination to Supreme Court," *Facts on File World News Digest*, Sept. 18, 1981: 670.
3. "Hearings Open on Bork Nomination to Supreme Court," *Facts on File World News Digest*, Sept. 18, 1987: 673-74.
4. Robert H. Bork, *The Tempting of America: The Political Seduction of the Law*, The Free Press, 1990.
5. *Ibid.*
6. "Bork Concludes Testimony at Confirmation Hearings," *Facts on File World News Digest*, Sept. 25, 1987: 689.
7. "Bork Refuses to Withdraw Supreme Court Bid," *Facts on File World News Digest*, Oct. 16, 1987: 756-57.
8. Robert H. Bork, *The Tempting of America: The Political Seduction of the Law*, The Free Press, 1990.
9. "Ginsburg Nomination to Court Faces Ethics Probe," *Facts on File World News Digest*, Nov. 6, 1987: 823-24.
10. "Supreme Court," *Facts on File World News Digest*, Dec. 18, 1987: 936.
11. The Associated Press, July 2, 1991.
12. Eric Woolson, "Grassley Puzzled by Ad Attacking Demos," *Waterloo Courier*, Sept. 6, 1991.
13. "Supreme Court," *Facts on File World News Digest*, Sept. 26, 1991: 717.
14. The Associated Press, Sept. 24, 1991.
15. "Judiciary Panel Deadlocks on Thomas Supreme Court Vote," *Facts on File World News Digest*, Oct 3, 1991: 734.
16. "Supreme Court Nominee Thomas Accused of Sexual Harassment; Confirmation Vote Delayed Amid Emotional Debate," *Facts on File World News Digest*, Oct. 17, 1991: 756.
17. "Grassley Stands Behind Thomas," *Waterloo Courier*, Oct. 15, 1991.
18. "Thomas Narrowly Confirmed as 106th U.S. Supreme Court Justice," *Facts on File World News Digest*, Oct. 17, 1991: 769.
19. Eric Woolson, "Grassley Sees Bright Spots in Bitter Battle," *Waterloo Courier*, Oct. 16, 1991.
20. "Senate Membership: 57 D, 42 R, 1 Undecided; Preelection: 57 D, 43 R," *Facts on File World News Digest*, Nov. 5. 1992: 831.

## "Seeing How High He Could Make the Rubble Bounce"

1. The Associated Press, "Former legislator considers run against Grassley in '92," *Waterloo Courier*, May 10, 1991.
2. Eric Woolson, "Squabbling continues in Welsh investigation," *Waterloo Courier*, Jan. 28, 1992.
3. Eric Woolson, "Lloyd-Jones: Grassley 'insensitive' to kids," *Waterloo Courier*, March 18, 1992.

4. Eric Woolson, "Freeburg goes up against Lloyd-Jones in Senate race," *Waterloo Courier*, May 15, 1992.
5. Eric Woolson, "Lloyd-Jones gets her two minutes of fame," *Waterloo Courier*, July 14, 1992.
6. Associated Press story, Sept. 14, 1992.
7. Eric Woolson, "Grassley Annihilates Lloyd-Jones," *Waterloo Courier*, Nov. 4, 1992.

**Public Service, Personal Gains**
1. Jack Bender, "Why pass up 'safe' race?" *Waterloo Courier*, Sept. 20, 1979.
2. The Associated Press, "Grassley lists income, issues tax challenge," *Waterloo Courier*, May 6, 1980.
3. The Associated Press, May 21, 1985.
4. The Associated Press, May 23, 1994.

**Grassley and the Media**
1. "The Best & Worst," *Washingtonian*, July 1982.
2. Eric Woolson, "Grassley cruises in race that might not have been," *Waterloo Courier*, Nov. 5, 1986.

**The Global Grassley**
1. "Lebanon," *Facts on File World News Digest*, Nov. 18, 1983: 870.
2. "Over 200 U.S. Marines Killed in Beirut Suicide Bomb Attack," *Facts on File World News Digest*, Oct. 28, 1983: 809, 813-14.
3. "U.S. Aircraft Bomb Syrian Positions in Lebanon; Two Planes Lost, One Crewman Killed and One Captured," *Facts on File World News Digest*, Dec. 9, 1983: 917.
4. Charles E. Grassley, "A Visit With Soviet Jews," *Saturday Evening Post*, September 1983.
5. *Ibid*.
6. Eric Woolson, "Harkin, Grassley split on Somalia troop vote," *Waterloo Courier*, Oct. 15, 1993.
7. Meta Gaertnier, "Culver attacked at meeting," *Waterloo Courier*, Oct. 29, 1980.